Teaching general practice

Teaching general practice

Edited by
Jack Cormack MD, FRCGP
General Practitioner, Edinburgh

Marshall Marinker MB, BS, FRCGP
Leicestershire Professor of Community Health, University of Leicester

David Morrell MB, BS, FRCP, FRCGP
Wolfson Professor of General Practice, St Thomas' Hospital Medical
School, London

Kluwer Medical   **London**

ISBN 0 903393 53 0

First published in Great Britain in 1981 by
Kluwer Publishing Limited, 1 Harlequin Avenue, Great West Road,
Brentford, Middlesex TW8 9EW

Printed in Great Britain

For Joy, Jeanette and Joyce

Contents

Foreword

'. . . The growing number of doctors who have become teachers of general practice' — so starts the introduction which follows this foreword. It is only 25 years since it was the common view that general practice could be neither defined nor taught. It seemed equally unlikely that learning about it or performance in it could be assessed. Yet we now plan that every GP should have the chance to be a teacher — not only for patients, as he always has been — but for his own colleagues. Our concept of continuing education now requires an active contribution from every doctor, resting on the belief that each has experience which is of value to others doing the same sort of work. Keeping up to date with relevant advances in specialist medicine is still necessary, but it is not enough. Something more is needed if the general practitioner's enthusiasm, intellectual development and critical sense are all to remain a match for the challenge of changing needs and changing knowledge.

We owe much of this flowering to the work of 'academic GPs'. They are often pilloried as unrealistic by the less imaginative of those from whose ranks they have emerged, who seem to pride themselves on being 'ordinary practical doctors'. This is to despise thinking.

This book is the product of academic GPs. So far from being unrealistic, it is highly relevant to all of us. It is about the learning and relearning of a practical profession which owes everything to thinkers and to using thought.

The material, marshalled within a framework which covers the search for standards and their assessment as well as the content and methods of teaching, bears, therefore, on undergraduate and on initial and continuing post-graduate education alike. The book contains many admirable contributions, and some will challenge any teacher who does not wish to go on learning.

I recommend it as a valuable spur to the enthusiasm of that growing numbers of doctors who are now becoming teachers.

JOHN HORDER
President, Royal College of General Practitioners

Contributors

J.H. Barber MD(Edin), FRCGP, MRCP(Glas), DRCOG

Has been Norie Miller Professor of General Practice at the University of Glasgow since 1974. Has special research interests in preventive paediatric and geriatric care and is joint editor of *General Practice Medicine* and *Towards Team Care*.

J.J.C. Cormack MD, FRCGP

Is a general practitioner in Corstorphine, Edinburgh. Formerly part-time lecturer in the Department of General Practice, Edinburgh University. After qualifying worked in mission hospitals in Labrador and Malawi. President of the Medico-Chirurgical Society of Edinburgh, lately Secretary of the Lothian Area Medical Committee, currently member of the panel of examiners of the Royal College of General Practitioners.

Author of *The General Practitioner's Use of Medical Records* and papers on medical records; editor *Practice: A handbook of primary care*.

Michael Courtenay MA, MB, BChir, MRCGP

Is a general practitioner in Battersea and Senior Research Fellow at the St Thomas' General Practice Teaching and Research Unit (part-time). Past President of the Balint Society, having been involved in Balint Group work as member and group leader for 23 years. Publications include research into family aspects of general practice.

Alastair Donald MA, MB, ChB, FRCGP

Is a general practitioner in Edinburgh. He is Regional Adviser in Postgraduate Education for General Practice in South East Scotland, and Chairman of Council of the Royal College of General Practitioners.

Michael Drury OBE, MB, FRCGP

Is Professor of General Practice at the University of Birmingham. His major interests are in practice organization and in therapeutics. He has written widely and is the joint editor of *Treatment* and the author of *The Medical Secretary's Handbook* (4th edition, 1981) and joint author of *An Introduction to General Practice*.

Michael D'Souza MD, MFCM, MRCGP

Is a general practitioner in Kingston-upon-Thames and a part-time lecturer at the Cardiothoracic Institute and the Department of Community

Medicine at St Thomas' Hospital Medical School. He has done research in respiratory disease and general health screening.

Charles Florey MD, FFCM

Is a Reader in Community Medicine in the Department of Community Medicine at St Thomas' Hospital Medical School, London. He has been involved in epidemiological studies of cardiovascular disease and diabetes and in the study of the effects of environmental hazards on health in the United States, the West Indies and in the UK. He has carried major responsibility for the planning and execution of numerous epidemiological studies. In his present position he has frequent contact with general practice through association with the General Practice Unit at St Thomas' Hospital.

Robin C. Fraser MD, FRCGP

Is Senior Lecturer in General Practice at the University of Leicester and also Secretary of the General Practitioner Research Club since its inception in 1969. His principal interests are in research methodology, medical audit, population denominators in general practice and the general practitioner – hospital interface.

Eric Gambrill MB, BS, FRCGP, DRCOG

Has been a general practitioner in Crawley, Sussex, for 14 years and is Course Organizer of the Crawley Vocational Training Scheme. He has been an MRCGP examiner for the past six years with a special interest in the modified essay question.

Keith Hodgkin BM, BCh, FRCGP, FRCP

Has been a general practitioner for 25 years in Redcar, North Yorkshire. From 1973 to 1978 was Professor and Chairman of Department of General Practice, Memorial University, Newfoundland, Canada. Also Sir Harry Jephcott Visiting Professor in General Practice, Dundee and Glasgow Universities. Author of *Towards Earlier Diagnosis*, joint author (with Professor J.D.E. Knox) of *Problem-Centred Learning* and recent articles on assessment and evaluation in general practice.

John Howie MD, PhD, MRCGP

Is Professor of General Practice in the University of Edinburgh. After working in general practice in Glasgow, he spent ten years in the University Department of General Practice in Aberdeen before moving to his present post in 1980. Has had a particular interest in research in general practice, particularly in the fields of antibiotic use and respiratory illness. Author of *Research in General Practice* published in 1979 by Croom Helm.

James D.E. Knox MD, FRCPE, FRCGP

Is Professor of General Practice, University of Dundee, and a principal in the medical school teaching practice. He has a special interest in the teaching and learning of communication skills in general practice.

Brian R. McAvoy MB, ChB, BSc, MRCP, MRCGP

Is a general practitioner in Northamptonshire and a lecturer in the Department of Community Health at Leicester University. He qualified at Glasgow in 1972 and after completing vocational training, spent a year as a Teaching Fellow in the Department of Family Medicine at McMaster University, Hamilton, Ontario. He has a special interest in role-play and simulated patients and their application in the teaching of clinical and communication skills.

Pauline A. McAvoy MB, ChB

Is a general practitioner in Northamptonshire and a lecturer in the Department of Community Health at Leicester University. She qualified at Glasgow in 1973 and after three years' training for general practice spent a year as a Clinical Fellow in the Department of Family Medicine at McMaster University, Hamilton, Ontario. There she gained experience as a counsellor in human sexuality and developed a particular interest in undergraduate teaching.

James McCormick MB, BChir, FRCGP, FRCPI, FFCM

Is now Professor of Community Health in Trinity College, Dublin. Was in general practice from 1954 to 1973. Has a special interest in the relationship of general practice to society, and published in 1979 *The Doctor — Father Figure or Plumber?*

Michael McKendrick MB, BS, FRCGP, DObstRCOG

Has been a general practitioner in Hexham, Northumberland for 20 years and Northern Regional Adviser (jointly) in general practice for the past six years. Concerned with the development of graduate medical education for general practice both locally, and nationally in the Royal College of General Practitioners. Special interests include assessment methods in vocational training.

Ian McWhinney MD, MRCP, CCFP, FRCGP

Has been Professor and Chairman of the Department of Family Medicine at the University of Western Ontario since 1968. Before that time, he was in general practice for 14 years in Stratford-on-Avon, Warwickshire. His book, *An Introduction to Family Medicine*, was published by the Oxford University Press in February 1981.

Marshall Marinker MB, BS, FRCGP

Was in general practice in Essex for some 15 years until 1974, when he was appointed to the Foundation Chair of Community Health in the University of Leicester. He is a member of the Council of the Royal College of General Practitioners and a past chairman of its Education Committee. His published work is concerned with medical education, clinical problem solving and the doctor–patient relationship. Editor *Practice: A handbook of primary medical care.*

David Morrell MB, BS, FRCP, FRCGP

Is Wolfson Professor of General Practice at St Thomas' Hospital Medical School. He spent five years as principal in general practice in Hoddesdon, Hertfordshire. In 1963 he was appointed Lecturer in General Practice in the University of Edinburgh and in 1967 Senior Lecturer in General Practice at St Thomas' Hospital Medical School. His first book *The Art of General Practice* was published in 1965 and he has since published extensively on patterns of illness in general practice and factors influencing the demand for primary medical care. He is an editor of *Practice: A handbook of primary medical care* and associate editor of *Laboratory: A manual for the medical practitioner.*

Ian M. Richardson JP, MC, PhD, FRCP, FRCGP, DPH

Is Mackenzie Professor of General Practice in the University of Aberdeen. Was an examiner for the MRCGP with special responsibility for the development of the MCQ paper. Main research interests are the measurement of the processes and products of medical education.

Nigel C.H. Stott BScHons, FRCPEd, MRCGP

Is a general practitioner in South Glamorgan and also works in the Department of General Practice at the Welsh National School of Medicine. Formerly Professor of Primary Medical Care in Southampton University and Senior Lecturer in General Practice in Cardiff. His research publications include work on clinical problems and educational methods with a special interest in health promotion and the rapidly evolving international discipline of Primary Medical Care.

Chris Watkins PhD, MRCGP

Is Senior Lecturer in General Practice in St Thomas' Hospital Medical School. He has been a principal in general practice in Kennington for the last nine years during which time he has been involved in undergraduate and postgraduate medical education.

His research interests include the factors which influence demand for primary medical care, the measurement of quality of general practice and the diagnosis and prognosis of respiratory illness in childhood.

W. Wayne Weston MD, CCFP

Is an Associate Professor of Family Medicine at the University of Western Ontario. He practised in a small village in Southwestern Ontario for ten years before becoming a full-time teacher of Family Medicine in 1975. Since 1977, he has co-ordinated a course on Teaching and Learning for the graduate programme in the Department of Family Medicine, University of Western Ontario.

John Wright MB, ChB, FRCS(Eng), FRCGP, DCH(Eng)

Is a general practitioner in Leeds and is Senior Lecturer in the Department of Community Medicine and General Practice at the University of Leeds.

Part I
Principles

1

Introduction
Marshall Marinker

This book is written for the growing number of doctors who have become teachers of general practice. Primarily it is intended to be of practical use to general practitioners concerned with the education of medical students and vocational trainees. We hope that it will also prove useful to doctors acting as course organizers or general practice tutors, and to other general practitioners who, whether or not they are formally engaged in the teaching of medical students and trainees, now wish to form groups in their own practices or postgraduate centres in order to look critically at the content of their work, and at the setting of standards for general practice and the monitoring of performance.

As in every multi-author book, what is presented here is a series of essays on different aspects of the subject. The editors, in addition to their role as authors of their own chapters, have tried to shape the book and choose the authors so as to present a coherent view of the content and tasks of teaching general practice.

Although written in the context of general practice in the United Kingdom, this book is intended to be of help and interest to all doctors in primary care practised in other countries, and who are now becoming involved in similar educational tasks. Throughout we have used UK terms to describe both teachers and learners, and these terms now require some definition for overseas readers.

The term 'medical student' is self-explanatory. We have tried to avoid the term 'undergraduate', because many of our medical students are graduates, and in some countries like the USA, the vast majority of medical students are graduates. The term 'trainee' refers to the young doctor who is either undergoing a three-year vocational training programme in general practice, or is spending one year in a training practice. Currently in the United Kingdom a vocational training programme lasts for three years, two of which are spent in junior hospital appointments, and one in a selected teaching practice. A large minority of doctors compose their own programmes, but the majority follow these programmes within a vocational training scheme and have the benefit of a three-year day release course which allows them to develop a group identity, and to undertake group learning and group projects. Elsewhere in the English-speaking world the equivalent term might be 'registrar in general practice' or 'resident'.

We have used the term 'clinical teacher' to refer to the general practitioner's teaching role within his own practice. The term 'trainer' in the United Kingdom refers specifically to this role in relation to vocational training. The term 'tutor' in the United Kingdom usually refers to a general practitioner who is responsible for the organization of a group of trainees, and for the conduct of a course or day release programme. Sometimes the term 'tutor' is applied to a general practitioner member of the academic staff of the medical school department who is responsible for teaching groups of medical students.

No two readers will use a book like this in an exactly similar fashion, nor would the editors wish to prescribe a 'right way' of using it. For the doctor who is a novice in teaching, who wants to catch something of the flavour of the task and to learn some of the basic language and assumptions of medical education in general practice, a first order of reading might be Part I, where the principles are outlined, followed by Part III, where there is an approach to the content of teaching. This might then be followed by a reading of Part II, where a variety of teaching methods are explained in relation to the content. The final chapter, The Teaching Practice, may then help the reader in looking at his practice organization in relation to the teaching tasks which have been outlined.

Some of the material here is intended primarily for use by course tutors — that is by general practitioners responsible for teaching groups of students or trainees. It is nevertheless important for the general practitioner teacher in his own practice to understand the scope and intentions of these small group learning tasks. This material is presented in some of the chapters in Part II, Methods, and in Chapter 46, Designing and running courses.

Assessment is the key to all educational tasks. Unless the learning is assessed, we can have no idea about the success of the enterprise. The form and content of assessment is nothing other than a restatement of the objectives to which the teachers have committed themselves at the outset of a course. The design of assessment predetermines, more than any other aspect of planning for teaching, the content and quality of the teaching and learning. For example a course for medical students may be largely composed of objectives concerned with aspects of whole person medicine and communication skills. It may be taught in small groups with the use of role-play and closed circuit television. But if the assessment consists of a fact-dominated multiple choice questionary, the learners will soon retreat to the library in order to cope with their own realistic interpretation of the objectives which they now see in terms of the way in which the course is to be assessed. It is a sorry paradox in most educational endeavours, that whatever the stated objectives of the teachers, the major objectives of the learners have to do with satisfactorily completing the assessments which are set.

Part IV, The search for standards, is aimed at the general practitioner who wishes to attempt some review of the care which he is giving to his patients. In recent years the term 'medical audit' has crept into use, although the editors dislike the term because of two unpleasant connotations. The first is that medical audit is concerned with a rather banal form of accountancy: with the tedious measurement and summation of events which do not tell us a great deal about the care provided. The second is that medical audit requires an auditor who will perform like an inspector or external assessor of the doctor's work. What is suggested in Part IV of this book is a series of exercises which may be undertaken by a small group of established doctors, or for that matter a small group of trainees in general practice, which will permit them to develop some basic demographic and epidemiological skills in looking at their practice populations, the events that take place and the possibility of measuring some aspects of the outcome of medical care.

What is perhaps more difficult is to draw up guidelines for the way in which small groups of doctors may come to a conclusion about acceptable standards of clinical practice. Value judgements are inevitable, nor can they, nor should they be eschewed when there is insufficient evidence from the results of empirical research. An attempt to examine the quality of evidence and the quality of opinions in case discussions is made in Chapter 15.

Perhaps the most controversial characteristic of this book has been the editors' choice of chapter headings for Part III, Content. When the Royal College of General Practitioners produced *The Future General Practitioner: Learning and teaching,* the authors of that book summarized the content of general practice under the following headings:[1]

Area 1. Health and diseases

Area 2. Human development

Area 3. Human behaviour

Area 4. Medicine and society

Area 5. The practice.

This categorization has continued to dominate the literature on general practice teaching both in the United Kingdom and beyond, since it first appeared a decade ago. We have made no attempt in this book to develop such a detailed system of teaching objectives for general practice. Instead we have taken what appear to us to be the most important aspects of medicine in the setting of general practice, around which clinical teaching can take place. But our list of chapters was never intended to be an exhaustive one. It was intended to be the list of topics we considered most important and most relevant, and at the same time a series of examples of the way in which a particular teacher tackles his subject. We might have chosen such headings as 'The care of the old', or 'Respiratory diseases in children', or 'Depression'. Such titles or focal areas for discussion are simply alternative ways of expressing the organizing of teaching from the clinical encounters of general practice. We hope that one of the advantages of a multi-author book is that the reader will be able to compare and contrast different styles and different preoccupations.

At the beginning of a new decade, we are keenly aware that change in medical technology, in educational technology, and in society itself is accelerating in an unprecedented way. This means that inevitably the view which we have taken, the approaches which we favour and the educational settings which we describe will change apace. In particular, medical education is likely to change in the following ways. With the development of a new information technology, facts will become much less important in medical education, and the importance and relevance of good clear problem-solving techniques will become more evident. Self-motivated learning, in particular the sort of exploratory learning which comes from project and small group work, will increasingly free the student in school and university from the shackles of the classroom. But in medicine, it is hard to imagine that anything will replace the clinical apprenticeship. Indeed in some new medical schools, for example in Canada, Australia, Israel and Holland, that apprenticeship begins in the first days at medical school. This encounter between the teaching doctor, the learning doctor and the patient remains the central event of medical education. It has, throughout, been our central concern in the making of this book.

Reference

[1] Working party of the Royal College of General Practitioners (1972) *The Future General Practitioner: Learning and teaching.* London: British Medical Association.

2
The language of medical education
Marshall Marinker

Introduction

In our own continuing medical education we assume that we cannot acquire additional professional skills without learning new concepts, and the language and definitions which describe them. For example in learning to respond to the problems of patients who suffer from the so-called auto-immune diseases, we have had to acquire new ideas and the words to describe these new ideas.

In order to discuss education, we have to use a professional language different from our own — the language of educationists. Inevitably, in extending the concern of the clinical teacher from medicine to education, it becomes necessary to use some of the special language, the so-called 'jargon' of educationists. Experience suggests that this jargon often causes irritation and dismay. Sometimes the irritation hides a deeper discontent with or rejection of the ideas which it describes.

It has to be admitted that in talking about education for general practice, the use of the language of educationists has sometimes been employed more to obscure the issues than to make them clear. There is always the danger that jargon can be used to give the appearance of certainty when there is in fact room only for doubt and good judgement. In the use of medical jargon, doctors have not been innocent of such ploys. If we asked an educationist to explain why a particular student had failed his examination, we might well feel puzzled, outraged and embarrassed to be told that the reason was either 'iatrogenic' or 'idiopathic'.

This chapter is concerned with some basic educational concepts and hence will introduce a few new terms which are then explained. It is possible to teach without knowing the language — many of our clinical teachers in the past did so, and there were distinguished and successful teachers among them. But knowing the language of education simply allows the teacher to think and communicate more purposefully about what he is trying to do.

Facts, skills and attitudes

There are a number of ways of defining what it is that the learner learns. A frightened looking 40-year-old train guard comes into the surgery and complains of severe pain in the back passage. The pain came on suddenly the previous evening and has been unremitting. History and examination reveal a perianal haematoma. The general practitioner explains the situation to the patient, the student or trainee, reassures the patient that the condition, although painful is not sinister, and then incises the skin and releases the haematoma. Afterwards, he discusses the patient's bowel habits and advises him on a high fibre diet to correct his constipation.

The student learns a number of facts: the natural history and presentation of the condition, its causes and its management. He learns certain social skills, for example how to explain things to a patient, how to reassure a frightened person. He learns certain manual skills — for example, how to incise the skin and evacuate the clot. But he also learns much about the attitudes of the doctor. Unlike facts and skills, attitudes will probably not be consciously taught, but will rather be 'caught' by the student. Both learning and teaching encompass at one end of the continuum memorizing and recognizing observable facts, and at the other end understanding and coming to terms with oneself.

Objectives

The aim of all medical education is to develop or change a set of behaviours. Learning about the pathology of the renal tract, about diagnostic radiology and bacteriology, about the experience of adolescence and the problems of communication, all help to develop a professional performance — for example, the way in which the doctor will respond to a young girl's complaint of painful micturition. The acquisition of facts, skills and attitudes shapes behaviour. What the teacher intends that the learner will learn are termed 'teaching objectives'. The objectives are called 'behavioural' when they are couched in terms which describe what it is that the learner must be able to do. That is to say, active verbs are used, like list, describe, compare, examine, and so on. 'The student should be able to detect and describe the typical changes of diabetic retinopathy.' When the objective is a very broad one covering a wide area of medicine, for example 'The student should be able to describe the natural history of diabetes mellitus' the terms 'aim' or 'goal' are sometimes preferred. But the terms of medical education are only flags of convenience. In this book we adopt the simple expedient of using the word 'objective' throughout.

Most educational programmes, for example a course in general practice for medical students, or a three-year vocational training scheme, may be described in terms of *topics* like Clinical Method, the Primary Care Team, or The Family. More helpfully, these topics may be described in the broad terms of a behavioural objective. For example, in my own department, the topic Clinical Method is expressed as follows.

'The student should be able to demonstrate the application of clinical method in the setting of general practice. There should be evidence that he recognizes the specific range of clinical information about the patient and the illness, the weight of probability in each case and the early and late stages of natural history, which are encountered in general practice.'

Here the specification of a broad topic into behavioural objectives focuses the attention of teacher and learner on the need to change behaviours in a particular direction.

In vocational training such curriculum statements are suggested in works like *The Future General Practitioner: Learning and teaching*, and the publication on *Specific Training for General Practice* by the Loewenhorst Group. It would be unreasonable to expect that each group of teachers, for example the tutor and trainers in a vocational training scheme, should recreate broad statements of objectives at the beginning of every programme. However it is important that such groups should look critically at these large objectives, in order to determine how relevant they remain. The very broadness of these more global objectives leaves much to the initiative of the individual clinical teacher, and allows the course tutor to determine in some detail the shape of his own programme.

Purists demand that all objectives be written in behavioural terms. Words like 'understand' or 'empathize' are shunned because they do not immediately suggest how they are to be assessed. But in defining many of the objectives concerned with attitude (see below), the search for behavioural objectives can be exhausting and the game is probably not worth the candle.

Some American medical schools have attempted the most detailed description of their courses in terms of behavioural objectives. But such exercises, while they are intellectually challenging and rich in material for academic debate, probably do little to improve the quality of teaching, which may become mechanistic and unimaginative, as teachers trek obediently from one objective to the next. Sometimes teachers and students alike may find it helpful to have such a detailed statement of objectives. An example, on the subject of 'The Family', is given on page 157, Chapter 22, which deals with this topic.

In the context of the teaching practice itself, the clinical teacher requires a knowledge of the broad objectives of the course and the way in which a topic may be sharply defined by the construction of behavioural objectives. The teacher has to develop the habit of thinking in terms of such objectives, and the importance of discriminating between the objectives of teaching and the objectives of health care in the consultation is dealt with in Chapter 3.

Methods

Method refers to such techniques as the lecture, small group teaching, the individual tutorial, the group project, and so on.

The lecture is an important method in university teaching, and has until recently been the standard technique in postgraduate education for general practitioners. It is a particularly useful way of getting across a body of facts to a large number of people. But in the report of the Royal Commission on Medical Education the view was expressed that the lecture was an inappropriate method for the teaching of general practice to medical students.[1] Nonetheless the techniques of the lecture are important and are dealt with in Chapter 9.

Small group teaching is very widely used in teaching medical students, vocational training and in the continuing education and self education of established general practitioners. Small group teaching is not a lecture given to a mini audience. It is a process of interaction, of mutual learning, in which the role of teacher or group leader is more often to question and direct than to give information. It is in this sort of learning that the uncertainties and ambiguities of clinical medicine can be explored in some depth. The method is described in some detail in Chapter 8.

A tutorial is a session with one or two students and a teacher. This is the most important method which the clinical teacher will employ, most often with one medical student or one vocational trainee. Because of the peculiar setting of general practice most often this tutorial will be intimately linked with the consultation. It is this complex and intimate relationship between the consultation and the tutorial which poses many of the problems and offers the greatest challenges and rewards to the general practitioner clinical teacher. This teaching is discussed in some detail in Chapters 5, 7 and 16.

The project is a way of 'learning by doing'. Here the learner is actively involved in problem solving: he is set a general problem which he must then define and specify, devise a way of answering his question and of defending the usefulness and truth of the answers which he gives. This technique is becoming increasingly attractive in the teaching of medical students, and may well form a major component of vocational training in the future. The management of projects discussed in Chapter 10, and the whole of Part IV of this book concerned with The search for standards are relevant.

Reading is an important part of the learner's experience. Chapter 13 describes the use of medical literature.

Settings

The term *setting* refers to the place in which learning may occur; examples of such settings in medical education are the library, the laboratory, the post mortem room, the hospital ward and the out-patient clinic. In general practice, the most important setting is the practice itself — its consulting rooms, records office, the homes of its patients. Aspects of the setting will include the workload of the teacher while he is teaching, the physical arrangement of the teaching consulting room, and the tasks and attitudes displayed by the members of the teaching practice team.

It will be clear that there are strong links between what is to be taught (the *objectives*), where the learning will take place (the *setting*), and how teaching is to be acomplished (the *method*). For example, learning the natural history of diabetes mellitus may take place by reading. Learning how to use the ophthalmoscope and how to recognize the changes of diabetic retinopathy may take place in the diabetic clinic, and rely on tutorial teaching. Learning about effective communication with the patient may, in part, be enhanced by a particular use of role-play.

In general practice, it is the consultation and the tutorial which is associated with it, that stands at the centre of the doctor's work as clinician and teacher. Much of what follows in this book centres on what goes on between the general practitioner, his patient and the student or vocational trainee in the setting of the practice.

Styles

Each of us has a preferred style of human interaction, communication and thus of teaching. Two contrasting styles are worth describing. First there is the so-called *didactic style*, more crudely described as 'telling and selling'. Here the teacher is authoritative, gives facts, expresses opinion and quotes sources.

In contrast the teacher who uses the *Socratic style* is more inclined to ask questions than to give answers. It is the learners who are invited to give answers or to look more closely at the nature of the questions which they are asking. Here the teacher gives few facts, rarely an opinion, but guides the individual or the group to further exploration of the matters being discussed.

Teacher:	'What else would you want to do now [with this diabetic patient]?'
Learner:	'I would want to examine the fundi.'
Teacher:	'Why?'
Learner:	'I want to look for dots, blots and exudates.'
Teacher:	'Good. What will you do if you find them?'
Learner:	'I would want to refer the patient to an ophthalmic surgeon.'
Teacher:	'What will you tell the patient?'

(Later in the
tutorial)   'Obviously you are unwilling to be frank with the patient. Why is that?'

Most teaching involves a blend of both styles. The teacher is rarely entirely didactic/autocratic in his approach to a particular topic. But an understanding of the different styles as well as a self awareness of one's own preferred style can be a help in developing the effectiveness of teaching. The didactic style is appropriate for the transmission of facts or the instruction of skills. But in the exploration of uncertainties and ambiguities, so necessary for the teaching of general practice, a didactic style can allow the teacher to hide his own uncertainties, to defend himself too successfully. This accomplishes very little for the learner. By the same token the Socratic style, while it may stretch the imagination and the intellectual work of the learner, can sometimes frustratingly deny him a straight answer to a straight question. This may defend the teacher from the embarrassment of his own ignorance, but again the learner gains little. It is the experience of teaching that medical students and vocational trainees will repeatedly call both of these bluffs.

Syllabus, timetable and curriculum

The term *syllabus* refers to the topics which are to be learned. Ideally these may be seen as a very elaborate set of behavioural objectives, though they will not be expressed in such a detailed way. The *timetable* sets out where the learner will be and what he will be doing from day to day in his course. It is the curriculum which binds these two ideas together. The *curriculum* attempts to relate the objectives both to the settings in which they will be learned and to the methods which may be employed. In constructing such a curriculum, the course tutor will bear in mind what is best learned in the practice itself, what can be expected from a long series of consultation tutorials, what work is best accomplished in small group, project work and in background reading.

Conclusion

In essence the language and ideas of medical education are quite simple. An adherence to a proper use of the language imposes a discipline in teaching which allows teachers and learners to come to an understanding about what it is that must be learned, where and how it may be learned, and how that learning is to be assessed. Techniques of assessment are dealt with in Part V of this book.

Reference

[1] Report of the Royal Commission on Medical Education (1968) Cmnd. 3569. London: HMSO.

Further reading

Working party of the Royal College of General Practitioners (1972) *The Future General Practitioner: Learning and teaching.* London: British Medical Association.

3
Clinical teachers
Marshall Marinker

Introduction

In the UK the whole of hospital medicine is geared to a tradition of teaching. The structure of medical staff is strictly hierarchical both in terms of the responsibility for patients and in the relationship of learner to teacher. The atmosphere of learning and teaching in this setting tends to be competitive; successful learning may lead to promotion, and in this sense a consultant/junior hospital doctor relationship contains within it the elements not only of teacher and learner, but also of employer and employee. In such a tradition learning is characterized by didacticism, anxiety and competition.

The organization of care within the hospital reflects the teaching tradition. The house physician has limited responsibility for the day-to-day care of the patients in his ward, the registrar may have responsibility for an overview of this care and for taking certain practical decisions in diagnosis and treatment, while the consultant will have a more strategic view of the patient's care and will be brought into the decision-taking process at particularly crucial points. In its essence, whether the ward is in a teaching hospital or not, the consultant's grand round combines teaching and care in its very structure and function.

The situation is totally different in general practice. The staff structure of modern general practice in the UK is almost entirely non-hierarchical: a small group of general practitioner principals have equal status in the National Health Service, will share equal status within the group practice, and each will take total responsibility for the care of a patient in the course either of a consultation or an episode of illness. Even the introduction of vocational training in general practice has changed this little. The trainee, although he is neither a principal in the National Health Service, nor a partner in the practice is very soon accorded responsibility for his own consultations. The setting of the general practitioner's consultation, the presentation of a clinical problem and the need for a rapid definition of the problems and the suggestion of solutions, make it almost impossible to divide responsibility. In the early days of the traineeship, the trainee's consultations may be observed by his trainer, but supervision very soon becomes a matter of the discussion and analysis of those consultations for which the trainee takes full responsibility. Because medical care is not hierarchical in the general practice setting, the relationship between teacher and learner tends also to be less characterized by authority and deference than by sharing and questioning. At least that is the natural consequence of setting medical education in general practice. For the clinical teacher in general practice this poses problems of identity and gives rise to all sorts of anxieties about competence.

Competence

It was Michael Balint who pointed out that since all general practitioners were trained by specialists, and since the general practitioner defers to specialists in the diagnosis or management of specific conditions which lie outside his own competence, the relationship between specialist and general practitioner continues throughout their professional lives to be characterized by elements of a teacher–learner relationship. For this reason general practitioners do not readily identify or accept their roles as teachers. Until the recent past there was little in their experience as medical students, postgraduate students or general practitioners to reassure them about their role. There were no effective role models.

A further area of anxiety for the clinical teacher in general practice is that he is not sure how much he knows. This is a particularly acute problem for the generalists in any subject. Most of his own education has been knowledge based and the possession of facts has been particularly highly valued. This continues to be true in the assessment of medical education which is still dominated by the assessment of the candidate's grasp of facts. Further, these clinical facts have by and large emerged from the researches of specialists.

What has not been so well defined is that fraction of these facts which are essential for the practice of generalist medicine. As an academic subject, general practice now attempts to assemble such a core curriculum. Examples of this are to be found in a number of current texts of clinical medicine in general practice. But although such core knowledge may be implicit in good general practice, the general practitioner may not yet be confident of the proper or expected boundaries of his own knowledge. Contact with learners like medical students and vocational trainees, whose knowledge base in certain areas of hospital medicine will certainly be larger than those of their teachers, heightens this sense of anxiety. The general practitioner teacher has to learn how much he knows, how much he has to give his student or trainee.

If learning and teaching in general practice are non-hierarchical and reciprocal, the clinical teacher's anxieties will quickly be allayed. As he becomes more confident in what he knows, and what he has to teach, he becomes more eager to learn from his students and to modify in this way his grasp of current medical concepts.

Another major anxiety is the conflict which the clinical teacher may perceive between his responsibility for his patient and his responsibility for

16

the learner. Like most of the anxieties about teaching, these are more acutely experienced in prospect than in the course of teaching itself. However, it would be dishonest to pretend that no such conflict exists, at least in the short run. If the general practitioner is to share his consultation with a student, the patient has to sacrifice a degree of privacy, intimacy and, for that matter, the undivided attention of his doctor. What the patient gains, though it may not be immediately obvious, is a consultation in which the act of teaching enhances the quality of the care. Perhaps the two most important determinants of health care quality have been the developing expectation of patients and the continuing pressure on clinical standards that is exerted by the open audit of teaching.

Defences

The clinical teacher in general practice may respond to these anxieties in a number of ways. He may defend himself, first, by becoming over didactic. In his anxiety to demonstrate a competent grasp of facts, he may seek to teach facts where such teaching is inappropriate, or where the facts are already well known to the learner. In the middle of winter a 60-year-old patient with chronic bronchitis and heart failure may ask the doctor for a repeat prescription of oxytetracycline. The clinical teacher may launch into a tutorial about the choice of antibiotics in this situation, the likely organisms involved and so on. But the medical student's knowledge of antibiotic therapy is likely to be no less complete than the general practitioner's. What he wants to ask, is why the general practitioner has failed to examine the chest. The general practitioner may have excellent reasons for this. He may be able to teach about the unreliability of chest signs in monitoring the progress of chronic bronchitis, but he will not know what it is that he has to teach until he allows his student to show him.

This will not happen unless the teacher opens himself to the possibility of criticism. The danger is that the clinical teacher will defend any adverse observation with the words, 'It is all a question of experience'. Of course experience is important. But the student has virtually none, the trainee very little in general practice. He can only judge the experience of his teacher in terms of the logic of his argument, or the effectiveness of the outcome for the patient. Good teaching therefore involves the teacher in a re-examination of his own experience, not simply in a restatement of it. If he can explore with the student or the trainee the reasons for holding opinions or taking actions which may have remained unchallenged and therefore unexamined for many years, again both teacher and learner will learn from each other, and the patient will be the beneficiary.

Another form of defensive teaching has in the past tended to distort the true contribution of general practice, both to basic medical training and to vocational training. Here the clinical teacher responds to his own anxieties about how much he knows and what are the boundaries of his competence by making special claims to knowledge of the patient's background, the information about the patient's past social history and family situation. Far from achieving the sort of balanced teaching about whole person medicine which is so important in general practice (see Chapter 17), this produces a distorted view of clinical medicine in general practice and gives rise to the criticism often heard from outside it that general practice is concerned only with trivial physical complaints and with an anecdotal approach to the social vagaries of people's lives.

Lastly, and most dangerously, the clinical teacher may fall into the trap of professional paranoia. There is a degree of paranoia in all professional groups. The traditional rivalry between departments of medicine and surgery, for example, often the subject of so much medical school humour, contains also quite serious complaints which each side makes of the other. The same tensions can be discerned, for example, in neo-natal units between the obstetricians and the paediatricians. Similar cold wars are waged on the clinical frontiers of psychiatry, geriatrics and other disciplines.

Because of the structural gulf between general practitioners and hospital staff, and because the work of the general practitioner so much influences the work of the hospital specialists, it is along this professional frontier that so many of the professional border skirmishes take place.

This is not to say that doctors working in the hospital and those working in the community do not have good relationships, cannot respect one another, or cannot co-operate in the care of patients. They can and do. But the tensions and mutual criticisms exist. Sometimes in the care of patients when the tensions are ignored and buried, it is the patient who suffers. The same will be true in teaching. The tensions have to be faced both by the doctors and by the students. These attitudes must be explored and examined so that they serve the needs of what is to be taught and learned. They should never be simply defended in order to serve the needs of the teacher's damaged ego.

Conclusion

The analysis of a task can offer explanations but it cannot convey the total experience. When every word has been spoken about movement, rhythm, patterns, pitch and tone, tempo and space, nothing has really been conveyed about the excitement and beauty of a first division soccer match or the Schubert Quintet in C major. Nor can the game or the music be played according to a tight programme of correct behaviour and response. At the root of all learning is self-understanding. At the root of all teaching is creativity, even joy. Medicine, as most of our students believe and most of us have found, is a profession of intellectual challenge and human relevance. Too often these feelings are choked out of medical education. If the clinical teacher in general practice can convey his scientific curiosity, his compassion for people, his enjoyment of the job, then all the goals of learning and teaching will be successfully achieved.

Further reading

Cormack, J.J.C., Marinker, M. and Morrell, D.C. (eds) (1976) *Practice: A handbook of primary medical care.* London: Kluwer Publishing.

4

Medical students
Marshall Marinker

Introduction

The medical student's attachment to a teaching practice is usually short
term, at the present time often no more than four to six weeks. This poses a
particular problem, for the general practitioner tends to think of
professional relationships and doctor–patient relationships as being long
term. This may mean that the teacher will feel some anxiety to accomplish
a great deal in a short time, and this anxiety may result in over teaching, or
a wish to say everything about each case that can be said. The student's
attitude to general practice, the way in which he values the work of the
general practitioner, or the importance of medicine in the community will
to a large extent be formed by his previous medical teachers — the vast
majority of whom will have been hospital specialists. The clinical teacher in
general practice may, therefore, feel constrained to become a propagandist
both for his practice and for the role of the general practitioner. The danger
is that such propaganda may result in unrealistic claims for the
effectiveness, efficiency and humanity of medicine in general practice
which may not be entirely substantiated by the student's experience.
However these ambivalent feelings can be usefully explored in direct
relation to the patients whom the student now meets and the clinical
problems which he attempts to resolve.

The vocational trainee in general practice is already a practising doctor.
When he meets a clinical problem he wants to ask the question, 'What shall
I do now?' For the medical student this is rarely the object of the exercise.
He is still learning basic facts and skills of clinical medicine, and he is much
more interested in the question, 'What is going on?' Even though,
particularly in the senior clinical years, the medical student may be given
some degree of autonomy in conducting consultations, he remains
primarily an observer rather than a decision taker. It is important that the
clinical teacher bears this in mind; the difference between teaching medical
students and trainees is not simply one of 'quantity' or 'level of
sophistication', but rather of orientation. In addition the clinical teacher
must bear in mind that the medical student comes out into general practice
in order to develop further his basic clinical skills and competences. He
may gain some insight into general practice as a way of life, but this is not
the primary intention of this stage of his education.

Problems of identity

When the medical student comes into general practice he may be faced with problems of identity. Wearing a short white coat in the ward of a teaching hospital, his role is easily established as a medical clerk or a surgical dresser. He fits neatly into the bottom rank of that health care and educational hierarchy described in the previous chapter. No such tradition exists in general practice. He is faced with problems of what to wear, and how he will be described to the patient. The student will have little difficulty in taking a history from a patient in a hospital bed, and carrying out a physical examination. Not only is this a part of the tradition of the hospital, but the hospitalized patient has already surrendered a great deal of his autonomy. He has become dependent and his care seems somehow linked with his compliance. The patient in general practice retains much more autonomy, and his compliance in teaching has to be renegotiated at each consultation. The way in which the patient is informed that a student will be present during a consultation, or that he may see a student independently of his doctor at some stage in the consultation, is discussed in Chapter 47. In establishing a relationship with medical students, the clinical teacher should be prepared at an early stage to discuss these problems of role, title and dress. When the student is introduced to the patient, by name, it must be agreed what description will be used — 'medical student', 'student doctor', and so on. It is, however, imperative that no deception be practised; such deception is not only an assault on the doctor–patient relationship, but also a destructive experience for the student. The question of the student's dress is often a vexed one. The problem here is to reconcile the expectations of the patient with the self-image of the student.

All these issues are best resolved by open discussion. Often they can be first raised in the form of a student work book. The following is an extract from the fourth year student workbook at Leicester University:

An introduction to the consultation

'It is the intimacy and privacy of the consulting room which permits the patient to "open up" to the doctor. In the hospital out-patient department, it is often difficult to maintain such an intimacy unless the doctor makes a special effort to exclude others from the room: the nurse who may be assisting in a series of physical examinations, a junior hospital doctor, a secretary who may be present to take clinical notes from dictation. In general practice, however, it is rare for a doctor and his patient to share a consultation with another, except with another member of the patient's family. Further, because both doctor and patient are aware that the framework of medical work in general practice includes the physical, psychological and social aspects of the problem, the patient may regard much of the information which he gives his general practitioner as being in one way or another secret, privileged, perhaps damaging to his own self-esteem or to the happiness of others. Because of this, your demeanour and appearance in the consultation must be such as to give the patient some confidence in your ability to keep confidences. This may involve some of you in personal sacrifices of individual style. It would be impertinent to prescribe what sort of dress you should wear when you see patients — if for no other reason than that this would only reflect the tastes of your teachers, which are themselves diverse and idiosyncratic! But it is reasonable to suggest that you dress in such a way as to reassure the patients that you meet. As long ago as the fifth century B.C. Hippocrates advised on the dress and demeanour of doctors. Despite much of the critique that sociologists make of the ''doctor role'', it remains important for the patient that the doctor should look the part. If the doctor does not look the part, the patient cannot trust that he will play the part — that he will be able to hear the full story, or that he can be allowed to make a physical examination. Looking conventional on such occasions may be thought of not as a defeat of youth, or a retreat from personal freedom, but rather as a facilitation of clinical skills.

'Whether the consultation takes place in the consulting room or in the patient's home, there are three broad roles that you may play. You may be primarily an observer of the consulation; you may participate in the clinical work and share the consultation with your clinical teacher; you may undertake a consultation with the patient alone, and in this sense ''fly solo''.

'It is impossible to be present during a consultation without becoming a part of the process. Your presence in the room must inevitably diminish the intimacy of the encounter and tangle the lines of communication. All three of you — patient, doctor and student — have to accept these limitations. The patient will already have been informed of your presence and have indicated his acceptance of the situation. Even so, during the always unpredictable course of the consultation, the patient may suddenly wish to talk about some private or painful aspect of his problem, or the doctor may perceive the need to explore some aspect of the patient's problem which he cannot do in your presence. When this happens — and you should be sensitive to the rare occasions when it does — some way has to be found to leave the doctor and patient alone. Quite often this can be done openly: the doctor may say, ''I would like to continue this consultation with Mr Brown alone. Would you mind leaving us?'' At other times the doctor may simply indicate that he would like you to go and take a history from the next patient, or look at the medical records of the patients still to be seen that morning. You should develop the interpersonal skills required to sense when doctor and patient need to be left alone together and to deal with the situation effectively.

'It is important to negotiate with each of your clinical teachers what role you are to play during these observed consultations. Where are you to sit? Much depends on the configuration of the consulting room, but ideally the student should be seated in such a way that he can observe both the doctor and the patient. Inevitably, many patients will address their remarks both to you and to the doctor. Some patients may seem to forget about your presence completely and carry out the whole interview as though you were not there. Others may turn full face to you, give you their history and even address questions directly to you.

'Each clinical teacher has his own preferred style of consulting and of teaching. Some may prefer you to question them while the patient is present, or may question you in the same way. Others may insist that any discussion of the patient's problem should be deferred until after the patient has left the room. Still others may prefer that you should both defer discussion until the end of a consulting session. The great advantage of discussing problems as they occur, or immediately after the consultation, is that you do not need to make notes at the time of consultation. Such note taking may be off-putting for the patient and sometimes even for the doctor that you are observing.

'It is fairly safe to predict that your strongest impression, when you start to observe general practice consultations, will be one of bewilderment. Some of the consultations will take on an immediately recognizable shape. That is to say, a patient will present a new problem, or restate an old one, information will be exchanged, and some resolution arrived at. But because of the nature of continuing care, and because of the episodic nature of many disease processes, many of the consultations that you witness will be no more than fragments from a continuum of the health care process. That is to say that consultations will appear to start in the middle of a problem and will end without any sense at all of a resolution having been reached.

'There is a further source of bewilderment. If you spend a morning in the psychiatric out-patient department, or the gynaecological, or the ENT, you can at least begin to observe what is going on in relation to some framework of pathology or therapeutics. General practice offers you no such frameworks. In the course of one morning, patients of either sex and any age may present with problems in any order which might be described in part as psychiatric, gynaecological, orthopaedic and so on. In addition the perspective of general practice places the physical pathology in the context of the patient as a person, and the patient in the context of his social setting. Although this may happen also when the patient is seen in hospital it is rarely central to the problem which is to be solved.

'Consequently, unless you can focus your attention on a particular aspect of a general practice consultation, it is very easy to get lost. There are a number of approaches to this problem.

24

'For example, you may want to look at a series of consultations in relation to one of the seminar topics, say, on prescribing or anticipatory care or whole-person medicine. Remember that not every consultation will furnish you with a good example of what you wish to study. It may well be that while you are concentrating on, say, the diagnostic process, a really excellent example of the interrelation of family problems will be presented and it would be a pity to miss the opportunity of looking at this particular case in depth. It is therefore important not only to have a specific focus in mind when starting a surgery session, but also to remain alert, so that you can take advantage of an excellent learning situation whenever it presents itself. To learn effectively from general practice, you have to become a learning opportunist.

'You will probably have access to the medical record on the doctor's desk during the consultation. There is a great temptation, particularly when you are being baffled by what is going on, to look for clues in the past notes. The clues are often there and it is often crucial to search the record. But it may be least appropriate to do so when the patient is with you, simply because, while your eyes are scanning the record sheets, they cannot be observing the behaviour of doctor and patient. The record will still be there when the patient has gone, but there will be no substitute for the observations that you have missed.

'Sometimes the clinical teacher will invite you to share the consultation, in the sense that you will be invited to perform some specific tasks. For example, you may be asked to confirm the doctor's own examination — to listen to a patient's chest or palpate his abdomen. Sometimes you may be asked to take the patient to another consulting room and take a more detailed history. Sometimes your clinical teacher may interrupt a consultation to send you and the patient into the examination room where you will be asked to carry out an examination ahead of the doctor. If you feel comfortable with this sort of sharing, more opportunities will be given to you.

'Towards the end of the course you may be invited to undertake the whole of the consultation independently and then to present the case to your clinical teacher. Similarly you may be invited to carry out follow-up visits to the home of a patient whom you have already seen in an earlier surgery session. It is in these shared and solo consultations that you may also begin developing your own note-taking skills.'

Conclusion

It is clear to most clinical teachers that the medicine which is taught and learned in the general practitioner's consulting room is in many ways different from that which the student experiences in the hospital ward. The nature of these differences is outlined in Part III of this book. By the same

25

token the form, style and atmosphere of teaching in general practice are often very different from the medical student's hospital based learning. Faced for the first time with the task of teaching medical students, many general practitioners revert to the role model of the specialist consultant clinical teacher of their own youth. This is to impose on the setting of general practice a form, style and atmosphere of teaching which is alien and unhelpful. As the clinical teacher in general practice develops a competence to teach what he knows, he will develop a form, style and atmosphere of teaching which reflects his practice. This may in itself constitute one of the most important lessons which the medical student can learn in general practice.

5
Vocational trainees
Marshall Marinker

Introduction

At the time of writing the period of vocational training for general practice which is actually spent in general practice itself is only one year. This short period, which dates from the introduction of trainee assistantship in 1950 seems to have become the norm, not only in this country, but in many European countries and in much of the English-speaking world. In the UK this one year represents only a third of the total period of vocational training; the majority of the time is spent in junior hospital appointments. This gross imbalance in our training programmes means that the trainee year in general practice is a period of intensive learning for the future general practitioner.

Knowledge and skills

Mention has been made in previous chapters of the bias of hospital teaching towards the accumulation of facts. In their penetrating study of vocational trainees in the UK, Freeman and Byrne found very little difference in the clinical knowledge retained by trainees and their trainers, although there were a number of areas where the trainees as a group were deficient.[1] The implication is clear that the clinical teacher in general practice does not need to be primarily concerned with teaching clinical facts. Trainee and trainer are as likely to learn facts from each other.

When the investigators attempted to assess the problem solving capabilities of both groups, the trainers achieved statistically significant higher scores than the trainees. The implication here is that the clinical teacher's major contribution to his trainee is in clinical problem solving. Further, the investigators compared the 15 trainees most highly rated by their clinical teachers in overall terms with the 15 most poorly rated trainees using a nine criteria continuous assessment tool (see Chapter 39). There was no significant difference between the scores of these two groups in terms either of knowledge or clinical problem solving skills, but there were considerable differences in the personality profiles of these two groups. The trainees classified by the their teachers as 'excellent' gave average scores for each of the following nine personality variables: rigidity; authoritarianism; social conformity; dominance; introversion; extroversion; aggression; self confidence; cynicism. The trainees classified as 'marginal' showed a profile of extremes. In particular they scored low on introversion and cynicism.

The writers comment that some psychologists have argued that many of the introversion/extroversion scales are, in fact, indicators of social adjustment. The implication here is that the trainee year may be concerned with aspects of social adjustment in clinical practice and with what Michael Balint, writing about established practitioners, called 'a limited though considerable change of personality'.

Learning

Many opinions have been expressed about the supervision of the trainee's clinical work during the first few weeks in practice. No clear directives can be given about how many shared consultations the trainee should experience before beginning to hold independent consultations. Most trainers will want to observe their trainees in action throughout the year of training, and this may best be achieved by shared consultations or by the analysis of tape recorded consultations and video cassette recordings (see Chapter 12). The majority of case discussions will be based on the trainee's own description of his consultations. It is in these regular tutorials between trainee and trainer that the most important learning and teaching will take place. Experience suggests that although much of this clinical discussion will take place in an *ad hoc* manner, special time must be set aside in the practice programme (see Chapter 47).

A detailed analysis of such tutorials by the London Teachers' Workshop suggests that in every tutorial there are two major objectives for the trainee.[2] The first is perceived by the trainee himself, and often comes from what the Workshop members described as a 'hot situation'. They defined a 'hot situation' as an aspect of the reported consultations which was either charged with emotion, or was intellectually challenging. Invariably, this objective could be couched in terms of, 'What should I do in this situation?' In this the trainee is much more action oriented than the medical student, whose focus of attention is most often removed from the need to take autonomous clinical decisions. This 'immediate objective' may be different from any of a number of other aspects of the reported consultation about which the clinical teacher might think it important to teach. For example, a teenage girl is brought to the trainee by her mother, a capable managing sort of woman who is a senior nursing officer. In the course of the case discussion it becomes clear to the trainer that the trainee has failed to elicit from the patient sufficient information either to confirm or deny a diagnosis of depression. But for the trainee, the major problem has been how to deal with a controlling mother. He has already identified two distinct patients in the consultation, but he does not know how to disentangle the muddle. The 'immediate objective' is best determined by sensitivity to the trainee's anxiety. The trainee's lack of knowledge about depression must be dealt with at another time, and in another way. Often an MCQ paper at the beginning of a traineeship will identify areas of clinical need which can be corrected by remedial reading or topic teaching (see Chapter 39).

A further interesting finding of the London Teachers' Workshop concerns what was termed 'the developmental objective'. Close scrutiny of many of these tutorials revealed that in addition to the 'immediate objective' concerned with the question 'What should I do?', there was a second and equally important objective concerned with 'How can I become this sort of doctor?'. Such objectives are concerned not so much the acquisition of more knowledge, or social skills within the consultation as with the acquisition of a sense of identity as a general practitioner. Here the issues were more often the ability to tolerate uncertainty, the challenge of retaining clinical judgement in the face of strong feelings about the patient and so on. In many ways the findings of the London Teachers' Workshop which was based on the experimental analysis of tutorials is supported by the contemporary work of Freeman and Byrne whose researches were based on objective data collected in a reliable sample frame.

Often the doctor in his training is placed in particularly vulnerable and difficult situations which would tax the clinical skills of his mentors. For example the junior hospital doctor probably has to deal at first hand with dying patients more frequently than at any other time in his future professional life. He does this at a time when he is still young, when his own personal experience of dealing with dying patients and with death is small, when he has to work under great pressure of time, and with patients with whom he has not had a long previous relationship. Similarly in general practice, the trainee has to cope with two unusual and difficult situations.

The first might be called the 'new doctor syndrome'. By this I mean that those patients whose problems are particularly intractable, or whose previous relationships with other doctors in the practice have failed, will turn to any new doctor in the practice and with unrealistic expectations. Most new partners in a practice are aware that they quickly collect a number of such difficult 'problem patients'. The trainee has to cope not only with this, but with the fact that at the most his doctor–patient relationship will not last for more than 12 months. Most often he has much less time than this. Little attention has so far been given to the peculiar constraints and challenges offered to the trainee by this short term contract. Teaching about the doctor–patient relationship, therefore, has to explore this sense of impending separation in all of the trainee's relationships with his patients. In this, the clinical teacher has much to learn from his trainee.

The second concerns the role of the trainees in the practice. Many of the tutorials analysed by the London Teachers' Workshop were connected with the ambivalent relationships between the trainee, his appointed trainer and the other partners in the practice, with whom he had both a colleague relationship and also a learner–teacher relationship. Time and again we were able to see that unresolved conflicts between the partners surfaced as problems between the trainee and his patient, or between the trainee and his trainer. In order to discuss such conflicts and to help the trainee grow as a future partner of another practice, the clinical teacher must often be prepared to look at aspects of his own personality, his own relationship with colleagues and the structure of his own practice in ways which will be revealing but may be painful. Once again the rewards of being involved in teaching are considerable both for the doctor and his patient. For the trainee–trainer relationship to be effective, both must be prepared to look at that relationship with some courage.

References

1   Freeman, J. and Byrne, P.S. (1973) *The Assessment of Postgraduate Training in General Practice.* London: HMSO.
2   Marinker, M. (1972) *Journal of the Royal College of General Practitioners, 22*, 551-559.

6

What is to be taught and learned?

John Wright

'What is to be taught and learned?' falls firmly into that category of question which simultaneously demands and defies an answer. (If you doubt the truth of this, sit for a few minutes with any curriculum committee of any medical school.) It recalls the dilemma of W.E. Gladstone, of whom it was said that by the time he had solved the Irish question, the Irish had altered the question. The practice of medicine remains the same yet changes: successive students and postgraduate trainees are very similar to, yet very different from, each other; time, resources and circumstances vary; and so, necessarily, do educational aims.

The present chapter will, therefore, attempt no more than to discuss some of the principles influencing the decision as to what should be taught to and learned by the student and the trainee in the context of general practice. The reader who is looking for a syllabus will need to seek it elsewhere.

Teaching and practice

Self-evidently, in any particular context some things are taught and learned more readily than others; and we need to be clear about the boundaries imposed on learning by the context and character of general practice.

Undergraduate teachers in general practice frequently express the view that, 'It is not our task to teach students clinical medicine — they must learn that in hospital'. In similar vein, postgraduate vocational trainees spend two of their three years' programme in hospital appointments. Both these imply a restricted role for teaching in general practice, concerned more with the art that the science of medicine. Both spring, in part, from the view that a compendious body of factual information is a *sine qua non* of future professional practice and that much of this factual information is best acquired in a hospital setting. By contrast, hospital based undergraduate teachers (even in the most conservative medical schools) often emphasize the need to concentrate on teaching the 'principles' rather than the factual content of medicine, and the General Medical Council's Recommendations[1] provide a list of educational aims for basic medical education many of which can be appropriately provided for in the context of general practice.

Plainly some re-thinking is needed about the areas of learning which the student and the trainee need to encompass, and the role which general practice should have in providing for them. Perhaps its limitations are not as great as we have sometimes thought.

Areas of learning

In assessing the capabilities of a student or trainee the questions which we commonly find we ask ourselves are, 'What does he know?'; 'How clearly does he think?'; 'What can he do?'; and 'How does he react?'. Clinical learning thus needs to embrace the learning of knowledge, of methods of thinking, of manipulative skills, and of attitudes.

However, in using these four broad areas as a guide to teaching we do need to remember how composite in character each of them is and how closely interlinked they are with each other. For example:

Knowledge does not only comprise the knowledge of 'facts' (including a knowledge of where to find knowlege) but includes also knowledge of working definitions, concepts, theories and methods useful in everyday practice.

Manipulative skills include a wide range of motor abilities varying considerably in their complexity — for example, the ability to use an otoscope effectively, administer an anaesthetic, or remove a patient's appendix. All are built on a background of factual knowledge (i.e. of how to perform them) and of cognitive skills (i.e. when or why to perform them).

Methods of thinking (the so called 'cognitive skills') include such abilities as those of observation; deduction (inference); analysis (identifying constituent parts); synthesis (recognizing relationships and combining parts in logical units); evaluation (making critical judgements); and communication (receiving and transmitting information). All these abilities are obviously composite in nature and psychologically complex. Like motor skills they are cultivated against a background of factual knowledge, the student using and manipulating the latter to develop his cognitive skills to the point where they become subconscious processes.

Attitudes, values and beliefs are conveniently grouped together, if only because the conceptual distinctions between them are the subject of wide disagreement. The three terms are often used without precise definition, and Miller remarks that, ' "Attitude" has almost as many meanings as there are people who use the word'.[2] However, within this spectrum of definitions, it seems to be generally agreed that attitudes are:
1. States of readiness or predisposition; feelings, for or against something, which predispose to particular responses. Thus, for example, an attitude has been defined as being 'a mental and neural state of readiness ... exerting a directive or dynamic influence upon the individual's response

to all objects and situations with which it is related'.[3]

Attitudes thus involve emotions (feelings) and knowledge (or beliefs) about the object, and emanate in behaviour.

2. Not inherited but are learned; and, though relatively stable, are modifiable by education.

The term 'value' is equally variably used. By some it is thought of as 'an estimate of worth' directed to more specific objects than is the case with attitudes. On this view, attitudes may result from one or more values. (For example, a doctor's attitude to night calls may result from the positive value he attaches to professional availability or to continuity of care, as against the value he attaches to an unbroken night's sleep.)

However contentious these definitions may be, what is less in contention is the importance of attitudes, values and beliefs to learning and practice. In remarking that, 'It is universally accepted that the development in medical students of "wholesome" or "constructive" or "socially approved" attitudes is one of the goals of medical education', Miller is expressing the view of many clinical teachers. Such a view, however, raises difficult questions. For example, what specific attitudes (or clusters of attitudes) are predictive of the way in which a doctor will practice? And if such are definable can their presence and their relevance be assessed reliably?

In the face of such questions, the teacher may well be tempted to sidestep this area of learning.

Education and training

In successive phases of the doctor's development, the emphasis accorded to each of these four areas of learning needs to be considered carefully, and the balance between them varied.

For the established practitioner, the balance of learning aimed at in continuing medical education will largely be determined by his own individual needs, varying from doctor to doctor and from time to time. For the postgraduate vocational trainee the balance must aim at providing for his foreseeable tasks as a general practitioner; and for the medical student, in contrast, at providing a foundation on which subsequent learning can be built — no matter in which branch of medicine he chooses to work after graduation. Learning thus proceeds from the general (for the student) to the particular (for the trainee); and from the particular to the individualistic (for the established practitioner).

In commenting on the difference of emphasis required in the undergraduate and early postgraduate period of learning, the Royal Commission on Medical Education remarked:

'...the undergraduate course in medicine should be primarily educational. Its object is not to produce a fully qualified doctor but an educated man who becomes qualified in the course of postgraduate training.'[4]

Similarly, we find ourselves habitually speaking of undergraduate *education* but of postgraduate *training*. This distinction between education and training — at first sight largely a semantic one — is in fact of the greatest practical importance, and is a major determinant of the patterns of learning desirable in the undergraduate and early postgraduate periods.

A moment's reflection will show that *training* (of the motor mechanic, the bricklayer, plumber or doctor) is primarily concerned with preparing the individual for specific tasks, i.e. with the learning of skills, and with knowledge insofar as it is necessary to those skills. It is designed to prepare the trainee to respond to a specified, foreseen set of situations, and its hallmark is thus its particularity. In consequence, given the job specification which a trainee will subsequently need to fulfil, it is not difficult to compile an appropriate syllabus of learning.

In contrast, *education* is not confined to preparing the student for specific tasks but is concerned with enabling him to respond appropriately ('intelligently') to unforeseen situations. To achieve this, education seeks to develop a capacity for 'lateral thinking' ('transfer') — the ability to apply the insights and methods of one subject to the problems of another; a capacity for critical analysis; and a capacity for intellectual synthesis. In short it involves a heavy emphasis on methods of thinking and on attitudes, and it regards factual knowledge primarily as a vehicle for developing these.

These differences of emphasis between education and training, and the way in which they complement each other, are shown in Figure 1. This diagram serves to underline three important principles.

1. Precisely because these various fields of learning are inseparably linked, learning needs to go on simultaneously in all of them from the time that the aspiring doctor enters medical school. At any stage in his career it is not a matter of 'either... or' but of 'both... and'. The important questions for the teacher, faced by a particular student/trainee at a particular time, are thus questions of emphasis and priorities.

2. Since learning is a continuum (punctuated though it may be by such hiccups as graduation, and postgraduate diploma examinations) the teacher's priorities must depend on what his student has already achieved.

3. That education provides the basis on which training is built. 'The true aim of the teacher', remarked Karl Pearson, 'should be to impart an appreciation of method rather than a knowledge of facts.' Until the embryonic doctor has learned to think clearly and critically, and has developed appropriate attitudes, no amount of training will create a

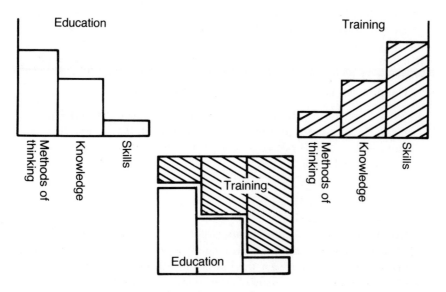

Figure 1

doctor who can be relied upon. Indeed, the more training the uneducated doctor receives the more dangerous he may well become.

Present experience, however, suggests that students often achieve graduation with a high level of factual knowledge but poorly developed cognitive skills. And although postgraduate training for general practice should not have to provide for the shortcomings of undergraduate education, in contemporary Britain it may sometimes, regrettably, need to do so.

What knowledge should be learned?

These differences in character of the undergraduate and early postgraduate phases provide us with broad guidelines to the spectrum of factual knowledge which the student and trainee should learn.

The medical student

Traditionally the undergraduate's curriculum has laid (and, in many medical schools, continues to lay) a heavy emphasis on factual knowledge.

In part this has been due to the fact that for nearly a hundred years (1858 – 1956) a university degree in medicine provided the entrance to licensed independent practice, and a social responsibility therefore rested on the universities to produce the 'safe' doctor. However, with the rapid expansion of factual knowledge and the equally rapid development of technical procedures, no student can hope, by the time of his graduation, to know more than a fragment of what is available. Equally important, much of the knowledge acquired by graduation is rapidly outdated. Any content-dominated curriculum which pays little heed to the development of cognitive skill cannot, therefore, hope to produce the 'safe' doctor.

The problem is not a new one. In 1925 Flexner wrote:

> 'A bare recital of the different subjects into which, for convenience, medicine has been broken up will dispose of the notion that any curriculum, however long or crowded, can contain or deliver to the student the knowledge, skills and techniques it would profit him to possess.'[5]

The learning of factual knowledge thus needs to be selective. On what basis is selection to be made?

Knowledge may be acquired with two different aims in mind. With the first, characteristic of training, it is related (as we have seen) specifically to the tasks which it is foreseen the individual will be called upon to fulfil. With the second, characteristic of education, it is regarded as desirable in its own right, providing a vehicle for the development of mental skills.

A body of precise factual knowledge is essential to the undergraduate student — for if he has not learned to be precise in this he will scarcely be precise in anything else. In everyday practice the content of factual teaching is often determined by the clinical problems presenting to the doctor at the time the student is present (and thus it commonly includes factual information regarding common conditions). But the actual content of knowledge is less important than the skills it is used to develop. The fact that individual teachers continue to argue endlessly about what factual content is, and what is not, 'essential' reflects an outdated approach to medical student education which insists on giving pre-eminence to factual knowledge rather than cognitive skills. *For the medical student the precise content is largely irrelevant; the purposes to which it is put are critical.* (However, the teacher needs to remember that the long-suffering student is likely to belong to a medical school which lays great store on factual knowledge, and subjects him regularly to examinations designed to do no more than test a voluminous factual recall.)

Postgraduate training for general practice

Here the situation is very different. The doctor has now elected to embark on a career in a particular field of medicine — general practice — and needs an appropriately tailored period of training. The aims of such training are to develop those skills which will be specifically required in his career choice and to achieve the factual knowledge on which those skills are based.

This factual knowledge — with much of which the trainee will be unfamiliar — has been usefully categorized under five headings:
—Clinical medicine
—Human development
—Human behaviour
—Social medicine
—Practice administration
The field is as vast as that of any hospital-based specialty and, like the latter, requires that decisions be reached on the minimum 'core content' which the trainee should have demonstrably achieved by the completion of his training period.

What methods of thinking?

What are the methods of thinking (cognitive skills) which doctors habitually (if subconsciously) use, and which the student needs to develop?

Sitting in with a doctor at any consultation (whether in hospital or in general practice), one will see him observing; communicating; following initial ideas (hypotheses); selectively collecting information (in history taking, examination, or investigations); arriving at an assessment (diagnosis); planning treatment, follow-up management or preventive care; or reviewing the clinical situation.

Each of these activities is made up of subordinate types of activity, so that an empirical list of the cognitive skills which the doctor needs begins to emerge.

Self-evidently, the list in Table 1 is illustrative, not comprehensive. However, the skills listed in it are skills which all doctors use in consultation. No matter, therefore, what clinical specialty he subsequently chooses after graduation, the student needs to develop (and the trainee to refine) them. Furthermore since they are skills which are used in every consultation, any consultation (whether for a whitlow or a phobic neurosis) can be used to illustrate them.

The need for a shift in educational emphasis, from factual knowledge towards methods of thinking, is no purely theoretical issue, but has considerable practical importance. Many of the current criticisms of clinical practice stem directly from an inadequate familiarity with the basic mental skills on which clinical method depends. Thus, for example, doctors are not infrequently charged with an inability to communicate effectively with patients; with an excessive use of investigations; with an undiscriminating acceptance of new treatments; with excessive prescribing; and with a neglect of preventive care. These criticisms are not without foundation: and the more highly trained the uneducated doctor becomes, the more likely are they to be compounded. Only the doctor who has learnt to think critically about what he does, and about the inherent limitations of

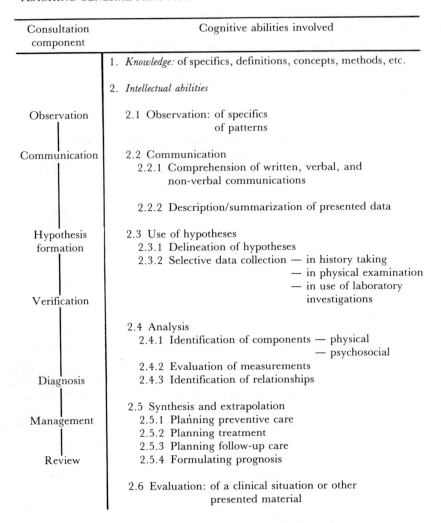

Consultation component	Cognitive abilities involved
	1. *Knowledge:* of specifics, definitions, concepts, methods, etc.
	2. *Intellectual abilities*
Observation	2.1 Observation: of specifics of patterns
Communication	2.2 Communication 　2.2.1 Comprehension of written, verbal, and non-verbal communications 　2.2.2 Description/summarization of presented data
Hypothesis formation	2.3 Use of hypotheses 　2.3.1 Delineation of hypotheses 　2.3.2 Selective data collection — in history taking — in physical examination — in use of laboratory investigations
Verification	
	2.4 Analysis 　2.4.1 Identification of components — physical — psychosocial 　2.4.2 Evaluation of measurements 　2.4.3 Identification of relationships
Diagnosis	
Management	2.5 Synthesis and extrapolation 　2.5.1 Planning preventive care 　2.5.2 Planning treatment 　2.5.3 Planning follow-up care
Review	2.5.4 Formulating prognosis
	2.6 Evaluation: of a clinical situation or other presented material

Table 1

clinical method, can be regarded as 'safe' in any meaningful sense of the word. If he has learned to do this during his undergraduate period, he has a solid basis on which to build his chosen postgraduate training. If not then the latter needs to start by providing for the shortcomings of his education.

Teaching in general practice

The trainer and the teacher of medical students in general practice alike undertake the majority of their teaching in a one-to-one relationship — one student with one teacher. This is one of the few situations in contemporary higher education where the tutorial system still persists. It is a privileged situation for both parties. It is also one which imposes considerable demands on the teacher.

If only for logistic reasons, it seems likely that the present pattern of postgraduate vocational training in general practice (with two years of its three-year period spent in a variable rotation of hospital appointments, often before the trainee has had any working experience of practice) will continue in the foreseeable future. Educationally, this pattern is often unsatisfactory. Repetitive service tasks take priority over educational needs, and continuity of supervision is inadequate to ensure that the trainee acquires the factual knowledge and specific skills he will need subsequently in practice. If training *for* general practice is indeed to be achieved by training *in* general practice then new thought will need to be given to the specific knowledge and skills which require to be learned.

Nor has the potential contribution of general practice to undergraduate education yet been properly developed — though this potential has increased out of all recognition in the past 25 years. In terms of factual learning, changes in the predominating patterns of morbidity (for example, the increasing predominance of chronic disease, of psychosomatic illness, and the problems of ageing), the greatly increased therapeutic armamentarium available to practitioners, access to diagnostic facilities, and the increase in specialization and cost of hospital care, have all converged to create this potential. If, as the General Medical Council suggests, it is necessary for a student to acquire knowledge and understanding of the normal growth and development of the human body; the aetiology, natural history, and prognosis of the common mental and physical ailments; normal pregnancy, the principles of antenatal and post-natal care, and medical aspects of family planning and of psycho-sexual counselling; the principles of prevention; human relationships and the interaction of man on his physical, biological and social environment; and the organization and provision of health care in the community, then the most natural place for the student to achieve this knowledge would seem to be in general practice.

Similarly, as a situation in which to develop the cognitive skills requisite in all consultations, general practice has, potentially at least, much to offer — since the problems with which it is concerned are open-ended and 'undifferentiated' (no presuppositions can therefore be adopted regarding their nature); present early, with a plethora of symptoms but few physical signs (often demanding, therefore, considerable skill in interpretation); and constantly require consideration of psychological, as well as physical, factors in their genesis.

Currently, however, such potential is largely either unrecognized or unused; and it will remain so until those of us who teach have thought more clearly about what it is that should be learned in general practice — by the medical student, by the vocational trainee, and by the established doctor.

Summary

'What is to be learned?' is to be thought of in terms of knowledge, methods of thinking, motor skills, and attitudes.

Education and training are different in their aims, the former being primarily concerned with the development of cognitive abilities, the latter with preparation for specific tasks. In Britain, with the advent of mandatory postgraduate training for all doctors, the university is freed from the responsibility of attempting to produce the fully trained doctor at graduation. The learning of factual knowledge in the undergraduate period needs to be recognized, therefore, as avowedly selective — being used as a vehicle for the development of cognitive abilities rather than of importance in itself.

Teaching and learning in the period of postgraduate training are primarily concerned with the development of the specific skills, and the acquisition of the specific knowledge, on which general practice depends. It is also concerned with further developing the trainee's critical faculties. Where development of the latter has been neglected in a student's medical school education, it will (for important practical reasons) become a priority aim of postgraduate training. At all times, the medical school teacher and postgraduate trainer alike need to recognize (and define) their students' individual strengths and weaknesses. There is no immutable curriculum.

References

[1] General Medical Council (1980) *Recommendations on Basic Medical Education*. London.
[2] Miller, G.E. *et al.* (1962) *Teaching and Learning in Medical School*. Cambridge, Massachusetts: Harvard University Press.
[3] Allport, G.W. (1935) 'Attitudes' in C.M. Murchison (ed) *Handbook of Social Psychology*. Worcester, Massachusetts: Clark University Press.
[4] Report of the Royal Commission on Medical Education (1968) Cmnd. 3569. London: HMSO.
[5] Flexner, A. (1925) *Medical Education*. London: Macmillan.

Further reading

Working party of the Royal College of General Practitioners (1972) *The Future General Practitioner: Learning and teaching*. London: British Medical Association.

Part II
Methods

7
Teaching in the consultation
W. Wayne Weston and Ian McWhinney

'The setting for learning in a medical school is molded by many things, but the major artisan is the teacher whose work penetrates to unnumbered patients who profit or suffer from encounters with his students. This responsibility is too heavy for tradition, inertia, or ennui to be allowed to dictate his actions — as a scientist he can do no less than prepare himself for this responsibility as carefully as he prepares to be a physician or investigator. The means are at hand. All he need do is use them.'

George Miller[1]

Introduction

Teaching in the consultation is teaching in the context of providing patient care. This form of 'teaching on the run' is complicated by two features: the teacher must attend to the needs of both patient and learner at the same time; and what will happen in any patient–learner–teacher interaction is frequently unpredictable. Fortunately, many of the skills required to teach this way are the same skills used by effective family physicians. The process of teaching parallels the process of care.[2]

The teaching and learning process

There are several varieties of learning outcome and each has specific conditions to facilitate learning.[3, 4] It is important for the teacher to recognize the difference between the types of learning in planning any instructional event.

1. *Verbal information.* These are ideas, propositions, 'facts' — the basic alphabet of knowledge. Without knowing the names of things, it is difficult to communicate with others in the field or to learn more complex knowledge. This material is most efficiently learned from lectures and reading and benefits from repetition. Family physicians are often amazed how many facts they know relating to family medicine which are new to their students. In this chapter the term 'student' is used for learners at all levels, from undergraduate to postgraduate. On the other hand, students often have more basic science facts at their fingertips than the family doctor, who never uses this particular information. It is important to keep in perspective that 'facts' are

essential building blocks of knowledge but that each discipline has its own body of important facts. If family medicine is incorrectly defined as simply a conglomerate of all the specialties, its practitioners will always be found lacking in 'basic facts'. However, when family medicine is seen as a unique discipline in its own right, it becomes possible to elaborate the core of knowledge that defines the field.

2. *Intellectual skills.* These are discriminations, concepts and rules — the ability to interact with the environment using symbols. Individuals possessing intellectual skills have a sufficient understanding of a body of knowledge that they can elucidate principles and identify novel examples of concepts. For example, the student will be able to discuss the patho-physiology of congestive heart failure and will be able to identify the features of heart failure in a new patient.

   This type of learning is facilitated by stimulating recall of previous related knowledge and guiding the new learning by a statement, question or hint. Concepts 'discovered' in this manner, as compared with being learned in a lecture, are more accessible to the learner when he needs to retrieve the concept in a new situation. Providing occasions for the learner to perform his just learned skill in connection with a new example is invaluable. For example, when a student encounters the concept 'pityriasis rosea' in the surgery for the first time, it is important for the teacher to help him discover the salient feature of this condition (herald patch, characteristic lesions, and natural history). His learning can then be consolidated by having him review this disease in a textbook or review slides of similar rashes.

3. *Problem-solving skills.* These are the skills by which an individual uses his verbal information and intellectual skills to deal with a situation which is novel to him at that time. Problem-solving is a complex process that includes the ability to recognize the problem, skill in generating alternative solutions and judgement in selecting an appropriate option. Attitudes relating to the content of the problem, self-confidence and comfort with uncertainty will all greatly influence the learner's ability to deal with a specific problem at a specific time.[5] Prerequisite intellectual skills and verbal information are needed to solve specific problems. The learner will need the skills to recognize when these prerequisites are missing and should be able to seek them out appropriately. There is no substitute for practice, using problem-solving skills in a variety of novel situations.

4. *Motor skill.* This is the ability to co-ordinate muscle movements in a smooth, regular and precisely timed fashion, e.g. performing a physical examination, suturing a laceration or inserting an IUD. The student

needs to know what the skill looks like. Written educational objectives or a description of the skill may help but a demonstration is even more helpful, especially for the novice. The student needs to learn each of the 'part' skills and also the order in which each part is performed. Learning is facilitated by repeated practice in a situation which provides feedback. Feedback is absolutely essential to effective learning of motor skills. The nature of the feedback should be varied, depending on the level of skill of the learner. A novice will need fairly detailed and specific feedback about his performance — what was done well and what needs more practice or additional skills. As the learner improves and develops a clearer idea of what a good performance looks like he will be more aware of his own shortcomings. At this stage he needs guidance to improve specific component skills and practice putting it all together. It is important to distinguish between application and acquisition practice. Acquisition practice occurs when a student is first learning a skill. It is useful at this stage in learning to practice one component of a skill at a time and to do it over and over again. Simulated patients and models are useful for this type of practice. But even real patients can be used. The student can be asked to concentrate on a specific part of the physical examination in a series of patients. Application practice is done to consolidate learning of 'part' skills in a co-ordinated and integrated manner similar to the manner in which the skills will be used in the application setting. It is important to recognize a student's level of skill. He should not be expected to perform a complex motor skill on a real patient, e.g. suturing a laceration, if he has not had an opportunity to practice the component 'part' skills first, e.g. tying knots.

5. *Attitudes.* These are internal states that influence the choices of personal action made by an individual. A number of attitudes have been identified as important for effective practice for the family physician. His commitment is to the person and not to the disease; he uses patient contacts as opportunities for prevention; he views his practice as a population at risk; he has a feeling of personal satisfaction from the intimate relationships with patients naturally developing over long periods of continuous care, as opposed to short-term rewards from treating episodic illness. Attitudes may be learned from an emotionally toned experience after following a course of action. For example, comfort with obstetrics may decline for a long period after a hair-raising delivery in which everything went wrong. This might be reflected in an over use of consultants, over-zealous investigation or giving up obstetrics.

Attitudes are also learned from 'models'. A model is an admired or respected individual. All of us have an unconscious tendency to model ourselves after our heroes. This is a very potent teaching tool in the family practice setting where there is often prolonged and intimate one-to-one contact between teacher and student. Unfortunately, modelling is largely unconscious and our students may pick up our foibles as well as our strengths.

The needs of the learner and the tasks of the teacher will vary with the desired learning outcome. Facts are effectively learned from books and lectures; principles are learned by struggling with the material and applying it to new examples; problem-solving is best learned by trying to solve problems in a variety of situations; motor skills are learned by practice in a situation which provides feedback; attitudes are usually learned by interacting with respected models. Hence the teacher's role varies from resource person to facilitator of learning, to manager of learning resources, to provider of feedback, to model.

The diagnostic-management process

A valuable parallel exists between patient care and teaching. Both can be seen as approaches to problem-solving[6] (see Figure 1).

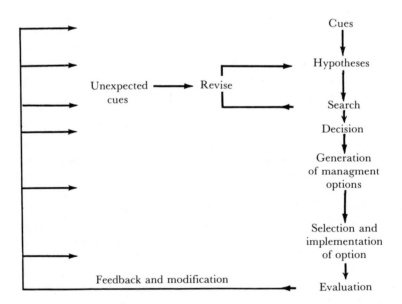

Figure 1. The diagnostic–management process

The patient/learner provides cues to his problems. The physician/teacher generates hypotheses based on these cues, obtains additional data which may turn up additional cues and lead to a revision of hypotheses and finally reaches a decision to stop searching and begin treating/teaching.

The decision to stop searching will be based on time available, the need for precision and the specificity of the problem label. The problem will need to be defined clearly enough that a management decision can be developed from it. The physician/teacher then considers a range of options in

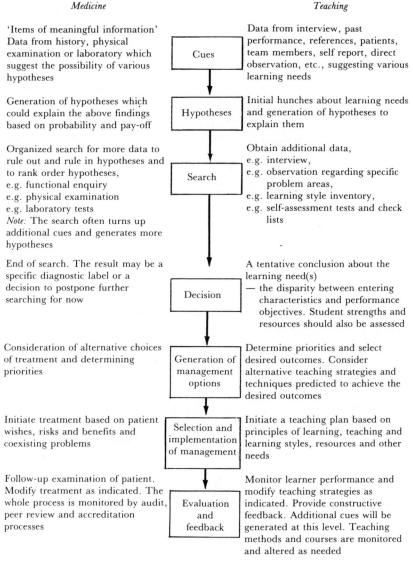

Medicine

'Items of meaningful information' Data from history, physical examination or laboratory which suggest the possibility of various hypotheses

Generation of hypotheses which could explain the above findings based on probability and pay-off

Organized search for more data to rule out and rule in hypotheses and to rank order hypotheses, e.g. functional enquiry e.g. physical examination e.g. laboratory tests *Note:* The search often turns up additional cues and generates more hypotheses

End of search. The result may be a specific diagnostic label or a decision to postpone further searching for now

Consideration of alternative choices of treatment and determining priorities

Initiate treatment based on patient wishes, risks and benefits and coexisting problems

Follow-up examination of patient. Modify treatment as indicated. The whole process is monitored by audit, peer review and accreditation processes

Teaching

Data from interview, past performance, references, patients, team members, self report, direct observation, etc., suggesting various learning needs

Initial hunches about learning needs and generation of hypotheses to explain them

Obtain additional data, e.g. interview, e.g. observation regarding specific problem areas, e.g. learning style inventory, e.g. self-assessment tests and check lists

A tentative conclusion about the learning need(s) — the disparity between entering characteristics and performance objectives. Student strengths and resources should also be assessed

Determine priorities and select desired outcomes. Consider alternative teaching strategies and techniques predicted to achieve the desired outcomes

Initiate a teaching plan based on principles of learning, teaching and learning styles, resources and other needs

Monitor learner performance and modify teaching strategies as indicated. Provide constructive feedback. Additional cues will be generated at this level. Teaching methods and courses are monitored and altered as needed

Boxes: Cues · Hypotheses · Search · Decision · Generation of management options · Selection and implementation of management · Evaluation and feedback

Figure 2. A comparison of the diagnostic management process in medical practice and teaching

treatment or teaching and finally makes a choice, implements it and then evaluates the outcome.

Examples of cues to learning needs are: the student frequently comes late for duties; he avoids part of the history or physical examination; he annoys and irritates patients, staff or teacher; he does not know what his peers know. Hypotheses that might explain some of these findings are: he lacks knowledge; he lacks specific skills, e.g. how to do a pelvic examination, hence he avoids doing them; he lacks confidence; he is not interested in a particular aspect of medicine; he does not see the relevance of the material of which he is deficient; he has personal problems. These hypotheses can be narrowed down by further observation of the student in his interactions with patients, surgery staff and teacher. Discussion with the student about the problems is essential. Feedback from the patients and staff and other physicians in the surgery is also invaluable. Once the learning needs are clearly identified, then appropriate learning experiences need to be developed to meet his needs based on an analysis of the varieties of learning (see Figure 2).

Teaching as a triadic relationship

'He must be secure enough in his professional performance to be able to widen his relationships to include a novice colleague and to master enough of his craft to function effectively with patients in spite of the distractions resulting from the novice's presence.'

Richard M. Magraw[7]

Teaching in the consultation involves a complex triadic relationship between teacher, learner and patient. The teacher in this context is responsible not only for the quality of the learning experience but also the quality of patient care. Sometimes the two aims seem to be at odds and the physician's discomfort in these situations may interfere with the student's learning. Physicians are often more reluctant to allow students to 'practise' on their patients than the patients are themselves. For example, physicians may falsely assume that their patients would not want a student to do a cervical smear on them. This may be a reflection more of the physician's discomfort than the patient's uneasiness. Most patients are willing to co-operate to benefit student learning as long as the student is appropriately supervised and not trying clumsily to do something for which he is ill-prepared. It is also important that the physican be visibly involved in the care.

Teacher and student may take on a variety of roles depending on the situation and the educational goals.

1. *Observation.* The teacher acts as a role model and provides the patient care. The student observes. This is especially useful to help clarify objectives by demonstration. New students benefit from this but so also do seasoned learners who are trying to learn from the teacher a skill that he has trouble clearly articulating.

2. *Partial care.* The student provides a portion of patient care, e.g. taking a history and performing part of the physical examination. This is especially suited to inexperienced students who need help with management decisions. It is also a useful format for acquisition practice.

3. *Collaborative care.* Teacher and learner together provide care, e.g. a conjoint family interview. This allows the student to see how it is done and to be actively involved at the same time. The teacher may gradually withdraw and give more responsibility to the student. The roles of teacher and learner need to be clearly understood and their relationship should be secure before attempting this approach.

4. *Supervised care.* The teacher provides 'backup' and may double-check portions of the history and physical examination, but the student provides the majority of care. This is appropriate for situations where the patient problem is within the competence of the learner. The teacher monitors the care for a variety of reasons — to respond to learner's questions, to provide feedback to the learner or to reassure the patient about the quality of care.

5. *Facilitator.* The teacher functions as a facilitator of learning rather than as a physician. The learner provides full care to the patient. This situation is appropriate where the patient problem is well within the competence of the learner. The teacher observes in order to provide constructive feedback.

Characteristics of effective role modelling[8]

1. The teacher exhibits enthusiasm for patient care.
2. He is self-confident in his abilities as a family physician.
3. He demonstrates awareness of his strengths, weaknesses and limitations.

4. He shares with his students his struggles and successes with patients as a model of continuing learning.
5. He uses himself as a role model:
    (a) to demonstrate physical examination skills,
    (b) to influence attitudes and values, e.g. honesty, dealing with uncertainty, genuine caring for patients,
    (c) to demonstrate interpersonal skills,
    (d) to demonstrate problem-solving skills.
6. He is open to criticism from his students; using it to enhance mutual learning.
7. In using himself as a role model, he uses a planned approach to teaching:
    (a) He prepares the learner for observation, suggesting what he is to look for in the consultation.
    (b) He assists the learner to understand the reasons for his actions.

Characteristics of effective supervision[9]

1. The teacher appropriately selects his patients for the learner, taking into account his level of skill and the learning task at hand.
2. He assists the learner to focus on specific learning objectives in an encounter with a patient.
3. He plans with the learner what role the clinical teacher will assume in a patient care encounter, e.g. consultant, observer.
4. He recognizes when patient care requires his direct intervention or active participation for the wellbeing of the patient.
5. He is accessible to the learner. It is essential that there are no barriers to the student seeking help from his supervisor, e.g. if he is afraid of being 'found out' he is less likely to ask advice when he is uncertain.
6. Parallel process.
    (a) The teacher recognizes the parallel processes between the teacher – learner and doctor – patient relationships in a supervisory role.
    (b) He is able to use these parallels in his relationship with the learner to enhance his understanding of the doctor – patient relationship.

Characteristics of constructive feedback[10]

Giving helpful feedback is the instructor's ability to describe to the learners their effective and ineffective behaviours and to show them how to improve their ineffective behaviour.
1. Feedback is descriptive rather than evaluative:
    e.g. 'You are rather weak in interviewing skills.'

    vs.   'I noticed that you avoided eye contact with the patient when talking about sex.'

2. Feedback is specific rather than general:

    e.g.   'You had better do some work on your clinical skills.'

    vs.   'You picked up well on the patient's back pain, but seemed uncertain how to explore the problem.'

3. Feedback focuses on behaviour rather than personality:

    e.g.   'You aren't interested enough in your patients.'

    vs.   'Your infrequent use of silence and open-ended questions reduces the chances of the patient telling you what's on his mind.'

4. Feedback involves sharing of information rather than giving advice. This encourages the learner to decide for himself how to handle the problem.

5. Feedback limits the amount of information to how much the recipient can use rather than overloading him.

6. Feedback is verified or checked with the recipient:

    e.g.   'You were terrific!'

    vs.   'How do you feel the interview went?'

    Even positive feedback may be confusing or unhelpful if the student thought that he really did a poor job.

7. Feedback pays attention to the consequences of feedback. The verbal and non-verbal responses of the student are noted. The student is asked to comment on the feedback.

8. Feedback avoids collusion:

    It is not always essential to provide brutally frank feedback — this may be harmful. However, it is vital not to provide meaningless and misleading or dishonest feedback:

    e.g.   'That was okay', when it was really poorly done.

Planning instruction[11, 12, 13, 14]

Planning instruction can be compared with planning for a trip.

Where are you going?

Determine the educational objectives. Broad objectives may be provided by a course organizer or university department. However, the individual teacher should critically review the objectives and 'flesh them out', based on his own setting and the types of students that he works with. In situations where no objectives are provided, the teacher must clarify in his own mind what it is he wants his students to learn from him. 'If you don't know where you are heading, there is a good chance that you will end up somewhere else.'

Where are you now?

What are the 'entering characteristics' of the student in knowledge, skills and attitudes? How well is he motivated? What are his expectations? What are his previous experiences in family medicine? What is his preferred learning style? Does he prefer to jump in and try new things and then read about it or does he prefer to read about it and watch someone else first? The discrepancy between the objectives and the entering characteristics equals the learning needs. Even students from the same school and the same class have vastly different abilities and learning needs. It is crucial to identify these so that the students are not put into situations where they are out of their depth. It is also important to identify strengths so that valuable time is not wasted practising skills already mastered while ignoring areas of deficiency.

How will you get there?

It is the teacher's job to develop learning experiences to meet the learning needs of the students. The variety of possibilities is limited primarily by the lack of imagination and flexibility of the teacher.

The student may not have a clear enough understanding of the task he is trying to learn. Written performance objectives may help but are often too vague for the novice to comprehend. He may need to see the teacher do it first fully to understand the task.

The nature of the learning task, as defined by Gagne, will suggest the type of learning experiences that are required. A student lacking information can be given a reading assignment; a student whose clinical judgement is deficient needs practice in problem-solving; a student who lacks motor skills needs practice in a setting that provides feedback; and a student whose attitudes interfere with his clinical performance needs to interact with a respected role model who exhibits the required attitudes.

How will you know when you have arrived?

Frequent monitoring of student performance is required to assure good quality patient care and also to measure achievement of educational objectives. Learning plans may need to be modified if new problems are identified. Students require feedback for motivation and encouragement, and to clarify their continuing learning needs.

Monitoring performance in the consultation[15]

Several methods for monitoring performance are available. The student may be observed directly by 'sitting in' or through one-way glass or closed circuit television. He may be asked to report his assessment after he has seen the patient, teacher and student then seeing the patient together. The consultation may be recorded on audio-tape or video-tape and reviewed with the student at another time. The records of patients seen by the student may be analysed. Finally, patients may be asked for an assessment of the student's performance. The choice of method will depend on a number of factors, among them the student's level of training, the availability of time, and the availability of resources.

In identifying strong and weak points in the student's performance, it is helpful to analyse the process of the consultation in the stages set out in Figure 1. Questions may be asked about each stage. Were all the cues identified? Failure to identify a cue may be due to lack of clinical experience (not knowing that the information is significant), poor interviewing technique, or to an inappropriate mental set. For example, the student may 'block out' a behavioural cue if he is rigidly pursuing a tightly structured interview.

Were the student's hypotheses based on a correct assessment of probability and 'pay-off'? Students coming to general practice for the first time have usually learned to base their hypotheses on the incidence of disease in highly selected hospital populations. Did the student consider enough hypotheses, or did he foreclose too early on a single hypothesis? For example, in a patient with a febrile illness, did he think only of a viral infection, without considering possible bacterial infections?

In his search strategy, were the questions, items of physical examination and investigations chosen with regard to their predictive value; were risks and benefits taken into account? Did the student do redundant tests when observation over time would have tested the hypotheses equally well?

Were the management decisions properly thought through? Can the student justify his decisions by reference to the balance of risks and benefits and to individual factors in the patient's personality and circumstances? Have the ethical issues been thought through? Has the management plan been properly explained to the patient? Have arrangements been made for follow-up?

Whether or not these questions can be answered depends, of course, on the method chosen for monitoring performance. The student's hypotheses can be identified in discussion after he has seen the patient, but a missed behavioural cue can only be identified if the consultation has been directly observed. The student's laboratory and X-ray investigations can be monitored by examining the records, but not his technique of interviewing and history taking. Students at different stages of their development will need different combinations of these methods. With most students, however, the teacher will need to use a selection of methods to monitor all aspects of performance. Although direct observation is time-consuming, it is a powerful method and, for most students, need not be used very frequently. Recording the consultation on an audio- or video-tape has the special advantage of allowing the student to monitor his own performance, with the teacher acting as a facilitator. It also enables the teaching occasion to be postponed until more time for analysis is available.

The student as a person[16, 17]

Above all else, the relationship between teacher and learner is the single most crucial variable affecting the outcome of learning. Good teachers have a desire to help others learn which transcends the problems that teaching creates. Teaching interferes with the physician's intimate one-to-one relationship with his patients. It slows him down. It exposes his weaknesses and areas of ignorance. It demands a positive regard for the learner as a person, even when his behaviour may infuriate the teacher.

It is essential that there is congruence between the process of teaching family medicine and the content of the discipline. For example, just as our commitment as doctors is to the person and not the disease, so, too, our commitment as teachers is to the person of the learner and not the subject matter. This commitment transcends individual learning problems or specific skills to be learned. It extends into the very being of the learner and challenges him to stretch himself to his limits. Such learning may require the learner to experience painful self-discovery or to make difficult personal changes. It requires the development of an intimate and trust-based relationship before such intensely personal learning and growth can occur. It is one of the very special privileges of teaching to share in the struggles of our students for growth and self-actualization.

References

[1] Miller, G.E. *et al.* (1961) *Teaching and Learning in Medical School.* Cambridge, Massachusetts: Harvard University Press, p. 296.
[2] Tiberius, Richard G. (1977) 'Interpretating educational concepts for the teaching family physician: some parallels between patient care and undergraduate clinical education'. *Journal of Family Practice, 5* (3), 395-398.
[3] Gagne, Robert M. (1977) *The Conditions of Learning,* 3rd Edition. New York: Holt, Rinehart and Winston.
[4] Gagne, Robert M. and Briggs, Leslie J. (1979) *Principles of Instructional Design,* 2nd Edition. New York: Holt, Rinehart and Winston.
[5] Haney, Allen C. (1971) 'Psychosocial factors involved in medical decision-making' in Robert H. Coombs and Clark E. Vincent *Psychosocial Aspects of Medical Training.* Springfield, Illinois: Charles C. Thomas.
[6] McWhinney, Ian R. (1972) 'Problem-solving and decision-making in primary medical practice'. *Proceedings of the Royal Society on Medicine, Section on General Practice, 65,* November, 934-938.
[7] Magraw, Richard M. (1973) 'Relationships between teacher, student, and patient'. *Journal of the American Medical Association, 224,* (2), 225-228.

[8] Irby, David M. (1978) 'Clinical teacher effectiveness in medicine'. *Journal of Medical Education. 53*, October, 808-815.

[9] Yonke, Annette M. (1973) 'The art and science of clinical teaching'. *Medical Education. 13*, 86-90.

[10] Bergquist, William H. and Phillips, Steven R. (1975) *Handbook of Faculty Development, Vol. I.* Washington, D.C.: The Council for the Advancement of Small Colleges (see Ch. 13, Helping Skills, pp. 213-234).

[11] Fabb, W.E., Heffernan, M.W., Phillips, W.A. and Stone, P. (1976) *Focus on Learning in Family Practice.* Royal Australian College of General Practitioners' Family Medicine Programme.

[12] Byrne, P.S. and Long, B.E.L. (1975) *Learning to Care, Person to Person,* 2nd Edition. Edinburgh: Churchill Livingstone.

[13] Mager, Robert F. (1968) *Developing Attitude Toward Learning.* Palo Alto, California: Fearon Publishers.

[14] Mager, Robert F. (1962) *Preparing Instructional Objectives.* Palo Alto, California: Fearon Publishers.

[15] Morgan, Margaret K. and Irby, David M. (1978) *Evaluating Clinical Competence in the Health Professions.* Saint Louis: The C.V. Mosby Co.

[16] Rogers, Carl R. (1969) *Freedom to Learn.* Columbus, Ohio: Charles E. Merrill Publishing Co.

[17] Zabarenko, Ralph N. and Zabarenko, Lucy M. (1978) *The Doctor Tree: Developmental stages in the growth of physicians.* Pittsburgh, Pennsylvania: The University of Pittsburgh Press.

8
Small groups
Michael Courtenay

At a time when small group learning methods are much in vogue it is important to review their proper place in medical education. They are expensive in terms of teaching resources and unless these are unlimited, small group learning should be reserved for those situations where it is particularly valuable.

The advantage of the small group is that it allows an interchange of knowledge, beliefs and attitudes between the individual members of the group. The interactions which are encouraged by the group leader explore motives, modes of thinking and the critical use of information. The members are enabled to apply principles and knowledge with which they are familiar to unfamiliar situations and to discuss misunderstandings and difficulties which they have encountered in their work. In the small group the members can practise their intellectual, verbal and social skills with each other.

Small groups can also be used for problem solving, for providing new information and for elucidating difficult concepts. The special characteristic of the small group, however, is the opportunity it provides for its members to interact and share their experiences. It is this function which will be particularly considered in this chapter.

Types of groups

Group work is sometimes arbitrarily divided into task centred and process centred. This is convenient in that the former is concerned with achieving specific objectives while the latter focuses on the way the group functions in the course of which the values and attitudes of the group members are explored. It is, however, an over-simplification of the way in which most groups work. In even the most controlled task centred group, the interaction provoked between members will lead to attitudes being expressed and examined, and the most free flowing process centred group will often start their deliberations with a specific problem.

The distinction is, however, useful in considering the role of the group leader and the way in which the different types of group evolve.

It is important to bear in mind the attitudes of the individuals who join a group. They will often have no preconceived ideas as to whether the group is task or process orientated. The ways in which they will react to each other are unpredictable as also is their response to the group leader. They may at once resent his authority or, alternatively, they may idealize him. Over the course of time their attitudes may change, and as the group matures they may rebel against him.

The leader of the group, be it task or process orientated, must be prepared to deal with these conflicts and tensions. He will try to identify with the group members and share their experiences. His role is perhaps best expressed by the French word 'animateur' rather than the English word 'leader'.

Task centred groups

Task centred groups are necessarily concerned with specific goals and the ground work must be prepared in detail by the tutor. This may involve a text, a sequence of problems, a preliminary mini-lecture, video-tape or film, a presentation by one or a group of students, a set of illustrations, folders of documents, research papers, or prescribed preliminary reading. The material should be provocative and challenging.

Problem-solving exercises are one of the many types of activity which can be used in this sort of group. Case material can be presented in a sequential manner in the way that a patient management question is set out, but by means of slides, or on cards if slides are not available; the group can then respond to the data presented in stages. The members may reveal that they do not recognize the relevance of the knowledge they possess in solving the group problem. If the tutor can cull from the group members a coherent pattern of facts and connections, they are often startled to realize how much they know and from this begin to understand how to make the knowledge usefully available at other times.

Basic skills such as interviewing can be practised, either through role-play or by a modified type of role-play in which the student conducts the interview which is recorded on video-tape and this is then watched by the group and discussed in detail. As they all participate in turn, no one is in a position of being able to criticize without being criticized, which usually prevents any student being hurt too much, though the tutor has a reponsibility to see that this does not occur.

Developing critical faculties can be achieved by getting the students to read a research paper. The skill of reading critically is often one that is ignored, and help with ways of appreciating the value of a piece of work by using the group to state their points of agreement and disagreement with the thesis, backed by evidence or reasoning can be very valuable to them for the rest of their professional lives.

Many of the methods described in Chapters 10, 11, 12 and 40 are used in the small group setting.

In general it is in learning to apply principles to both familiar and unfamiliar situations that the task centred group is most appropriate. The ways in which the group leader may achieve this overall objective are many and varied. His role is to determine in advance the lessons he wishes his group to learn, and yet, during the discussion to remain open to opportunities presented by the group to develop any useful and relevant points. He should be sensitive to the interests of the group and allow them to explore promising lines of discussion without straying too far from the original objectives. He must take some control of the more talkative members and encourage the more reticent. He must be aware that what is exciting to one member may be profoundly boring to another and try to keep the group moving productively together.

In task centred groups, the leader is much more authoritative than in the process centred groups; at the same time he must beware of talking too much. The work of the task centred group is fairly well defined. The leader's role is to catalyse the interactions between group members which ensures that the work is done.

Process centred groups

Most tutors will be relatively at ease with task centred group work, but process centred group work requires a different approach for a variety of reasons. These groups are occupied with free, associative discussion, with little direction from the group leader. They proceed slowly and therefore require more time. In these groups the leader does not predetermine his learning objectives, but promotes the interaction of members of the group. The group is challenged to develop its own discipline and in due course to set its own objectives. The leader's role is that of encouraging and ensuring that the group in general keeps to its own rules. He is more like a referee who ensures that the game proceeds smoothly and without fouls, than the leader of the task centred group who may be compared with a coach, who rehearses his group along well tried pathways.

This sort of group can be used for developing professional skills and communication, understanding personal bias and can lead to creative problem solving. It can promote understanding, which has both a personal and group dimension. Understanding is something an individual does in terms of the grasp of a relationship. In a process centred group each member contributes his understanding and ideas and may modify them in the light of the contribution of the other members. It is through the discussion that he relates their viewpoints to his own. This method of learning will be unfamiliar to most group members. It may require considerable adjustment to their preconceived ideas which can be painful and may threaten the progress of the group. The ultimate objective is that the group members should obtain a greater understanding of themselves and their potential and that this should promote good discussion and effective problem solving and management.

Before discussing the ways in which the group may be formed and developed, it is worth considering the role of the individual group members and the leader of the group.

The individual group member

Every member of the group learns and contributes to the learning of all other members. Most individuals join a group with very vague concepts of what this will mean for them. They may be prepared to make a commitment to regular group work but may be startled to find that rather than receiving authoritative advice, they are left to struggle with each other in the group in determining how the group should develop. The individual may be challenged, not just at an intellectual level, but on a personal and emotional level about his behaviour and his pattern of work. He will almost certainly go through periods of self-examination and wondering whether the group is helping him to mature as a doctor or simply destroying such confidence as he possesses. At this stage, he needs the support of other members of the group and the group leader until he can interpret intellectually lessons which he may have learned painfully at the emotional level.

The leader of the group

The leader must be concerned about every individual and try to ensure that each grows both professionally and personally. He must respond to the way in which each member behaves in the group as well as being aware of the working of the group as a whole. Do the members help each other? Who are the questioning ones and the silently approving ones? Who is ignored and who arouses hostility? Are one member's contributions over-valued? Who sits next to whom? Talkative members sometimes hog the limelight, quiet members are not heard, and may become resentful.

The leader of the small group must have knowledge of the field of work in which the group is operating in terms of its task, and have experience of work in small groups. Both are essential. Someone who is extremely skilled in group dynamics may be useless in a group dealing with field work he does not know. Michael and Enid Balint who pioneered group learning methods for general practitioners in the 1950s were unsure at first whether leaders other than psychoanalysts could function properly, but were always sure that psychoanalysts who were unwilling to learn about general practice would be ineffective. Latterly, groups have been led by general practitioners who have had enough group experience to absorb the necessary understanding of group dynamics.

The leader has a double identity in the group and has to be particularly careful about the attitudes and values he brings into discussion and how he behaves as a person. Most leaders talk too much, even though they may repeatedly resolve not to do so. Sometimes frank teaching may be appropriate but the temptation of 'telling the group what' must always be resisted. It is sometimes hard for the leader to be patient, but it is the nature of the exercise to have to allow time for the group to learn from themselves and an attempt to shorten the process may actually destroy it altogether.

Any authority the leader may have must be concentrated on the responsibility for enabling the group to become a growing one. Any group discussion follows a pattern of words and silences. The leader must allow a silence to spread if it is an important moment. It is all to easy to break it with anxious interjections. The discussion may be moved forward at times by projecting an image which somehow crystallizes the groping efforts of the members for a way forward. Too much agreement may bring the discussion to a halt. The silent member must be observed to see if he is taking something in. The talkative member's capacity to listen is assessed. All the rules are only an aid towards self-discipline in the work of the group but some are useful. Too much personal exposure by a member may have to be headed off. Cynical attitudes must be discouraged. Most importantly the imagination must be allowed to range freely without being ridiculed.

If possible, rigidity must be reduced and a freer style of communication encouraged so that insight may dawn, especially into the personal bias which every member (including the leader) brings to the group. In this way, an atmosphere of freedom can develop during the work. This is the group focusing on the professional problems it is discussing and not ostensibly on each other's problems in the expectation that every member will learn something about himself without being threatened and so be enabled to grow a little in maturity. Group interpretations should be used sparingly, even by those skilled in making them.

It must be remembered that any group members coming together may have collective expectations of what they will get from the leader and these may be quite different from the goals that the leader hopes the group may achieve. In the process of the group's work, the leader's goals must be accepted by the group as both more real and more satisfying than their own initial set, and this acceptance must not be sought at an unacceptably high price of frustration and hostility towards the leader. At the same time, the leader must always be open to learning something from the group, for only in this way can he remain sincerely a member of the group as well as their leader.

Leading a small group may seem to have been described in terms of great difficulty. The leader requires training and skill and perhaps a capacity to blend intellectual and emotional understanding at almost the same time. But, so too does the general practitioner in his work with patients. It needs time, because the nature of group process needs time. But it is not magic and can be learned by those who are motivated to do so and enjoy working with others in small groups to a professional end.

Formation of a process centred group

A group should ideally be formed of members selected by the leader. But, in most cases this is impossible. The leader is usually faced with an assortment of trainees or doctors, not of his own choosing and whom he must get to know as quickly as possible. He will observe their dress, manner, whether they are talkative or silent, who they sit next to and so on, in order to make a preliminary assessment of the members.

The size of the group may be equally beyond the leader's powers to determine. A small group may be between six and 12 people. Fewer than six tends to put a great deal of pressure on all the members, and the absence of a single member has a great effect, usually negative. A group larger than 12 tends to be unwieldy, in that the time for each member to have his say is reduced and may raise frustration to unendurable levels. This often causes fragmentation with sub-groups having a conversation while the rest of the group is engaged in the mainstream of the work.

Preparing the setting

Process centred groups are less structured than task centred groups and in consequence need a more stable setting. Meetings should be regular, at the same time, in the same place and if possible with the same furniture arranged in the same way. Chairs must be reasonably comfortable and ventilation adequate. With groups of more than 12, the circle of chairs tends to be too large. A large number of people may also produce fug, especially if some members smoke, and this may make the group sleepy and inattentive.

A large table is a great barrier to the exchange a process group is seeking and it is best to have no furniture at all within the circle although a small table may be useful if, for instance, a recording of the meeting is being made, so that there is a stand for the microphone.

The first meeting

The group mostly assembles in an irregular fashion. Individuals begin to arrive and engage each other in conversation. When a certain number has collected, not uncommonly, a silence falls on the group. Desultory conversation may break out with awkward silences recurring. The leader becomes a focus for attention. He is aware that he is expected to do something. At this point he may confide his anxieties to the group, thus sharing them at an early stage in the formation of the group. Alternatively, he may remain aloof, awaiting the assembly of the whole group. Whatever approach the leader takes the first meeting is always a testing occasion.

Once the group has assembled he must introduce himself in terms of his educational role and professional experience and invite each member in turn to give a brief account of his learning or professional experience to date. The leader must then explain the broad outline of his strategy with regard to the work of the group. This is not easy — if he is too specific he will either restrict the work of the group members too much, or give the impression that he is going to be directive. If on the other hand, his outline is vague or sketchy, he may induce a high level of anxiety related to the uncertainty of the members as to what the work is all about.

Most process groups start with actual case discussion, though it must be remembered that it is the group interaction to the reported professional relationship which is of the greatest importance in the work of this type of group. The members of the group are concentrating on their view of this reported relationship and their remarks occur naturally in that context. They are unaware that most of their responses reflect their personal values and way of expression. It is to this that the leader must pay the keenest attention. If he is too concerned with case material himself he will fail in his function.

Some leaders feel that they must involve all group members as soon as possible. Others will wish to observe the natural pattern of talkative and silent members for a while, before deciding whether this balance should be altered in any way.

The development of the group

The development of the group commonly follows a recognizable pattern. This is well described by Cockburn and Ross.[1] They recognize various stages in the development of the group which include appraisal, anxiety, conflict, dependency, etc. Each group is of course unique and the way in which these different stages affect the members varies as does the response of the leader.

At the first stage, the member's appraise each other's attitudes, backgrounds, status and intelligence. They are reluctant to expose themselves, being wary of involvement and fearful of non-acceptance. They are uncertain about the learning method and uneasy about the role of the leader.

The leader must now start to unfold the ground rules of his method, allowing a bold member of the group, perhaps, to start a presentation, but watchful of all that goes on. He, too, has anxieties as he may lose the confidence of the group because this teaching method is strange to most group members and the lack of direction is usually alarming. It is rare for a group to fail rapidly, but while some groups seek a way forward, employing their interactions, others resist accepting responsibility. If the discussion becomes blocked, some groups will review the situation and see what they have achieved, while others will cease to discuss and become angry with the leader's apparent ineffectual authority.

It is at this stage that the leader needs all his skills for group work. Conflict is almost inevitable but he must be able to recognize whether this is healthy and likely to lead to ultimate cohesion or whether it is destructive, leading to the dissolution of the group. Over the first few weeks the leader will be watching these developments.

In a growing group there is open disagreement as attitudes become clearer, differences are exposed and personal conflicts emerge. Resolution can often be achieved by stressing common ground, or finding a new synthesis. Gradually, involvement and identification of each other's problems grow and knowledge is assimilated through the experience of emotional learning. The discussion ranges more freely and more widely and new themes emerge. Group standards begin to develop. Discussion is disciplined and productive.

In the failing group, in contrast, there is increasing assertion of individual positions. Sub-groups may form. Some members may withdraw and others display studied indifference or even aggressiveness. The group will fall back on insisting on dependency on the leader while at the same time expressing frustrated hostility. They may escape by transferring responsibility. A substitute leader may emerge or pairs may form within the group. This may give temporary relief to the group but prevent the leader from realizing his role. In the failing group control is never taken by the group as a whole. Rarely, groups simply fail to mature and must be disbanded.

A group which has successfully grown together must, in due course, face the problem of termination. Over periods of months or years a group may become introspective and concerned with its own existence and does not wish to die. In these cases the leader must prepare for the end of the group some time before it is disbanded.

This portrayal of the successful group as compared with the failing group illustrates two extreme examples. Most groups fall somewhere in-between. There may be periods when they may become bogged down, when perhaps they may lose one or two members, but they then rally to do useful work.

Conclusion

The task centred group is relatively easy to run and is appropriate for undergraduate students, trainees, and for continuing education. It can beplanned to work together for periods as short as four weeks or for many years. It can set and re-set its objectives as it matures and its success can usually be measured against these objectives.

The process centred group seeks to produce more far reaching effects on those taking part. It challenges their beliefs and attitudes and abilities to work one with another in order to explore developing relationships. It is not suitable for short term work with undergraduates. It has been used with trainees over a period as short as one year, but it is particularly valuable as a continuing educational experience during the early years in general practice.

Reference

[1] Cockburn, B. and Ross, A. (1977) *Working Together*. Lancaster: School of Education, University of Lancaster.

Further Reading

Bion, W.R (1968) *Experiences in Groups*. London: Tavistock Publications.

9

The lecture
John Howie

The remarkable drop in prestige of the formal lecture has affected teaching in general practice more than in most other disciplines. In postgraduate education this in part reflects the general swing from hospital-based to general practice-based teaching, but the trend has been exaggerated because most general practitioners lack experience not only in delivering but also in planning and preparing lectures. Despite the proper modern emphasis on one-to-one and small group teaching, good lectures still have an important place, sometimes setting the scene for group work or more general discussion, but often because a well-structured talk is sometimes the best way of allowing a speaker to reach a large audience in a reasonably personal way.

Both vocational training and continuing education would be much the stronger if more of the many general practitioners with something individual to say about their ideas and their methods could be encouraged to talk to trainee meetings, to groups of their established colleagues or to audiences of hospital doctors. There is no reason why anyone who can qualify as a doctor should feel the techniques beyond him, and this short chapter attempts to give a few hints first on planning and preparing, and secondly on delivering a lecture. The chapter concludes with a brief comment on the related theme of the use of audio-visual aids, dealt with more fully in Chapter 12.

Planning and preparing

Objectives

As in any form of teaching, the essential starting point for preparing a lecture is the definition of objectives. At least all lecturers have in common their past experiences as members of audiences and know how true it is that concentration falls precipitately after the first seven to ten minutes of a lecture. Also, unless notes are taken, only a very few points of fact are retained longer than minutes after they have been made. I believe the lecturer should decide on not more than three factual objectives for his talk; if he insists on making more, he should try to group them so that he can end by summarizing his talk on the basis of three main points. Almost as important is deciding, as an extra objective, what kind of overall impression he wants to leave with his audience. Concepts such as enthusiasm, humanity or orderliness of thinking can be effectively communicated, and may in the end be the most important message taken away from a teaching session. By default, it is equally possible to communicate pomposity, dogmatism, over-confidence and intellectual disarray simply because these are all styles which people subconsciously use to cover lack of preparation.

Outlines

A good lecture must be personal. It should use illustrative material from the lecturer's own experiences, whether these be clinical, the results of original work or the interpretation of the work of others. The younger the lecturer the greater the risk of using anecdotes from clinical experience — these are not necessarily invalid but often come across as inappropriate. Quotations from the work of others has a correspondingly small part to play in the lecture given by 'an authority' whose own views are usually what the audience want to hear. Using a single sheet of paper, the outline should now be sketched in; the skeleton I use is usually along the following lines.
1. An opening which is personal to the audience I am addressing, including reference to the theme and the factual objectives I want to cover.
2, 3 and 4. Separate paragraphs dealing with each of my main issues (usually three) in turn, and noting the main illustrative material to be used for each.
5. A final part which summarizes the factual material which has been presented and leads into a final comment which may focus the audience on any overall conceptual point I have been trying to make.

Details

The outline I have sketched allows the balance of the talk to be decided and this will dictate the time to be given to each heading as well as the number of slides or other illustrations that will be needed or appropriate at different points. Apart from the occasional very formal lecture where a longer prepared script is read more or less verbatim, most lectures will vary between about 15 and 25 minutes in length and this allows time both to develop the main issues chosen and to portray the style the lecturer wants; this amount of time is usually short enough to allow the audience's attention to be held — given the proper use of illustrative aids. The main decision to be taken is how detailed the notes to be used by the speaker should be. This — as is everything to do with speaking in public — is personal to the individual. In general, the more that a lecture is read, the less likely it is that it will be memorable. An excellent compromise, useful both for the inexperienced speaker and for the regular lecturer on an occasion where his theme is new or his audience unusual, is to write out and if necessary read, the first page or two (about two minutes per page) and the last page or two. Notes, in whatever detail necessary, should be prepared to assist delivery of the rest of the talk. As well as being written on cards or on paper, they may of course be put on slides for the benefit of lecturer and audience.

No lecture should ever be given without proper preparation. If the talk is a new one, it should be planned at least a month in advance to allow time to consult necessary references, and for preparation of visual aids. No matter how familiar the theme is to the speaker, the needs of different audiences are always individual; the greatest mistake is to feel that notes or a text used on a previous occasion can be taken out at an hour's notice and used as they stand. It is wrong to believe that experienced speakers do not need to prepare; they do. It is, however, true that because they are used to speaking and usually know their topic well, they can prepare unusually quickly. The first-time lecturer rarely gets caught out by under-preparation. But the occasional speaker, gaining in confidence and becoming over-committed, all too often does.

Delivery

Anyone who does not feel nervous at the thought of, and especially immediately before, giving a lecture, ought to! The extra adrenalin is on balance an asset and should not be a cause for worry; if preparation has been adequate, everything should be all right. Delivering a lecture includes making preliminary enquiries and, if possible, an on-site inspection before the talk starts. How do the lights work, do you need to use a microphone, where should you stand to avoid interfering with the line of vision to the screen (particularly if an overhead projector is being used) and is there chalk for the board and a pointer for slides? Although the size of an audience can never be guaranteed, it is usual to be able to find out whether it is likely to be in the 30 or under range (where informality is necessary), between 40 and 80 (where informality becomes more difficult), or over 80 (where informality is likely to be inappropriate). It is a help to know the probable mix of the audience both in terms of experience and specialties. It is a help to know of any authorities in your field who will be present, to know who may oppose your views, and about any other particular awkwardness you may be faced with. It is always helpful to know whether you are part of a course of lectures, either on the same day or over an extended time, and to use this information in your introduction to set the scene to your advantage.

Always have notes with you — even if only in your pocket. It is a mistake to believe that this is a sign of weakness. If, at any point, you lose the track of your message, then consult them properly before resuming. The audience will prefer this to having to endure a long series of repetitions or irrelevancies while you feel your way back to dry ground. It is often easier to find your way again if using notes rather than a text, as it is often difficult to find the right point to resume reading after a digression from the prepared script. If you do expect to use and to depart from a prepared text, asterisk or underline suitable points at which re-entry will be possible and natural. When speaking, remember that the less formal a talk, the less is it necessary to stay in one position throughout its delivery; however, undue movement is distracting and should be avoided, as of course should the repetitive use of pet words or phrases.

At the start of your talk it is a good idea to address a few general remarks to the Chairman and audience; these should be friendly and can help greatly to win the empathy of the audience — who usually want to be on your side. Avoid apologising; never say you cannot think why you have been asked (an insult to your host) or that you have nothing to say, or that you were thinking last night what to say (an insult to your audience). Be positive; say what you are going to say, say it, say what you have said, sign off and sit down.

A little bit of humour is often appropriate and usually welcome. It should, however, fit with what you are saying and be carefully selected. Racial, religious and 'blue' jokes should be avoided. It is also courteous to dress smartly and essential to appear punctually. Speak for the length of time you have been given — alternatively for less time than has been allocated, and certainly not for longer.

Discussion

The last issue to be considered when lecturing is the degree to which audience participation should be encouraged. The inexperienced speaker is probably better to give his talk first and answer questions afterwards, but with a bit of experience and an audience like a day-release trainee course it is often valuable to allow a lecture to develop more along the lines of a structured tutorial. Once again careful thought in preparation and careful selection of visual aids helps the lecturer regain the floor at the time and place in his session that he chooses.

Questions and answers during or after the talk can cause difficulty if empathy between speaker and audience has been poor. Avoid becoming involved in personalized dispute; criticize ideas or interpretations but tread carefully before debating motives or ethics.

Visual aids

As well as acting as an aide-memoire for the speaker, appropriate visual aids can increase the effectiveness of any lecture. Because visual stimuli are often more effective than auditory stimuli, as much care should be taken in planning their use, as in deciding what to say. Quantity, quality and content all have to be right. As a simple generalization, ten slides or their equivalent is the maximum appropriate for a half-hour talk. In constructing slides, detail should be discarded in favour of simplicity. Overhead projector material has the advantage of being more quickly prepared and not requiring professional help. But poorly done it is a distraction from what may otherwise be a good talk. Remember that many overhead projectors distort because of errors of angle of the screen, and that freehand drawing during a lecture is only rarely other than untidy. The skilled use of a blackboard remains one of the best visual teaching assets and the prospective lecturer should learn its proper use. No other medium better allows the step-by-step construction of a message which will remain on view after the talk has finished. Similarly, an appropriate and simple handout may be given to supplement a lecture; give it out before or after — not during your talk. On the whole, stay with one audio-visual method during a lecture; duplication tends to confuse.

Some people find strange ways of enjoying themselves, and giving lectures may be one of these. Well done, the lecture not only provides a valuable service to groups of colleagues, but can genuinely be an enjoyable and stimulating activity. The more the care given to its planning and delivery the greater the chance that both audience and speaker will enjoy and benefit from the occasion.

Further reading

Evans, M. (1978) 'The abuse of slides'. *British Medical Journal, 1,* 905-908.

10
Managing a project
Robin Fraser

Introduction

Much of the time spent by students and trainees is taken up with the acquisition of knowledge and skills within the constraints of a set curriculum. This may afford little opportunity for the integration of individual initiative, self-learning and the application of knowledge derived from different disciplines. Project work can help to provide this extra dimension. Central to the concept of project work is the collection of data in a form capable of analysis. This usually requires creative but disciplined thinking, good organization, communication skills and the ability to evaluate in a critical way the work of oneself and others — qualities essential for the provision of good clinical care.

Definition

The Chambers Dictionary defines a project as 'a scheme of something to be done'. An alternative listed definition is 'a speculative imagination'. A working definition of a project could be 'a scheme of something to be done arising from a speculative imagination'.

Guidelines for teachers

General organization

Projects may be carried out individually or in groups, and the subject matter may be self-generated or imposed by the teachers. Because of the constraints of medical school curricula, most student projects are carried out by small groups of students working co-operatively, and the topic is selected by the teachers. It is suggested that no choice of topic be offered to medical students working in groups as they tend to spend most of their time deciding which one to choose! Trainees, on the other hand, have wider opportunities for individual enterprise carried out in greater depth over a longer period of time on a subject of their own choice.

Medical students may, however, carry out individual projects during an elective period of study, and trainees may benefit greatly from a group approach with fellow trainees or groups of trainers. The choice of individual or group work for a trainee will be determined by the nature of the topic to be studied.

Choice of topic

The choice of topic, whether teacher or learner selected, may be 'open' or 'closed', and must take account of the differing needs and maturity of the students or trainees.

An open topic would indicate a broad area of study. For example, 'The use of antibiotics in general practice'. A closed topic would more closely limit the area of study. For example, 'Are antibiotics appropriately prescribed by general practitioners in the treatment of sore throats?'

The students will usually be obliged to observe and evaluate the work of others, whereas trainees will have greater opportunities for self-audit. For example, a group of students may be asked to answer the question, 'Does general practice provide adequate anticipatory care for children?' The group would be able to monitor the contribution of the practice team in health education, prophylaxis and screening, but they would be confined to the role of observers.

The trainee, however, is in a more advantageous position. Not only can he monitor the practice team contribution but he can also compare and contrast his personal experiences, thus adding an extra dimension to the project.

Time allocation and feasibility

It is most important for students, trainees and teachers to realize that the questions posed in any project must be capable of producing reasonable answers within the time available.

For undergraduates working in groups, we have found at Leicester that approximately three to four hours per week per student is a reasonable period of time to devote to the project. In a group of 12 students over a four week period this amounts to approximately 144–192 hours, and it is surprising how much material can be generated in this time.

The amount of time trainees devote to the project will be much more variable and it is difficult to lay down precise guidelines. A trainee who identifies an area of study through his own interest and curiosity will be motivated to spend considerably more time on the project than a trainee who is unenthusiastic about project work. Time allocation will also depend on the degree of sophistication of the project. Some trainees may prefer to do a series of small projects, while others may prefer to do one large study extending over one year or more. The exact time allocation would be a matter for discussion between trainer and trainee.

It is essential for the individual or group to decide at the outset what strategy to adopt in investigating any particular topic. If the topic was expressed in broad terms then one approach would be to investigate all aspects in a fairly superficial way. An alternative approach would be to concentrate on a smaller sub-area and investigate in some depth. For example, in the 'anticipatory care of children in general practice' project one group may measure the contribution of all members of the practice team to all aspects of anticipatory care to arrive at a fairly superficial overall picture. An alternative strategy would be to identify, say, immunization procedures, and to investigate thoroughly all aspects of this single area.

Assessment

Some form of assessment of any project will be necessary whether group or individual projects are undertaken. The degree of sophistication and detail involved in any assessment will obviously relate to the scope of the study undertaken and whether it is to be formally marked or not. It is impossible, however, to allocate marks to individuals taking part in a group activity because of the problem of disproportionate contributions within the group. In this latter instance, assessments can be used as a teaching aid in providing the group with critical feedback.

Suitable headings under which assessment could take place might be:
1. Originality.
2. Identification of specific aims and the extent to which these were achieved.
3. Method employed including definitions of terminology and evaluation of factors causing errors and/or bias.
4. Clarity of presentation, verbal or written.
5. Extent to which conclusions reached were justified by the data collected.
6. Extent to which further questions were generated by the work.
7. Extent to which the students or trainees learned from errors committed in the course of the project.

Student guidelines and project briefing

A project briefing should be held at the beginning of the attachment or, if possible, a week or so before to allow more time for reflection and planning. The briefing should provide only the necessary details and the teacher should avoid directing the group towards a particular course of action as this will interfere with the group's initiative and ingenuity. The teacher should, however, be prepared to answer in a 'non-invasive' way, questions generated by the group throughout the planning and operational stages of the project.

The essential tasks to be accomplished at the briefing session are as follows:

1. *The educational objectives should be outlined.* The project aims to give the students experience of:

(a) Planning and working together as a group — so much of medicine involves teamwork.

(b) Identifying and assessing relevant background information, for example from libraries, literature and colleagues — something all doctors have to do throughout their professional lives.

(c) Simple data collection from their practices — this highlights the need for and value of factual information and perhaps sows the seeds of self-audit.

(d) Presenting information to professional colleagues — this demonstrates the value of concise and relevant communication.

2. *General strategy.* Give the students the project topic for their consideration. Advise them that it is essential that they decide at an early stage within the group just how they are going to tackle the subject matter, make some plan for task allocation within the group and make provision for regular group meetings to discuss progress. State that there is a variety of ways in which the subject matter may be considered and that there is no one 'correct way'. Remind them that they may make use of relevant literature, practice medical records and registers. They may also draw on their clinical experiences in the consultation and elsewhere, and further information may be derived from patients or clinical teachers by interview or questionnaire. It is important to stress, however, that the initiative and choices must come from themselves.

3. *Time allocation.* As indicated this should be of the order of three to four hours per week per student outside the normal teaching schedules. It is important that this guidance is given to avoid the risk of over-enthusiastic students neglecting their other clinical teaching.

4. *Presentation of project.* Indicate that they will be expected to present to the clinical teachers, and perhaps fellow students if there is more than one group involved, an account of the findings at a time to be specifically set aside. Explain that the structure of the presentation and how many members of the group will be involved in the actual presentation will be for themselves to consider. If appropriate indicate that slide projectors, overhead projectors or photocopying facilities will be available to them if they wish to use them. A strict time limit should be allocated for their formal presentation, followed by time for discussion. In addition they may be expected to present a succinct written account of their project.

5. *Assessment.* Explain that the project work will not attract marks which would count in a student's overall assessment as it is impossible to allocate marks fairly to individuals taking part in a group activity. Depending on the circumstances it is reasonable to advise the students,

however, that they may be asked questions about the project as part of an oral examination, if that oral examination is already part of their assessment procedure.

6. *Post briefing discussion.* The teacher should then allow the students approximately three-quarters of an hour to answer any questions which have arisen from their discussions.

Some students find their introduction to project work a perplexing proposition, and endeavour to subvert the teacher into providing a plan of action for them. The teacher is advised to endure what can be an uncomfortable experience by responding only to the problems identified by the students. He must at all costs resist the temptation to 'take over' the project. He should encourage the students to think and use their initiative, otherwise the value of the project to the students will be diminished. In retrospect most students are grateful for this non-directional approach as it allows them 'to get more out of the project'. A small minority of students will remain resentful of project work throughout.

Student reaction

A formal enquiry by questionnaire[1] of the opinions of fourth year medical students regarding their perceived value of project work produced the following results. The students worked in groups of eight with an imposed topic and no formal marks were awarded. Seventy per cent of students thought that the project was 'worthwhile and allowed me to gain fresh insight into the difficulties and constraints of organizing observations in general practice'. Comments ranged from 'very stimulating' to 'a complete waste of time'. They appeared, predictably, to achieve and value the project more when they found the topic relevant although challenging. Teachers should bear this in mind.

Trainee guidelines

For smaller scale projects the teacher's role will be little different from that relating to undergraduate groups, except that relationships will be closer as the teacher will be working on a one-to-one basis with the trainee over a prolonged period of time. As the trainee will be choosing a topic of particular personal interest the teacher may require to do some background studies to acquaint himself with the subject matter, as it may not necessarily reflect his particular interests. In the event of the project being a highly sophisticated study, the teacher may wish to collaborate with one or more members of the academic staff of the local university department. This would be of particular value if statistical or computer analysis were to be required. If the quality of the project is sufficiently high the trainee should be encouraged to submit a paper for publication.

Conclusion

As an educational exercise project work can be challenging, rewarding and perplexing for students, trainees and teachers alike.

Reference

[1] General Practice Course Assessment, 1979-80, University of Leicester, (unpublished).

11
Role-playing
Brian and Pauline McAvoy

Simulation techniques have long been recognized as valuable teaching tools in the training of such diverse groups as aircraft pilots, management personnel and the Armed Forces. One of their main advantages is that they enable the learner to practise and develop complex skills in a safe setting.

Role-playing is one such technique which has particular relevance to medical education. It has the benefit of allowing the participants to 'learn by doing', but avoids putting patients at risk from exposure to practitioners lacking in knowledge and experience. Although role-playing cannot replace direct clinical contact, there are situations where it may be a more appropriate vehicle for learning. These include psycho-social problems, e.g. bereavement or sexual difficulties, and acute medical or surgical emergencies, e.g. chest pain or abdominal pain. By giving the learner the opportunity to be 'in the driving seat', role-playing can provide valuable experience and enhancement of clinical competence and confidence.

Topics

Role-play can be employed at any level of medical teaching, although the objectives for undergraduates, trainees and established principals may differ.

It provides a method of exploring the following areas:
1. Knowledge
    (a) The consultation — its structure and variants.
    (b) Problems of communication — verbal and non-verbal.
    (c) Differential diagnosis.
    (d) Investigations.
    (e) Therapeutics.
2. Skills
    (a) Interviewing.
    (b) Social and interpersonal.
    (c) Problem-solving.
    (d) Management.
3. Attitudes
    (a) The difficulties of being a doctor.
    (b) The difficulties of being a patient.
    (c) Ethical issues, e.g. contraception, abortion, confidentiality.

In addition, role-play can give the learner valuable insight into his own attitudes and behaviour, while allowing him to experiment with alternate courses of action without risk to patients.

As each role-play develops, the 'doctor' will realize that a wide variety of behavioural and clinical responses is possible. It is important to emphasize to the learner that the object of the exercise is not to discover 'right' or 'wrong' solutions, but to facilitate examination and analysis of the consultation, and the behaviour and responses of the doctor and the patient.

Method

The technique of role-playing involves two individuals who take the parts of doctor and patient respectively, and attempt to recreate a consultation. The material can be drawn from an actual encounter which has been recently observed or participated in, or from a hypothethical encounter based on previous experience, e.g. a schoolgirl requesting the contraceptive pill or a busy executive asking for a check-up. The former source can give the role-player a greater opportunity to 'get under the skin' of the patient he is portraying, thus presenting the doctor with a more realistic situation.

Role-playing is not the same as play-acting. It does not require so much acting in the physical sense as a feeling for the part of the patient. The role-player who is the patient soon finds that he or she is able to interpret not only the appropriate difficulties of communication, but may also come to feel something of the patient's own confusion, reticence and fears. The individual who takes on the role of doctor becomes so absorbed by the problem he or she is trying to solve, that clinical anxiety will largely oust any vestiges of performance anxiety.

What characterizes a role-play consultation is that it grows naturally from its own situation and information. In this sense there is no script, only a working scenario. The consultation starts with a clinical problem posed by the patient and what develops is left largely to the creativity of the role-players.

One variant of this technique is the use of a simulated patient. Unlike role-players, who are members of the learning group (students or trainees), simulated patients are individuals (often actors) who have been carefully programmed to take on a specific role. That is to say they become well versed in the presentation of a particular clinical problem, are fully acquainted with the psychological and social components of the clinical situation, and are skilled in reproducing a wide variety of responses within the consultation. The use of this technique allows the development of clinical skills in a more structured situation than is possible in role-play, but because of the personnel and training required it is more suited to university-based teaching.

However, role-play is eminently suitable as a teaching tool for use in the general practice setting. It can be used as readily with small groups of learners as with individual students or trainees. In the former situation the general practitioner teacher can act as one of the role-players or as a facilitator for the group discussion. With his own trainee or student he can participate directly in the role-play, usually taking the part of the patient. This enables him to present a variety of clinical problems, and to observe directly the knowledge, skills and attitudes of the learner.

It is important to realize that there is no need for a role-play to be pre-arranged or set aside as a formal teaching session. It can be effectively used in the course of an informal case discussion over morning coffee, or while driving to a visit.

Advantages

Role-play provides an excellent vehicle for the exploration of knowledge, skills and attitudes in a 'no risk' situation. Learners can examine and test alternative courses of action without fear of harming or upsetting patients.

The student or trainee can also gain valuable insight into his or her behaviour and attitudes, and can experience what it is like to be in the patient's place. Indeed, Chekhov, himself a doctor, said he would devote a substantial portion of medical students' time in training to make them realize what it was like to be a patient.

Criticisms

One of the commonest criticisms levelled at role-play is that it is 'unreal', an elaborate device for creating artificial situations. However, as pointed out by Byrne and Long, it is not intended as a substitute for reality but is simply a safe introduction to reality.[1]

A more valid criticism is that not all learners are able to 'tune in' to the atmosphere of a simulated consultation. In practice, however, this is a rare occurrence, as the participants rapidly become absorbed in their roles, irrespective of the setting or the presence of observers.

Another criticism is that role-play is only appropriate for psycho-social problems, since physical signs cannot be readily reproduced. This problem can be easily overcome by briefing the participants beforehand to break from the role-play when the doctor wishes to perform a physical examination. He then asks the patient specific questions related to his examination, e.g. What is the blood pressure? Is there any tenderness in the epigastrium? The patient answers the questions directly, avoiding prompting the doctor or providing him with unsolicited information. Once the 'examination' has been completed, the role-play is resumed. The use of this technique allows a full range of physical, social and psychological problems to be explored.

Practical application

The following example may serve to illustrate the potential teaching opportunities offered by role-play. The general practitioner teacher plays the patient who consulted him at one of his recent surgeries, his student or trainee the doctor.

Mrs B, a 62-year-old housewife, opens the consultation by saying, 'I don't want to waste your time, doctor — I know you're so busy. All I want is a tonic — I've been feeling so tired recently'. She remains diffident and apologetic, but on direct questioning by the doctor reveals a six-month history of alternating diarrhoea and constipation, with one stone weight loss. She continues to play down these symptoms, 'I'm sure everything will be all right if I just have a pick-me-up'.

Physical examination reveals evidence of pallor, recent weight loss and a fullness in the left iliac fossa.

The doctor suggests referral to hospital for further investigation but she makes several spurious excuses for 'not having time' to attend. When pressed further she asks, 'Is it serious, doctor?'. He replies, 'There now, Mrs B, let me do the worrying, that's what I'm here for'.

The consultation ends with Mrs B receiving a prescription for a tonic and reluctantly agreeing to further investigation.

It is often helpful in discussing a consultation to look upon it as having three parts: the opening, the middle and the closure. Using this framework, the following issues might be raised:

1. Opening:
   (a) introductions and strategies for reducing anxiety;
   (b) control of the consultation — the use of leading questions;
   (c) the use of silence.
2. Middle:
   (a) history-taking;
   (b) appropriate physical examination;
   (c) differential diagnosis;
   (d) extent and timing of appropriate investigations;
   (e) coping with uncertainty.
3. Closure:
   (a) control of the consultation — was the patient allowed to talk enough?
   (b) how much should the patient be told — sharing anxieties;
   (c) how much responsibility should the doctor take?
   (d) methods of terminating the consultation.

Conclusion

Although role-play has been long established as a teaching method in numerous spheres, it has, until recently, been notably absent in medical education. Once initial inhibitions have been overcome, it can offer an excellent opportunity for learning to both undergraduates and postgraduates, enabling them to explore their knowledge, skills and attitudes in a safe setting. These simulated consultations can be used to integrate the learning of knowledge, skills and attitudes which can complement and enhance learning from real patients.

Role-play is adaptable, informal, requires no special equipment or training, and is thus a particularly valuable teaching method for the general practitioner.

Reference

[1] Byrne, P.S. and Long, B.E.L. (1975) *Learning to Care, Person to Person,* 2nd Edition, Edinburgh: Churchill Livingstone. pp. 67-79.

Further reading

Marinker, M. (1972) 'A teachers' workshop'. *Journal of the Royal College of General Practitioners, 22,* 553.

Working party of the Royal College of General Practitioners (1972) *The Future General Practitioner; Learning and teaching.* London: British Medical Association, pp. 225-227.

12
Audio-visual aids
James Knox

This chapter aims to set out basic principles to help the general practitioner teaching in the setting in which he is most familiar — his own general practice. It follows that complex technology applicable to the large classroom and special teaching centre will *not* feature, though reference will be made to video-cassettes because they are likely to become more readily available in the 1980s.

The matters considered here are *aids* to teaching and learning; they are subsidiary to the teaching and learning, and should be viewed only as agents useful in *promoting* learning. It is my experience that the strength of clinical teaching often lies as much in the impact of the situation and of the patient as in the teacher or any gadgets with which he may be surrounded. A useful starting point might be that most familiar of audio-aids, the telephone.

Telecommunications and teaching

There are several ways in which the telephone can be harnessed to assist the medical trainee or student.

Taking a turn as 'receptionist'

Many trainers already invite the trainee to stand in for a receptionist for, say, a morning, with the simple remit of answering calls. He would be required to record their nature, to classify them (as calls relating to appointments, home visits, repeat prescriptions, etc.) and indicate the responses he deemed appropriate to each. The resulting material is likely to make for a useful seminar on these and related topics.

Tape recordings of telephone calls

Some practices employ telephone answering machines on which the caller records a message. Simple replay can be a revealing process in which possible dangers of this method can be brought home, e.g. the caller who appears (erroneously) to believe that the recorded message is a 'live' telephone conversation.

Recording calls for teaching. Equipment (see Appendix) is now readily available which will capture telephone conversations on a cassette tape-recorder. Experience in using this method with out-of-hours calls shows that it provides a rich source of material which raises numerous issues of fundamental importance. These include ethical considerations of the procedure, capturing the basic elements on which priorities have to be decided (and these may include life-and-death issues), dealing with the guilt-ridden anxious relative out-of-hours, and many frankly clinical problems. The replaying of information obtained in this way can be a painful experience, revealing sometimes more about the doctor than the patient.

The telephone can be used in numerous other ways: most trainers will already give advice at long range in the course of the day-to-day work relating to patients. Advantage can be taken of 'hot' situations to put across other elements relating to the *principles* of the issue concerned as well as specific advice on the particular problem, for example, the trainee confronted by unexpected death on making a routine return visit, and who telephones for advice in this situation.

Long-distance learning

An extension of the use of the telephone in teaching at a distance is the 'dial-a-message' services available in certain centres (e.g. 'DAMES' — the Dundee service). By dialling a certain number, the (doctor) subscriber can obtain a two-minute recorded talk on a current topic thought to be of interest. Such gratuitous information is probably of limited value, unless it happens to be related to a subject that is engaging the doctor's interest at the time.

Experiments have been conducted in areas where geography and long distances pose problems in continuing education for general practice. The most spectacular of such enterprises is the use made of orbiting satellites in the 'Telstar' project in Newfoundland and Labrador to relay postgraduate meetings 'live' to receivers in remote areas.

A tape-recorder in the practice

The ordinary cassette recorder can be used in teaching in general practice. Articles on different aspects of the subject are appearing with increasing frequency, e.g. 'Ethical considerations',[1] 'Methods of analysing the content of the recording'[2] and 'Relating patient knowledge to what goes on in the consultation'.[3] It is evident that considerable potential exists in the use of tape-recordings of consultations to learn from one's own interviews. To obtain the most from this, at least three factors should be kept in mind:
1. The patient's permission must be obtained after explaining why the recording is desired; occasionally the parent or responsible relative may be the appropriate person to grant this permission, which can be

incorporated into the tape recording itself. Although the point has not yet been contested in court actions, it may be safer to obtain this permission in writing.

2. Tape-recordings take as long to replay as record. An early lesson learned from this work was the surprisingly large non-verbal component of a consultation (i.e. time taken up by physical examination, writing prescriptions, practical procedures, etc.). So some editing is usually necessary. This can be done both during the recording of the consultation (switching off the recorder during such procedures as physical examination) or on the subsequent replay. Judgement may need to be exercised in this, however, because silences may be of major importance in teaching and learning about the consultation in general practice (see Chapter 20).

3. Positioning of the recorder/microphone is important to pick up significant signals and to reduce background or extraneous noise. Proximity to the speakers (preferably nearer the patient), unobtrusiveness so as not to direct attention unnecessarily to the device, and accessibility of controls (volume, stop, start) are the relevant factors to be considered.

It was this simple device which provided Byrne and Long with the material for their book, which provides a useful approach to consultation analysis in general practice.[4]

Problems in using tapes in teaching

One of the problems of using this type of material for teaching lies in the tendency we all have, as doctors, to listen to the clinical content and fail to hear the 'music' of the consultation. The trainer himself needs to grasp the fact that every consultation has an anatomy and a physiology — sometimes, too, a pathology. Once this concept has been mastered, virtually every recorded interview has a teaching potential.

A second problem in teaching of this nature is the fact that there is not necessarily one 'correct' way of conducting a consultation. It follows that prescriptive teaching along the lines of 'how to do it' has little part to play in the training method. It is more a question of 'if one uses this line in the consultation, then that kind of response is likely to follow'. Each doctor develops his own style, and it may be a matter of helping the trainee to develop a repertoire on which to draw and a sense of appropriateness to match individual situations.

A third problem stems from the personal element in the consultation, namely the material produced by one centre may not always fully meet the demands of individual doctors. There is, on the other hand, a great field for producing material for one's own use both in self-learning and teaching on a one-to-one basis.

A fourth problem concerns the very real difficulties posed by evaluating what has been learned, and assessing the worth of the teaching material itself. This is probably the main reason why the literature contains very few reports on the subject. Nevertheless, I am convinced of the usefulness of this relatively simple method of creating awareness of the complex issues involved in consultations, surely an important first step in training on the subject.

Video-tape

The importance of the consultation as the central issue in clinical medicine has long been recognized, with attention being focused on the verbal exchange between doctor and patient. It is, however, only within recent years that the importance of other aspects — the so-called 'non-verbal communication' — of general practice has been recognized. Progress in teaching on these matters has had to await the introduction of new techniques, and it is in this field that the video-tape recorder has made such an impact.

The video-recording is now being widely used in undergraduate teaching by departments of general practice, and as equipment becomes more available its role in vocational training is being clarified. The previous chapter (Role-playing) and Chapter 20 (Communication between patient and doctor) suggest a number of ways in which video-tape can be used as a tool for teaching.

All the problems associated with sound tape-recordings apply also to video work, which has a few additional added constraints, not the least of which is cost. Partly for these reasons a special organization — the Merck, Sharp and Dohme Foundation — was set up to assist in the production of teaching material. The reader is referred to the article by Sabbagh for a fuller description of the aims of this venture.[5] Because viewing of video material can be such a useful device for one individual (and probably even better when two people — trainer and trainee — are involved), details of video play-decks, for use with ordinary domestic television sets, are set out in the Appendix.

Other audio and visual material

Slides and tape-slide presentations are increasingly used and, because of their important contributions, deserve some comment. The Graves Medical Recording Foundation has a wealth of material on a very wide range of topics. A simple battery-operated slide viewer and an ordinary cassette player are all that are required in the practice setting. The material can, of course, be presented to larger audiences, and can form the focus of effective teaching in a group comprised of members of different disciplines in medicine and nursing. Increasingly, pharmaceutical firms are turning to this type of presentation in genuine educational efforts of a non-promotional nature.

The growth of postgraduate education affords more frequent opportunities for general practitioners to present original work to large audiences. Slides and the overhead projector can prove very valuable aids on such occasion, but their use requires care, both in preparation and in presentation of material.

Slides

In the absence of the ready availability of professional slide-making facilities, the hard-pressed general practitioner may be tempted to make his own slides, using a camera. Such an approach calls for considerable skill; whenever possible the help of an audio-visual aid department should be enlisted (and most university Departments of General Practice are willing to assist). Material to be presented on a slide should be typed on paper backed by a reversed carbon paper to intensify the image. The projected message must be kept simple, with no more than six lines per slide, and complex 'railway timetable' formats avoided. Information on one slide may be supplemented by simultaneous projection of a second slide (preferably in pictorial form) alongside the first. The 'diazo' technique of slide preparation provides a blue background, which cuts down glare, and the process is less expensive and more convenient than methods previously employed. The disadvantage of using conventional methods of projection is the need to plunge the audience into darkness and this, with the aftermath of a good meal, can prove a formidable obstacle to all but the most accomplished orator. The hazard may be surmounted by the simple technique of rear projection, in which the magnified image is shone at the audience though a translucent screen; the judicious use of mirrors cuts down the physical distance between the projector and screen. This method of projection can be used in daylight.

The preparation of slides may not be a prime concern to many in general practice, but the closely related subject of clinical photography deserves mention, if only because of the numerous opportunities presented to us in our day-to-day work. There are many evanescent clinical conditions which can thus be captured and later used for teaching — slapped cheek disease and hand, foot and mouth disease are two examples. The series in the journal *Update*, entitled 'A camera in general practice' contains much helpful advice.[6] The Royal College of General Practitioners has instituted the Ian Stokoe Award, one of the aims of which is to promote this hitherto underused visual aid in teaching.

The overhead projector

One advantage of this device is the fact that the speaker may continue to face the audience and point out *on the machine* (*not* on the screen) the salient features of his presentation — an elementary fact that seems to escape many inexperienced in the use of this aid.

Acetate transparencies can be made beforehand using coloured felt-tipped pens and washable ink. Again, messages must be kept simple, with as few lines as possible, and in writing large enough to be easily visible from the back of the room.

A further advantage of this aid is the facility it affords to avoid 'information overload' — by judicious masking, and by overlaying second or even third acetates on the first, it is possible to pace the build-up of projected information to suit the talk, and the audience.

In using both slide and overhead projection, it is always worthwhile to inspect the venue of the presentation beforehand, and where appropriate, to brief (and be briefed by) the projectionist.

It is worth remembering that both slides and acetates can *distract* attention when the point has been made, if the image is left still projected on the screen.

Conclusion

Teaching and learning methods in general practice are evolving rapidly; because of the nature of the task, much will continue to depend on the situation involving the trainer, the trainee — and the patient.

The scope for audio-visual aids in general practice teaching is not as wide as in other teaching, but there is room for experiment with, study and above all further purposeful evaluation of, the use of aids.

The sound tape-recorder probably has the greatest potential because of cheapness and wide availability, but its use fails to illustrate an aspect of doctor–patient communication increasingly seen to be of importance in learning.

Future developments are likely to involve greater and more frequent use of video-recording. At present, production of teaching material rests with a small number of individuals working in special centres. The value of teaching material thus produced is probably limited, but the worth is likely to be enhanced when it can be generated by those who themselves will use such material to meet their own needs. This is likely to come about during the present decade.

References

[1] Royal College of General Practitioners (1980) 'Non-verbal communication in

general practice'. *Journal of the Royal College of General Practitioners, 30,* 323-324.

2 Bain, D.J.G. (1976) 'Doctor – patient communication in general practice consultations'. *Medical Education, 10,* 125-131.

3 Bain, D.J.G. (1977) *ibid, 11,* 347-350.

4 Byrne, P.S. and Long, B.E.L. (1976) *Doctors Talking to Patients.* London: HMSO.

5 Sabbagh, K. (1979) 'Audio-visual materials for general practice training — The MSD Foundation'. *Journal of Audiovisual Media in Medicine, 2,* 114-117.

6 Woodward, J. (1976) *Update, 13,* 401-409.

Further reading

Byrne, P.S. and Heath, C.C. (1980) 'Practitioners' use of non-verbal behaviour in real consultations'. *Journal of the Royal College of General Practitioners, 30,* 327-331.

Davis, R.H., Jenkins, M., Smail, S.A., Stott, N.C.H., Verby, J. and Wallace, B.B. (1980) 'Teaching with audio-visual recordings of consultations'. *Journal of the Royal College of General Practitioners, 30,* 333-336.

McRae, R.K. (1975) *The Overhead Projector,* Medical Education Booklet No. 4. Dundee: ASME.

Royal College of General Practitioners (1975) 'Tape recording consultations'. *Journal of the Royal College of General Practitioners, 25,* 705-706.

Taylor, R.J. (1977) 'Television in general practice'. *Update, 15,* 489-494.

Verby, J., Davis, R.H. and Marshall, R.T. (1979) 'Television in general practice'. *Journal of Audiovisual Media in Medicine, 2,* 56-58.

Appendix

Equipment for recording telephone calls

Telephone answering machines

For example, 'Ansafone'. Such equipment allows a previously recorded statement to be played and a message to be received for replay later. 'Ansafone' may be rented, details available from:
Ansafone Rental Ltd,
Lyon Way,
Frimley Road,
Camberley,
Surrey.

Telephone recording microphone

This equipment picks up changes in the electrical field of the telephone and is not dependent upon sound waves as such. The microphone is placed over the area of maximum field change on the base of the telephone, and not on the ear piece. It may be plugged into a suitable tape recorder having an appropriate five pin microphone-receiving socket. One relatively cheap device is the Japanese SMC TP-1.

Video-play decks

Since several manufacturers produce machines of each format of video player/recorder, the types are listed by format and not manufacturer. Local video dealers will be able to supply a suitable machine of each type. The format used in any particular case will depend on financial constraints and the amount and type of tapes of external origin to be used. All the types except 3. are cassette types.
1. Philips 1500 Series (VCR): Now obsolete though still available; 1 hour playing time; colour; much used in past.
2. Philips 1700 Series: Also now obsolete though still available; 2½ hours playing time; colour; little used.
3. Half-inch EIAJ Reel-to-Reel: Quite common in education; machines still available though obsolete; 75 minutes playing time; normally monochrome; moderate cost; good cost/quality compromise. Also a cartridge version available, but not common.
4. U-Matic: Semi-professional/professional; 80 minutes playing time; colour; much used in education establishments because of quality/reliability.
5. VHS: Most common machine in the UK; domestic format; 3 hours

playing time; colour; low cost; being increasingly used because of cost/quality benefits.

6. Betamax: Fairly common; domestic format; 3¼ hours playing time; colour; low cost; not so common as VHS but similar cost/quality.

7. Philips 2000: New format; domestic type; 4 hours × 2 playing time; colour; low cost; very new and difficult to predict format's future.

The MSD Foundation (Merck, Sharp and Dohme Ltd)

This is based at Tavistock House
      Tavistock Square
      London WC1H 9JP (Tel. 01-388 5946)

Acknowledgement

The technical information above was furnished by Mr R.A. Stewart, Audio-Visual Services Unit, University of Dundee.

13
Libraries and literature
John Howie

A decade ago, only a minority of those involved in training would have seen the subject matter of this chapter as meriting a chapter in a book of this kind. Several developments have changed this position: general practice now has a steadily increasing literature of its own, some as textbooks or monographs, some in the form of the scientific or philosophical material published in journals, and some in news-sheet format, where news and educational material are included in one and the same issue. There are also more and more practices with rooms available to store and display this material and indeed there is now a good case for regarding the possession of such facilities as part of the basic credentials of a teaching practice. Finally as more emphasis comes to be placed on teaching trainees to think more critically about the work of a practice, so more emphasis is being put into research, which of course implies the careful analysis of the available published work on the issue being studied. This chapter looks in turn at the topics of stocking a practice library, regular reading, and searching the literature as part of a research project.

Practice library

Books

Books may be required for reference when particular clinical or administrative problems arise, for more general reading in order to gain a breadth of insight into what general practice or being a general practitioner encompasses, or for occasional reading as monographs about a particular subject. Many of the reference books which a library might stock are written by specialist authors and a suitable range can easily be constructed. These days, specialist textbooks are reprinted or revised frequently and although small print advances will often not matter too much, it is probably better avoiding the outlay of large sums on reference books which will date quickly. Paperbacks are, of course, one way of saving money — but they wear easily if frequently handled. Textbooks on general practice written by general practitioners are now widely available; choosing between them is perhaps invidious, but *Practice*[1] has sold best at the expensive reference end of the market while individual general practitioners have produced inexpensive, perceptive and readable introductions for the trainee or medical student attached to the practice. A library should contain a selection of monographs to let readers see what can become and be made of special interests in general practice. The 'best buys' can be judged by reading book reviews, concentrating on what is 'between the lines' as much as on what is actually printed. A reasonably varied stock can be built by spending under £50 (1980) a year after the initial stock has been invested in. The Royal College of General Practitioners provides a pamphlet indicating some of the books available for a practice library and this source is a helpful way of deciding where to start.

Journals

In most practices in the UK the *British Medical Journal* (BMJ) and *Journal of the Royal College of General Practitioners* (JRCGP) will be available and can be donated to the library. In other countries, similar journals such as the *American Journal of Family Physicians*, the *Canadian Journal of Family Practice*, and so on, would be appropriate. There is much to be said for regular reading of journals of general practice from other countries. Other periodicals (including, for example, *Update, World Medicine,* the newspapers, *MIMS* magazine, *Drug and Therapeutics Bulletin* and *Prescribers' Journal*) also arrive in regular bulk deliveries, and current and immediately past issues should be attractively displayed, while older issues are filed in such a way that they can be easily retrieved if required. Back numbers are an essential part of any library which has hopes of fulfilling its proper function. Unless these are bound they soon become disordered or lost; facilities for filing or binding can be relatively cheaply obtained, sometimes from the publishers themselves. If a library is being properly developed, a catalogue of the books and journals held should be prepared, one partner or a secretary should act as librarian and clear rules about removing material from the library should be prepared and enforced. Nothing is more frustrating than lost material.

It is truly said that the trainee learns more from his patients than from books or references. I am particularly attracted to the idea (not, I regret, my own) of placing photocopies of interesting and instructional matter inside the folders or envelopes of patients to whom articles apply. In this way reading can be related to patients rather than topics and learning enhanced many times over. Where space for storage or display of journals is not available in a teaching practice, this may be an attractive solution for trainer and trainee.

Regular reading

General practitioners probably read less than doctors in most other disciplines. Partly this is because so little of the working day is spent in office-type surroundings where reading is easy. When evening comes, the doctor is tired and, even if he does sit down to read, his ability to read critically is likely to be significantly reduced. Into the bargain, he must inevitably have difficulty is selecting what to read as almost anything can be said to be within his territory.

A choice has to be made on the balance to be struck between general and specialist literature (for example BMJ and JRCGP) and between educational material (for example *Update* and *Prescribers' Journal*) and newspaper material. Any reading policy which consistently ignores any of these types of literature will risk distorting perspectives, and will in the end defeat the main purpose of reading — namely the broadening of both knowledge and understanding.

Probably no two doctors read the same as each other; my own policy is to skim the titles of each issue of the BMJ and JRCGP and read only what interests me. I usually read a fair selection of the correspondence, but often little else. In a good week, I will read most leading articles and the summaries of other articles which I might otherwise overlook. In a year I also read three or four monographs written by or for general practitioners. These give valuable insights into how other colleagues think about their work or one aspect of it and this is probably the most enjoyable and informative way for the occasional reader to widen his interests. Many would say that doctors would benefit if they read more widely outside the field of medicine; I suspect that this, too, may be sounder advice than the more conventional educators believe.

Searching literature

As more trainees attempt to include simple research exercises as part of a training year, the need for simple advice on searching literature for *useful* references is increasing. It is, however, important to put literature searching in perspective. A full review is a time-consuming exercise which may all too easily become an end in itself, defeating the more important aim of trying to collect and interpret some personal observations. A detailed review is of course an essential part of a major research interest and I have suggested elsewhere[2] how this may best be approached. For a trainee project or for a first attempt at original work, the aim of any literature search should be no more than to put the proposed idea in a somewhat wider setting than that of a single doctor in a single practice. (Anyone who looks long enough at the literature will realize that few contributions are really new; that is not, however, a reason for not repeating past ideas, as frequently the results are either not repeatable or different background influences to the study result in subtle but important changes in the findings.)

As a starting point, when time is restricted or access to reference libraries perhaps difficult, the RCGP library services are of particular value. As well as offering a photocopying service, many standard lists of references on everyday themes are already available. These allow the investigator to collect quickly a number of standard papers usually in accessible journals and written in English. Each paper will have its own list of references and aggregating these will quickly indicate the principal papers and main workers in the field. Cross-checking and study of any papers not already listed will allow the review to expand quickly; once papers are seen to be becoming repetitive it is reasonable to stop. For a first review, it is probably reasonable to stick to a five-year survey of *published* work (which will reflect the new or current ideas of up to ten years before) and to keep to mainstream general journals (BMJ) or specialist journals (JRCGP) relevant to the topic. A few points are worth remembering. Perhaps the most important is that reference lists are self-perpetuating and it is easy for a valuable reference to be overlooked because its title has not attracted reviewers to it. Once passed over it will probably remain missing. Secondly, useful starting references for a project may be found in non-science literature (*World Medicine* or *The Times* for example) or may be buried in Royal Commission Reports or similar volumes. These also tend to escape routine literature search. The solution to some of these difficulties is to review literature prospectively as well as retrospectively. Reading with a particular purpose is always rewarding, but of course cannot be the main method for a study to be completed in a short time span. It does, however, have its place as an embryo interest develops into a more mature research programme. Finally, never quote references you have not read for yourself; and quote only from originals and not from abstracts.

There are other reviewing or abstracting services as well as the one provided by the RCGP — which, incidentally, is available to non-members of the College as well as to members. FAMLI (Family Medicine Literature Index) is a new service designed to help the indexing of general practice literature in the way Index Medicus does for all medical literature; it is too soon to say how useful it will become. MEDLARS (Medical Literature Retrieval Service) is a computer-based service which is unjustifiably expensive for almost all general practice purposes. In any case, reviewing by the research worker himself with his own priorities in mind is usually better than having someone else do the work. For anyone who does not know how to use the standard reference and indexing volumes in a library, the proper approach is to ask the librarian for guidance. Requests of this kind will always be welcomed and will, in both the short and long term, usually save time for all concerned.

Conclusion

Many criticisms are made of modern teaching because too much emphasis is given to theory and too little time is spent seeing patients. Reading is sometimes regarded as a distraction from, rather than an aid to, learning the job of being a general practitioner. As in everything, balance is necessary and this chapter suggests some of the ways in which libraries may be constructed, and the literature used to provide this balance for both education and patient care.

References

[1] Cormack, J.J.C., Marinker, M. and Morrell, D.C. (eds) (1976) *Practice: A handbook of primary medical care.* London: Kluwer Publishing.
[2] Howie, J.G.R. (1979) *Research in General Practice.* London: Croom Helm, pp. 36-43.

14
Topic teaching
J.H. Barber

Although topic teaching has, for many years, been an accepted form of hospital-based undergraduate teaching, it is a less common but perhaps more appropriate educational method for both undergraduates and vocational trainees in general practice. Topic teaching can be described as the selection of a clinical or other topic relevant to the group that is being taught, and its subsequent exploration through the presentation and discussion of all important facets of the topic.

Characteristics of topic teaching

There are several characteristics that set topic teaching apart from almost all other educational approaches. The subject matter is treated in a holistic way which allows exposure to the topic in both breadth and depth. Although it is more usually found in a lecture with a large class of students and several lecturers, topic teaching is most appropriate to small groups of not more than 12 people, in which active participation can be achieved. It is thus generally unsuited to one-to-one teaching, either in the undergraduate or in the vocational training field.

Undergraduate topic teaching is most commonly found as part of hospital-based teaching. The topic chosen is usually a clinical one such as coronary artery disease, peptic ulcer or diabetes, and a number of presentations are given by different specialists on related areas that are appropriate to the discipline. The lecture hour may be fully taken up by such presentations or discussion can be stimulated by a question and answer session, for which the students may or may not have had prior warning in preparation. A typical topic teaching session would be as follows:

Topic: Peptic ulcer.
Speakers: 1. General practitioner. Subject: the presentation and management of peptic ulcer in general practice.
            2. Physician (gastroenterologist). Subject: the investigation and management of peptic ulcer in hospital.
            3. Surgeon. Subject: the surgical management of peptic ulcer.
Audience: A class of first or second clinical year students. Active participation may be variable and is dependent on the degree to which the speakers adopt a didactic approach, the time left available for discussion, and the willingness, and preparedness, of students for a question and answer session.

The range of other specialties that can take part in such a session is considerable, and clinical and laboratory disciplines, such as pathology or radiology can all contribute when appropriate to this comprehensive approach to a topic.

Topic teaching in general practice

The form of topic teaching that has been detailed above is clearly less suited to the education of undergraduates and vocational trainees in general practice. Practice, being both general in its scope and holistic in its outlook, does not readily subdivide into specialties and the format of a didactic presentation — albeit with some learner initiated questioning — is contrary to the current views of the importance of learner participation in education in general practice. Topic teaching, however, as an educational method can be readily adapted to general practice and can achieve its basic aims.

Topic teaching can be either subject or patient centred and there are a number of different formats. In the three variations described below, students or trainees play an active part in the presentation of different aspects of the topic and thus require prior warning of their area of responsibility, guidance in the selection of their source material, and sufficient time to prepare their contribution to the session.

Subject centred teaching

The topic chosen must be appropriate to the learning needs of the participants. Contributions are expected from both learners and teachers and the aim is to give a comprehensive review of the topic (usually a clinical one) as it affects general practice and general practitioners. This format is best suited to the small group.

Example

Topic: Hypertension in general practice.
Chairman: General practitioner.
Expert: Physician specializing in hypertension.
Speakers: Three of the group are selected as opening speakers each giving a resumé of current thinking and practice in different areas of hypertension.

Preparation time with the availability of textbooks and published articles is thus essential. The areas selected can include:

1. The incidence and prevalence of hypertension in the community; the natural history of the condition.
2. Different methods of identifying hypertension in general practice and the content of programmes of investigation.

3. Current views on the treatment of hypertension and its
outcome.

Content of session:	Three ten-minute presentations by members of the group followed by comment by the expert and chairman, and open discussion.

Subject/patient centred teaching

Although again more suited to small group teaching, this format can also be adapted to one-to-one trainer/trainee education. The aim is similar to that of the first variation. A clinical topic is selected, again one that is relevant to the learners, but the choice is limited to conditions such as chronic respiratory illness, epilepsy or incontinence. These conditions may present in all age groups, although there are differences in presentation, approach and management at different times of life. Source material would include relevant textbooks and published articles but more impact can be obtained if patients in the practice are introduced as specific examples. The appropriate patients should be identified some days prior to the session so as to allow each speaker to interview his patient and prepare his presentation.

Example:

Topic:	Diabetes mellitus.
Chairman:	General practitioner.
Experts:	(optional) Paediatric and adult physicians, specializing in diabetes.
Speakers:	Three of the group are selected as opening speakers, each of whom presents the case history of a patient in the practice. There is little to be gained by having the patient present at the teaching session, although there will be instances when this is appropriate. The patients selected and presented could include:

1. A child or adolescent with diabetes.
2. An adult with longstanding diabetes.
3. An elderly person with maturity onset diabetes.

Content of presentation:	This should be structured and could include:

1. The mode of presentation and the subsequent investigation of the patient.
2. The initial and subsequent management.
3. The long-term management and the probable course of the condition.
4. The effects of the illness on the family unit.
5. Problem areas in the overall management of the patient.

Patient centred teaching

This format uses an identified patient or family group to illustrate a number of aspects of management that are in general appropriate to the topic as a whole. Again it is more suited to small groups but involves learners to a much less degree than is the case with the other two variants. The aim is to give a comprehensive cover to a general topic through the detailed description of the management of one example.

Example:

Topic: Mental subnormality — a child with physical and mental retardation.

Speakers: General practitioner, health visitor, social worker, with representatives of any other professional or lay organizations that have at any time been involved with the patient or family. Thus, an educationist, school teacher, consultant paediatrician, or others may be involved, and in situations like this it may be useful if the family also are represented.

Each speaker gives a brief account of his personal involvement with the patient and the family, his unique contribution to the care, and areas of possible overlap or conflict with other disciplines. The presentations should highlight possible problems and difficulties as well as attempting to give solutions. Open discussion should be encouraged to allow a full examination of the holistic approach to the care of such a patient in general practice.

Conclusion

The three examples of topic teaching given above are in general appropriate to both undergraduate students and vocational trainees in general practice. The educational effect of topic teaching is enhanced by the use of the learners as teachers, by the need for members of the group to spend time in a detailed study of a patient or family, and in the use of appropriate published material. Care, however, must be taken to structure the content and method of the teaching in a way that is appropriate to the needs and experience of the learners and in the way it fits in with the overall objectives of their teaching in general practice.

15
Case discussions
Marshall Marinker

Medical audit is most often described in terms of an epidemiological exercise. Observations are made within a population framework, and the analysis of these observations is statistical. When questions are asked, they are asked in such a way that the answers may be expressed numerically. To make a judgement about the quality of an answer, we have to assure ourselves about the reliability and validity of the data collected, and the appropriateness and accuracy of the statistical manipulations which have been employed. The answers to such questions are statements about probability. The truths which are revealed are general statements about populations, and they can have no more relevance to the individual patient than this. If the individual patient is a heavy smoker, the results of epidemiological studies simply show that he now belongs to a population of whom it can be said that there is a considerably increased risk of suffering from a number of known conditions.

There is also a long tradition of medical audit which is concerned not with populations, but with the individual patient, his illness and its management; here the focus of attention is summed up by that much abused term 'the case'. In hospital medicine bedside teaching remains the traditional small group approach to such audit. In contrast the clinico-pathological conference usually takes place before an audience.

In general practice, case discussions may be a regular feature of practice meetings — a form of self-audit and continuing education. Case discussions are often part of the teaching of medical students and trainees.

Such case discussions usually have the following form. First there is a narrative, a description of how the problem presented: information is given from the clinical history, from the physical examination and subsequent investigations. There is then a discussion of the problems presented, and an exchange of information and opinions. But how is the quality of all this to be judged? You cannot apply statistical principles. Somehow those taking part in case discussion have to develop and apply other (that is to say non-statistical) criteria for judging quality. Without such a discipline, the case discussion can become nothing more than a meaningless exchange of impressions and prejudices. When this happens, no useful learning can take place. Worse still, there is the danger that such case discussion, because it can so easily simulate a rigorous and disciplined exchange, may actually reinforce a belief in unproven facts and a confidence in bad habits.

The group

In general practice, case discussion takes place most often in small groups. The *group leader* should be someone with skills in small group work (see Chapter 8). He may sometimes take on the role of *resource person* also, but this is not necessary.

When the small group is composed of medical students, there is usually no problem about identifying the leader — most often he is the course tutor. But if the group is composed of trainees, there is no reason why one of the trainees himself should not be elected as group leader. Here a trainer or the course organizer would act as a resource person. Sometimes a specialist may be invited to join such groups, in order to take him on this role.

There is much to be said for having a formal record of such case discussions. In addition to a group leader and resource person, the group may wish to identify a *reporter*. Reports from such discussions must rely heavily on the ability of the reporter to take notes during the discussion, and on his memory. Experience suggests that such reports should be written or dictated as soon as possible after the end of the meeting. They should also be circulated to all the participants within a few days so that amendments and corrections can be incorporated into the record.

There are a number of different techniques for selecting cases for discussion. One of the most searching is the so-called 'random case analysis'. Here the group decides that at its next meeting it will discuss one or more preselected cases, for example 'the third person to be seen next Tuesday morning'. Members of the group must guard against all forms of avoidance or frank cheating. There should be no means whereby a course member is able to predict or manipulate the appearance of a particular case.

Another method consists of the discussion of a particular type of case, for example children admitted to hospital or women referred for hysterectomy, or adults with more than four weeks off work because of back pain. Here, part of the strength of the case discussion lies in the comparability of one case with another. 'Entry criteria' are clearly very important: the group must define precisely what minimum number of characteristics must be present for the 'case' to form part of the discussion. The problem is analogous to that of selecting patients for a clinical trial.

Perhaps the commonest method, and a very valuable one, is to discuss 'difficult cases'. Here there is no need to define 'entry criteria'. Each doctor may have his own reason for regarding a particular problem as difficult, and may be allowed to present the story.

Judging the quality of the narrative

The presenting doctor may begin with a description of a patient and the salient points in the history. But how reliable is this account? In the hospital setting, the patient is often presented in person at the clinico-pathological conference. Although he may often be presented as an object, so that clinical signs can be demonstrated, he is sometimes in a position to comment on the doctor's history, or may even be invited to give the history himself. This rarely happens in the general practice case discussion. In deciding about the quality of the doctor's narrative, therefore, the group may wish to have access to the patient's notes, and to check the doctor's memory of the patient's story by recourse to the sequential notes in the record, to copies of the letters written to the hospital and replies from hospital doctors. More recently some groups have used tape recordings of actual consultations (see Chapter 12) in order to look critically at the reliability of the history. Often the patient's statements can be checked against notes and letters, and inconsistencies can be explored. The method may be imperfect, but it remains important to arrive at a reliable account of the march of events.

Judging the quality of opinions

A particular patient is described as suffering from an exacerbation of chronic bronchitis. A course of oxytetracycline is prescribed, but a week later the sputum is still purulent and the patient is now in heart failure. One of the doctors says, 'That is hardly surprising. I always use amoxicillin in this sort of situation — it is the drug of choice'. A number of other opinions may be expressed.

'It would have been as well to look at the appearance of a chest X-ray.'

'We really ought to ask for a sputum culture — it is poor practice simply to rely on the appearance of the sputum.'

'This sort of patient ought to be taking oxytetracycline throughout the winter months.'

How are we to judge the quality of these different opinions? The first step is to recognize them as opinions, that is to say they are statements of belief, and their provenance may be largely unknown. The group then has to ask the following sorts of questions:

1. Is the opinion based on empirical research? This may sometimes require a search of the literature (see Chapter 13).
2. Is there any evidence which links the appearance of the sputum to the presence of micro-organisms?
3. Is there anything to choose between one broad spectrum antibiotic and another?

In many instances, particularly in general practice, it may not be possible to challenge the quality of an opinion in terms of the results of empirical research. Here the argument must turn on the application of medical logic. Dr X suggests that the chronic bronchitic patient should have an X-ray whenever his sputum becomes purulent. How many X-rays is this likely to involve? In what way would the doctor act differently if the X-rays showed either increased markings or a small area of consolidation? Would the recommendation be a sensible way of picking up early carcinoma of the bronchus, or tuberculosis? Such an examination of the opinions expressed may often reveal areas of ignorance in general practice which cry out for further research. More often because few general practitioners have the skills or motivation to carry out systematic research, this sort of case will drive the doctor back to a consideration of first principles, and to the application of some sort of clinical dialectic (see below).

Judging the quality of clinical work

Donabedian[1] describes three aspects of the quality of care. The first is *structure*: for example the number of doctors in a health centre, the doctor–patient ratio, the number of consulting rooms, typewriters, items of diagnostic equipment and so on. The second is *process*: how often is a relevant family history taken, or a blood pressure, or a urinalysis performed? The third is *outcome*: what changes resulted from the doctor's clinical work? In the last analysis it is the quality of outcome which really counts. However favourable the doctor–patient ratio, however sensitive and appropriate the investigations, what really matters is whether the patient benefits from all the activity.

Orthopaedic surgery provides an excellent example of the utility and possibility of measuring outcome. Here it is possible to measure the difference in the performance of limbs and joints before and after surgery. Such measurements are not readily available in the setting of general practice: Part of the difficulty lies in the complex interaction between physical, psychological and social factors, in the conditions with which the general practitioner must deal. 'Before' and 'after' measurements are based on a mechanical model of disease; it is much more difficult to apply such measurements to the management of bereavement, or the counselling of a young woman who has just been given an ileostomy. A further cause of difficulty is the nature of so-called minor illness. Most of these conditions — acute backache, upper respiratory tract infections, gastrointestinal upsets — have uncertain causes, last for only for a few days, cause short-term discomfort and disruption of life, and leave little, if anything, by way of permanent damage. With so short a natural history, before and after measurements probably record nothing more than the natural history of the complaint. Lastly, a large part of the general practitioner's work is concerned with the management of chronic diseases. Conditions in this group have a natural history stretching over many years, and that history is usually marked by the ebb and flow of symptoms. Before and after measurements here are unreliable and may predicate nothing about the quality of care.

Despite the reservations expressed by Donabedian about judging the quality of process, case discussions in general practice must address the problem of assessing the quality of the processes of care. In other fields of human activity, for example sport, the qualities of process are given at least as much analysis as the quantities of outcome. In soccer, for example, although the final score is all important, a team is judged also by the style of its play, the intelligence of its strategies and the way in which the manager develops his players. The analogy is not as strained as it may appear. Good quality performance is most often found in teams which win games. It is more likely to bring success on the field than poor performance. In general practice where cure (as opposed to the management of spontaneous recovery) is much less common than care, it is simply nihilistic not to recognize the difference between good and poor quality work.

In the pursuit of clinical standards members of a case discussion might submit a case under review to the following sort of catechism:

1. *Has the problem been effectively identified?*
   Here the skills of clinical method (see Chapter 16) may be assessed — the accuracy of the history, the appropriateness of the physical examination, the selection of investigations. Any one of these issues may be critical. The skills of communication (see Chapters 20 and 26) must also be examined. There will be no easy answers. What constitutes 'a problem'? A patient may be found to be suffering from chronic bronchitis. But the 'problem' may have as much to do with fears of loneliness and social isolation as with the onset of cardiac failure. The notion of efficiency is suggested in the following questions.

2. *Has the problem been resolved in the shortest possible time?*

3. *Has the number of problem solving steps been reduced to a minimum consonant with safety?*
   The answers to both these questions will be open to wide discussion. Clearly it is important to diagnose, say, acute appendicitis or meningitis with as little delay as possible. But at what cost? Two examples may suffice to highlight the difficulties.

   James, aged three, was brought to the surgery by his anxious mother. He had been feverish for a day, and had vomited twice. A week ago the mother had telephoned with an exactly similar story concerning James' four-year-old brother. The locum general practitioner had prescribed penicillin V without seeing the child, and the symptoms resolved within two or three days.

   At this first consultation with James, the doctor could only elicit a history of feverishness and listlessness. Apart from a temperature of

100°F, there were no positive physical signs. He temporized. The next day the picture was unchanged, and he sent a mid-stream specimen of urine to the laboratory. There were still no positive physical signs. On the third morning the mother reported that James had again been feverish through the night and was now very listless. Examination revealed only some general lower abdominal tenderness. The child was then admitted to hospital, and the paediatrician decided that the most likely diagnosis was a urinary tract infection. He sent a second specimen of urine to the laboratory. That afternoon a so-called 'routine' chest X-ray revealed a small patch of consolidation in the lung. This resolved quickly when James was given penicillin. How is the quality of this care to be judged? If James' mother had telephoned the locum doctor, she would almost certainly have been given penicillin right away.

Joanna Black is 45 years old and married to a man 12 years younger than herself. She complained of atypical chest pain, and the description suggested no organic cause. She began to weep then, and said that her own mother had died suddenly at the age of 45. Now she feels old, less attractive than she was five years ago and, although her husband has given her no reason to doubt, she wonders whether she is still as attractive to him as she used to be. When the doctor probed further, she said that she was frightened of dying. In the course of a physical examination, the doctor found only one abnormality — a blood pressure of 180/110. The urine contained neither sugar nor protein.

In the course of case discussion it becomes clear that the doctor chose to ignore the raised blood pressure for three months, during which time he counselled the patient, only returning to the problem of her blood pressure when he judged her ready to deal with the threat of a major health problem. Subsequently he found that the average of three diastolic pressures was 118. How is the group to judge the quality of his problem solving? Was the delay in identifying the problem of hypertension justifiable or too dangerous?

4. *Has the simplest technology been employed?*

5. *Has the optimum medication been selected and monitored?*
   (See appendix to Chapter 25.)

6. *Has the management caused the minimum harm or risk of harm to the patient?*

7. *Has there been optimum use of health care personnel?*

8. *Have health-care and family-care been fully mobilized?*

9. *What realistic criteria of success were adopted, and were they achieved?*
   This last question forces the group to look at the possibility of clinical management by objectives. How can realistic objectives be set? Must they always be negotiated with the patient, and how should this be

done? What would be realistic objectives in the case of an elderly man suffering from Parkinson's disease, and how would these be measured?

Conclusion

Perhaps the most important gain from case discussions is the habit of critical thinking. So often definitive answers will elude the group. Elsewhere in this book much has been made of the virtue of tolerating uncertainty. It is a virtue born of necessity, but critical thinking in case discussion demands of the members of the group that they place limits on this uncertainty.

Particularly in the setting of general practice, the student or trainee may find it difficult to accept the case discussion as a part of scientific medicine. Because the data are often expressed as qualities rather than quantities, and because the thought processes are not clearly mechanistic, the judgement of the clinician may be seen as simply a point of view, perhaps no more than a habitual leap in the dark. Medawar[2] criticizes this mechanistic approach to clinical discussion in which '...no place has been found for flair and insight, and the enrichment that long experience brings to clinical skills'. He criticizes those who claim that medicine is born of a marriage between an *important* scientific element, and an *indefinable* [my italics] artistry and imaginative insight. Such clinicians, he says '...spoil everything by getting the bride and groom confused. It is the unbiased observation, the apparatus, the ritual of fact-finding and inductive mumbo-jumbo that the clinician thinks of as "scientific", and the other element, intuitive and logically unscripted, which he thinks of as a creative art.'

The good case discussion must achieve a balance between concern for the quality of evidence, and a concern for the doctors' creative use of imagination, insight and intuition. It is this balance between creativity and criticism which marks the best of case discussion, and which makes it such a powerful tool for learning.

References

[1] Donabedian, A. (1979) 'The quality of medical care: a concept in search of a definition'. *Journal of Family Practice, 9,* 277-284.
[2] Medawar, P.B. (1969) *Induction and Intuition in Scientific Thought.* London: Methuen.

111

Part III
Content

16
Clinical method
Marshall Marinker

Introduction

Many general practitioners are diffident about their role in teaching basic
clinical method. The reason for this diffidence probably lies in the disparity
between the way in which they were taught about clinical method as
students, and the way in which they now practise. For the most part
medical students, past and present, are taught their basic clinical method
on the hospital wards. The models used, the so-called 'good clinical
material' are patients who have either already been diagnosed as suffering
from a major and recognized disease, or patients in whom it has become
necessary to exclude the presence of such diseases. The student is taught to
carry out a complete history and a complete physical examination. There is
a concentration on accurate information and replicable skills. The
possession of knowledge is important, and this knowledge is often displayed
in terms of the range of technical investigations which are readily available.
This is very different from clinical problem-solving in the setting of the
general practitioner's surgery.

It is, however, these very differences which constitute the strength of
clinical teaching in general practice. The clinical method which the good
general practitioner employs is, of necessity, based not on certainty and the
possession of knowledge, but on an ability to deal with uncertainties and to
solve problems when many facts are unknown or perhaps unknowable.

The medical student may be asked how long he believes it would take
him to clerk a new patient. He will have been taught not only to elicit a
history of the patient's presenting symptoms, but to ask systematic
questions about other possible symptoms, and the physical examination
will include a check of all the major body systems. It is unlikely that even
the most experienced clinician, faced with the most co-operative patient,
could complete such a task in less than 45 minutes. Yet the average
duration of the consultation in general practice is some six minutes, as is
the average duration of the follow-up appointment in the hospital out-
patient department. Clearly, some other sort of clinical problem-solving is
taking place. But what is it? And is it scientific medicine?

The system-by-system approach bears a strong resemblance to what, in
science, has been called inductive reasoning. That is to say, theories,
explanations and causes are uncovered as a result of a thorough inspection
of all the facts associated with the problem to be solved. Until all the facts
are gathered the observer is discouraged from taking short cuts, from

guessing the answer in advance of the evidence, because to do so would be to introduce bias and hence error.

But clinical work in the general practitioner's surgery, as in the physician's consulting room, bears little resemblance to this inductive way of information gathering. Real clinical problem solving, like real scientific discovery, is not inductive. It is best described as hypothetico-deductive or guessing and testing. This simply means that the clinician makes an informed guess about what is wrong with his patient and then tries to see if his guess will fit the facts of the patient's symptoms and signs. In the words of Sir Peter Medawar, 'Imaginative conjecture and criticism, in that order, underlie the physician's diagnosis of his patient's ailments'. [1]

The following diagram represents this clinical method:

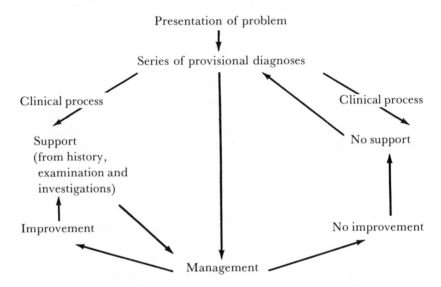

Usually the clinician can deploy his knowledge and skills without bothering to reflect on what he knows, how he knows it, and how he applies that knowledge. For example, a 35-year-old man, with heavily nicotine-stained fingers, comes to see the doctor for the first time. He is gaunt looking, a travelling salesman, and he looks down at heel. His breath smells not only of tobacco but of peppermint, and there is a chalky substance around his lips. He gives a long history of indigestion, points to his epigastrium and says that the pain becomes unbearable two or three hours after he has eaten. He has only come to see the doctor because he has started to vomit.

The doctor may come to a diagnosis of duodenal ulcer with pyloric stenosis, and much else besides concerning the patient's life style, his anxieties, and his problems with job and family. The symptoms suggest duodenal ulcer. The appearance of the patient's clothes, manner, and what he reveals in his history about his life style, may suggest levels of anxiety or depression and a consumption of cigarettes or alcohol which are part of the picture. What characterizes clinical method in general practice is its economy. The application of hypothetico-deductive thinking means that in this situation the clinician, general practitioner or hospital consultant is unlikely to take a detailed history referrable to the cardio-vascular system, or to auscultate the heart, or to assess the function of the cranial nerves. The student should develop the habit of submitting both the doctor's diagnosis and his treatment to some critical analysis of the way in which the problem is solved. For example, in this case the general practitioner may arrange for a barium meal, or refer the patient to a consultant surgeon. He may prescribe a simple antacid, or a tranquillizer. He may give advice about diet, smoking and the consumption of alcohol. His management reflects a complex set of assumptions about the nature of the disease and its aetiology which cannot simply be summed up by the words 'peptic ulcer'. Quite often one gets a clearer indication of the nature and range of the patient's problems from looking at what the doctor prescribes, than from looking at what the doctor describes as the diagnosis.

The student may wonder why a child, who is described as having an 'upper respiratory tract infection', has been given penicillin V. There may be a number of reasons for the prescription which do not appear in the cryptic diagnosis. For example Howie has pointed out that the use of these diagnostic labels hides much information about the clinical history of the patient, his social history, or even the presence and distribution of physical signs. There may be a history of recurrent bronchitis or otitis media, or the doctor may have detected added sounds in the chest. Sometimes the penicillin which is prescribed for an infection in a child is intended as a tranquillizer for an anxiety in the mother.

The diagnosis, like any other scientific statement, is a matter not of certainty but of probability. In general practice the patient's symptoms and problems are presented for the first time to a 'health care worker'. They have not been sorted out in relation to the likely nature of the disease, whether it is a gynaecological or surgical problem, a medical or psychiatric one, acute or chronic, life-threatening or temporarily incapacitating. Accordingly, there will be a difference between general practice and the hospital clinic in the importance given to a particular symptom or clinical sign, or the likelihood that it has serious implications.

For example, a young man who complained of a cough as his major symptom would almost always be subjected to a chest X-ray if he was being seen by a doctor in the hospital out-patient department. The majority of people complaining of cough in general practice have a mild upper-respiratory tract infection, and a chest X-ray would not be indicated. The general practitioner, however, would bear other probabilities in mind. If the patient were an immigrant worker from a group where pulmonary tuberculosis is much more prevalent than in the indigenous population, a chest X-ray would be clearly indicated. Most of the patients who present with such common symptoms as sore throat, headache, backache or tiredness, will not in the first instance require detailed investigation, only an appropriate history and a limited and focused clinical examination.

The general practitioner's decision to treat or to investigate further is based on a knowledge of the patient, the distribution of diseases in the population and an estimation of how safe or unsafe it may be to delay taking a decision.

Routines, rituals and dramas

Although Medawar's comment on the similarity between clinical and scientific method throws light on the processes of the consultation, the statement is also something of an exaggeration. Clinical work is not really the same thing as scientific exploration. Diagnosis is not always a discovery of something new, but most often the recognition of something already well known. In this sense, clinical work is largely a matter of pattern recognition.

What characterizes the idea of a disease is its sameness. For instance, measles is a particular collection and sequence of body changes. But each individual and his social situation is unique. The pattern may therefore be approached from an unusual angle, or it may be possible to discern only a few of the salient features, and these may bear a resemblance to other conditions. In this sense, the process of making a diagnosis is not unlike that of solving a particular form of television quiz, where the viewer is presented with a vague and undifferentiated shadow of an object, often taken from an unexpected angle. As more of the object is included in the picture and the focus sharpens, the viewer can guess the subject of the photograph. This is very different from such an exercise as painting by numbers or joining the numbered dots in a children's picture puzzle book, which the classical teaching of clinical method suggests.

Professor John Morris, in a paper on aspects of the person in social life, describes three sorts of human encounters: routines, rituals and dramas.[2] Consultations in general practice can be classified in a similar way.

Type I: routines

Usually both the situation and the patient are familiar to the general practitioner, and the type of problem is a common one. A three year-old child is brought into the surgery and the mother explains that the child has been crying all night. The child looks hot, has a nasal discharge and the doctor makes an 'educated guess' that the child is suffering an infection of the middle ear. Otitis media is far and away the most likely explanation of .

this presentation and the general practitioner will test this by examining the ear drums.

Type II: rituals

Here the clinical content of the consultation may be hard to discern. Usually a repeat prescription is issued because of some disease or some unexplained symptoms which were first dealt with in the past, sometimes years in the past. The repeat prescription has a psychological or symbolic significance for the patient, long after it ceases to have any pharmacological intention. In this sort of consultation there seems to be no attempt to solve a problem, but rather to reaffirm a relationship, albeit not a very close one.

Type III: dramas

Morris judges an encounter as being dramatic when it fulfils the following three criteria. First, the situation must be novel within the person's experience. He goes on to say that this does not mean that every aspect of it must be quite unfamiliar, but that important aspects of it are new. Second, the activity, or its outcome, must be important. Third, the outcome must be in doubt.

In Type III consultations the problems which are presented to the doctor may be novel or presented in a novel way. Both the activity of the problem-solving, and the outcome for the patient, are important and uncertain. An obese woman of 50 presents with double vision and an obvious squint. The diagnosis of diabetes mellitus with a neuropathy of the sixth cranial nerve will not come readily as an informed guess. In addition, the patient may have been terrified of a brain tumour, and must now come to terms with another major disease. There is no familiar pattern to be recognized from the fragments of what the patient presents.

The problems presented in Type I and Type II consultations may be resolved by pattern recognition. The problems of Type III consultations will be elucidated by a more formal application of the scientific method, that is to say of hypothetico-deductive thinking. The process may take some time and may extend over more than one clinical encounter.

The systematic clinical method which is analogous to inductive thinking has almost no place in clinical problem-solving, although it remains a useful way of learning the components of history-taking and physical examination. Doctors take this kind of history and make this kind of examination most often for the purposes of examination for life assurance. Very rarely, when the resolution of a problem is not arrived at by guessing and testing, doctors fall back on this sytematic approach. The results are disappointing.

119

Teaching in the consultation

When a consultation is shared with a medical student or trainee, the general practitioner has the unique opportunity to explore and develop the skills of clinical problem-solving. This will not happen, however, if the teacher's own anxieties betray him into taking up one of the following two defensive positions. The first is that he will display, at times boastfully, his own knowledge: a knowledge of clinical facts, a compendium of differential diagnoses and, most seductive of all, all sorts of facts that the general practitioner already knows about his patient, his family and his relationships. The second, is that the shared consultaton may become a *viva voce* in which the teacher pretends to an assessment of the learner's knowledge.

If a shared consultation with a learner is to be fruitful, the objective of the exercise must be made explicit. The student or trainee is told that he will be asked to share in the clinical process, that he will be asked to take part in the history taking, deciding on an appropriate physical examination, and a suggestion of differential diagnoses and so on. If this sharing is seen by the student to be an inquisition, then things may go badly adrift. The student will lose confidence and will begin to distrust the intentions of the clinical teacher. Questions like 'What would you like to ask this patient?', may be interpreted as 'There is one clever question which will elucidate the diagnosis. Do you know it?' 'Is there any other examination you would like to make at this time?' may be interpreted as 'There is a gross physical sign staring you in the face and you cannot see it'. The learner–teacher relationship quickly deteriorates into an adversary relationship, answers become defensive and the student or trainee will simply learn some technique for self-preservation in a tight corner.

Worse still, the patient loses his central place in the exercise. Instead of teaching enhancing the quality of the patient's clinical care, the patient's role and his clinical problem are set aside. The patient is invited instead to become a witness to the clinical teacher's inquisition. This model is not unknown to generations of clinical students, but it is destructive of the learner, it demeans the patient and suceeds in the end only in defending the teacher against any self-understanding.

Mr Jones is a 60-year-old, thin, anxious-looking bank clerk. He presents with a persistent pain in the right upper arm following a fall some months ago. 'Is there anything you want to ask Mr Jones?' The history of a minor fall is given and the doctor comments that the patient has hardly attended the surgery over a period of ten years. 'Is there anything else you would like to ask?' would be followed by, 'What sort of physical examination do you think we ought to carry out?'. An examination of the upper arm reveals an area of tenderness and swelling at the lower end of the humerus. The student looks perplexed and suggests tentatively that the opportunity should be taken to check the patient's blood pressure. The clinical teacher commends this idea and suggests that the student look at the patient's hands. They are heavily nicotine stained and there is clubbing of the fingers. 'Is there anything particular about Mr Jones's health that you want to ask now?' The student elicits a history of chronic cough with sputum which has recently become blood-stained. 'Is there any further examination that you want to make now?' The student may indicate that he wants to listen to the chest, look for lymphadenopathy.

At every stage of such a shared consultation, the clinical teacher must monitor the response of both the patient and the learner. Does the patient still feel that his problem is of central concern? Is he confused about who is his doctor? Has the consultation become impersonal, an intellectual exercise in which the patient himself has become some sort of object, a part of a clinical jigsaw puzzle? When this threatens to happen, it may be important to rescue either the patient or the student and to reaffirm the central intention of the consultation, which is a resolution of the patient's problem.

The teacher may have to decide how much further he will allow the student to continue to bear the burden of the consultation. In the case of Mr Jones, a diagnosis of bronchial carcinoma is very likely. If the physical exaination takes place in an examination room separate from the consulting room (often a useful way of gaining time for private discussion with the trainee or student in mid-consultation) the doctor may say, 'It is clear that you have made a diagnosis. What further steps would you want to take in order to confirm this? What shall we tell the patient?' In response to the student's answer the teacher may ask, 'Why do you want to be guarded in what you say?' Again in response to the student's answer the doctor may ask, 'How does Mr Jones's previous record help you to decide what to do?'

The thrust of teaching about clinical method refers much more to the 'why' of decision taking than to the 'what' of clinical knowledge. Moran Campbell makes the point that both clinical teachers and learners would help each other a great deal if they asked more often, 'What is in your mind?'[3]

This form of Socratic or reflective teaching about clinical method will apply equally to the shared consultation, the observed consultation, and the analysis of role-play. In small group discussion, perhaps the most useful technique is the serial interruption of the learner's narrative. The medical student or trainee is asked to present a case. He may begin by saying 'Mr Jones is a thin, anxious bank clerk who has not been to see the doctor for 15 years. There is a note eight years ago, that he was off work for two weeks with a sprained ankle, but otherwise nothing.' At this point the group leader may interrupt the narrative and ask, 'Mr Jones is a very infrequent attender. What possible explanations might there be?' When the student or trainee describes the presenting complaint, the group may be invited to discuss the possible causes of painful swelling of the upper arm following a fall. In this way, looking at probabilities, and possibilities, the members of the group create their own problem-solving pathway and may well explore a number of clinical possibilities, and their further elucidation, in the course of the discussion. In this way a seminar on clinical problem-solving starting from the presentation of Mr Jones, may move quite far from Mr Jones's actual problem, with advantage.

The so-called facts of clinical medicine and the theoretical frameworks which underpin them will change considerably during the professional lifetime of the students and trainees whom we teach. What will not change are the criteria by which they will judge the quality of their own thinking and that of their colleagues. In the future, a vast electronic information system will largely replace our present reliance on textbook, journal and library. Such information may well be available on a visual display unit on the general practitioner's desk, at the touch of a button. In such a professional future, how much the doctor knows will be much less important than how well he thinks. Teaching about clinical method should be a training in scientific method, the uses of probability and the rigours of logic. These have always been a part of good general practice.

References

[1] Medawar, P.B. (1969) *The Art of the Soluble.* Harmondsworth: Penguin Books.
[2] Morris, J. (1972) 'Three aspects of the person' in R. Ruddock, (ed) *Six Approaches to the Person.* London: Routledge & Kegan Paul.
[3] Campbell, E.J. Moran (1976) 'Basic science, science, and medical education'. *The Lancet,* January 17, 134-136.

Further reading

Feinstein, A.R. (1967) *Clinical Judgement.* Baltimore: The Williams & Wilkins Co.
Marinker, M. (1976) 'Clinical problem-solving in general practice' in J.J.C. Cormack, M. Marinker and D.C. Morrell (eds) *Practice.* London: Kluwer Publishing.
Working party of the Royal College of General Practitioners (1972) *The Future General Practitioner: Learning and teaching.* London: British Medical Association, Ch.3, 21-47.

17
Whole person medicine
Marshall Marinker

Introduction

The term 'whole person medicine' has come into use over the last two or
three decades as a motto, a banner to proclaim that medicine is concerned
with more than a bio-engineering concept of man. But the motto is a
dangerous one. Even after a relationship extending over many years
between a perceptive doctor and a patient prepared and anxious to reveal
large areas of private life, it is unlikely that the doctor's view of his patient
can encompass the whole person. If the clinical teacher implies that such
relationships and understandings are available to him in his practice, he
will not only mislead the student or trainee, who may see through the
deception quickly enough, but he may discourage the learner from setting
himself much less ambitious but much more fruitful objectives.

If the clinical teacher persists in such fictions, the student or trainee may
relinquish any realistic hopes of coming to some understanding of patients
as people, because of the limitations of time, skill and most of all appetite
for such intensive exploration. In this sense the exaggeration in the term
'whole person medicine' defeats the object of the exercise: the learner is
discouraged because he is taught that the task is impossible.

Even more dangerous, the fiction of whole person medicine encourages a
view of the doctor–patient relationship in which the doctor is accorded a
very manipulative role. In military terms, to know the whole person is to
command all the passes. The patient is then allowed no secrets, no parts of
his body or personality which he may hide from the doctor.

The intention behind this fiction, however, is benign. It is not that the
doctor should try to understand and evaluate the whole person, but rather
that the general practitioner should 'compose all of his diagnoses
simultaneously in physical, psychological and social terms'.[1] This
statement, first propounded in *The Future General Practitioner* and now taken
to be part of the core objectives of all general practice teaching, is still
greeted with rapturous enthusiasm by some clinical teachers, and with deep
hostility by others. The reasons for this hostility stem from two widely held
misunderstandings.

The first is that in all cases the physical, the psychological and the social
aspects of the problem have equal weight. They do not. But it is always
difficult to ascribe appropriate weighting. A three-year-old child is
diagnosed as having bilateral otitis media. The student may be asked about
the criteria for this diagnosis, and the relative merits of different antibiotics

explored. But along with questions about the likely need to combat haemophilus influenzae, there may be other questions to be discussed. It is one thing to select an appropriate antibiotic, another to have confidence in the patient's compliance with treatment. The mother may be anxious, even over-anxious. But the anxiety may be geared to the behaviour of the child rather than to the prognosis of the disease. She may therefore only administer the medicine for as long as the symptoms last.

A clinical history almost always extends beyond the symptoms of the disease. For example, the mother may mention that the child sleeps in the parents' room. The student should be alerted to the many possible reasons for this, and shown how the information may be a part of a whole person diagnosis that reaches beyond the pathology of ear infection. Problems like overcrowding, over-protection of the child, or even the child's presence in the parental bed as a symptom of the parents' sexual unhappiness, may not be a part of this consultation. But it may be an important part of the consultation tutorial.

A second misreading of the so-called triple diagnosis is that all diseases have psychological and social causes, as well as physical ones. Even in the so-called psychosomatic conditions like duodenal ulcer or asthma, a directly causal relationship cannot be ascribed with any confidence.

A young woman with asthma may have all sorts of anxieties — perhaps a fear of taking university examinations, or feelings of anger with her mother, which she cannot express or resolve. Here, the importance of the psychological component of the diagnosis is not related to a theory of causality but simply to a widening of the options open to the doctor who responds to the problem. If the asthma is provoked only at particular times of stress like taking examinations, or spending the weekends at home, treatment for the disease may include not only the continuous use of cromoglycate but also the exhibition of diazepam at the appropriate times. Whole person diagnosis is not simply an intellectual game, not an excuse for prying into the private lives of those who seek help. It is simply a way of making that help more relevant and sometimes more effective.

Not all social data can be used in the consultation. The fact that chronic bronchitis is more prevalent in social class V than in social class I does not help the clinician much. He cannot change the prognosis by changing the social class of his patient. But some variables associated with social class, like work or previous education, may be important components of whole person diagnosis and treatment. For example, the office worker with chronic bronchitis may be able to continue far longer in his employment than the factory worker. It is these aspects of clinical medicine to which the student and trainee must be sensitized.

More recently the term 'triple diagnosis', has been preferred to 'whole person medicine'. This suggests that the three aspects of the diagnosis should always be considered at each consultation, although in very many consultations work will be concentrated on one aspect only. These three aspects may be expressed as the physical, the psychological and the social, or using my own model of Unhealth: disease, illness and sickness (see Appendix).

A newly diagnosed diabetic woman may or may not need insulin. A view of the retina suggests retinopathy. Is it accelerating and is urgent treatment now mandatory? The disease has also changed the way in which she feels about herself. As an athlete and a successful sports teacher, physical fitness was both an occupational necessity and a personal ideal. The discovery that she is a diabetic now begins to affect her self-image and her relationship with her lover. Some hints of this may appear in the consultation. Is it appropriate for the medical student and the trainee to open up this area with the patient? And if so, what are the boundaries of his role as doctor? How far is he expected to go? Years later intermittent claudication may make it impossible for this woman to continue in her job. Now she is the sole support of her sick widowed mother and a brother who has Down's syndrome.

An American physician, Karl Menninger, writing about changing concepts of disease some 30 years ago wrote, 'A middle-aged Puritan spinster appears with a chancre on her lip. Isn't this a simple diagnosis? I don't think so. Nor would you if I told you the circumstances of how she acquired that chancre, whom she acquired it from, how she happened to select that type of man, or why she had permitted him to kiss her. Her sickness cannot be accurately diagnosed as syphilis. She did not come to me because of it. What she came to me for was a more serious thing. She was so depressed about the implications of the infection that she now wanted to kill herself. What is the name of that disease?'

These views of the patient and the problem are best taught by example. In this sense the triple diagnosis should be a part of every clinical discussion, but the clinical teacher must keep a sense of appropriateness. To discuss issues of stigma or the sick role when this diabetic presents with ketosis resulting from an unsuspected pneumonia, would be to reinforce other teaching which the student or trainee has received — that doctors would do well not to venture beyond the bio-engineering view of their task. But it is equally inappropriate to discuss the possible relationship between the control of blood sugar on the one hand and the rate of vascular degeneration on the other, when this woman presents because, 'I broke up with my man last month and now my diabetic control has gone hay-wire...'

Teaching

A number of structured small group discussions have been used specifically to enlarge the student's understanding of the triple diagnosis. For example one student or trainee may present a patient to the group, and then three other members of the group are invited to enlarge the discussion. The first member is invited to explore aspects of the physical dimension of the problem. The second to explore the patient's likely feelings and their consequences, while the third looks at the patient's social setting and the likely interaction between disease, patient and society. An elaboration of this method is described by Medalie.[2] Here the small group concentrates not on different aspects of the patient's life, but on different aspects of the doctor's role. Again one student or trainee introduces a patient. The group leader then accords to different members of the group the role of primary physician, personal doctor, family doctor, community doctor and so on. Each of these members then explores the problem, usually by further questioning of the presenter, who may himself need recourse to the clinical records, in order to look at the implications of the clinical problem from his assigned point of view. The discussion which follows may highlight all sorts of conflicts of perspective and interest. An epileptic young woman whose control has been precarious in the past, wants to leave home because she cannot cope with her mother's depression. Her mother's concern has been suffocating her for years, but the mother–daughter relationship is seen by the mother as the only fulfilling part of her life. The daughter's compliance in taking her anticonvulsant therapy has not been good in the past. Freed from her mother's control and suffocation, she may well develop as a person but there is a danger that she may start having fits again. The young woman has now been given permission to hold a driver's licence, and this is crucial to her work. These problems emerged in the course of the consultation when the mother asked the trainee for a repeat prescription for her daughter's anticonvulsants and her antidepressants. At the same time she thought that her breasts were becoming lumpy and wondered if the trainee would mind examining her.

Teaching about the triple diagnosis is not simply concerned with enlarging the learner's view of medical problems in order to include psychological and social variables. For the medical student this may indeed be the most important task. But for the trainee and for the general practitioner who wants to look at whole person medicine in his continuing education, for example in a Balint group or something similar, there is an additional and more important task. The doctor has to learn how to cope with all this information, and how to take decisions about priorities and appropriateness. In this the study of the patient begins to encompass a study of the doctor himself.

References

[1] Working party of the Royal College of General Practitioners (1972) *The Future General Practitioner: Learning and teaching.* London: British Medical Association.

[2] Medalie,J.H. (1965) in a sympsium on the Art and Science of General Practice. *Journal of the Royal College of General Practitioners 9*, Supp. 2, 20-43.

Further reading

Magraw, R.M. (1966) *Ferment in Medicine*. Philadelphia and London: W.B. Saunders Co. pp. 1-83.

Appendix

In teaching about the problems which patients bring to doctors I use a model of 'unhealth'. The following description is quoted from my chapter 'Health and unhealth' in *Practice*.[1]

Modes of unhealth

There are three sorts of departure from health which the individual experiences, and society recognizes. As doctors, we respond, and differently, to all three, but an imprecision in differentiating one from another can lead us into all sorts of therapeutic traps.

The first mode of unhealth is disease. This is a pathological process, most often physical as in throat infection or cancer of the bronchus, sometimes undetermined as in schizophrenia. The quality which identifies disease is a deviation from structural and functional biological norms. It is true that the concept of biological norms only takes us a little way. In a now famous controversy about hypertension, Platt held the view that high blood pressure was a distinct disease entity.[2] He believed that we could say either that the patient had hypertension or that he did not, in much the same way as we can claim that a patient either has or does not have influenza or an inguinal hernia. Pickering argued that blood pressure was a biological measurement that is continuously distributed in the population; that blood pressure was a measurement like weight or height. The general practitioner is aware that in his practice population there are not two distinct groups, one thin and one fat, but rather that the weights and heights of his patients are continuously distributed: those at either end of the scale he recognizes as being 'underweight' or 'obese'. Pickering demonstrated that the same is true for measurements of blood pressure: in statistical terms the distribution is not bi-modal but uni-modal.[3] The Bedford survey of diabetes mellitus revealed a similarly continuous distribution of blood-sugar measurements.[4] The cut-off point, the moment when the label switches from healthy to unhealthy can no longer be sharply marked. It is negotiated in relation to a host of factors. These include the believed prognostic significance of the measurement at a particular moment in the life span of the individual; the ability of the individual to avoid the predicted consequences; the availability of a specific remedy; the morbidity of the treatment in terms of unwanted side-effects of drugs; the social cost; the future dependence of the individual on health care and so on.

There is an objectivity about disease which doctors are able to see, touch, measure, smell. For this reason diseases and their management are the central facts of a medical education. Even though every disease is a unique event in the life of a unique individual, diseases are studied as ideal textbook models. The presence of a disease reveals itself to the doctor, in so far as the unique event in the patient resembles the ideal model the doctor recognizes from the literature. It is in this sense that the patient has been described as the accident of the disease.

The second mode of unhealth is illness. Illness is a feeling, an experience of unhealth which is entirely personal and interior to the patient. It most often accompanies disease, but may be entirely absent in the early stages: for example, tuberculosis, or cancer, or hypertension. Sometimes illness is experienced where no physical disease can be found. Doctors (and sometimes patients too) find this state of affairs hard to tolerate. Often the problem is 'resolved' by instituting a plethora of investigations, and when these have not yielded the description of a recognized disease, labelling the patient with a psychiatric disease like 'hysteria' or 'neurosis'.

The third mode of unhealth is sickness. If illness is an interior and personal experience for the patient, sickness is the external and public display of unhealth. Sickness is a social role, a status, or a negotiated position in the world. It is a bargain struck between the person henceforward called sick, and the society which is prepared to recognize and sustain him. The security of this role depends on a number of factors. The most important is to be in possession of a disease. Sickness based on the presence of illness alone is a very uncertain status.

Disease alone, however, guarantees nothing. The status accorded the sick person is influenced by the disease from which the individual suffers. The chronic sick are much less secure than the acute; the old than the young; the psychiatric than the surgical. The role of the doctor may be to cure diseases or to relieve illness: in contrast, society recognizes and legitimates sickness. At every consultation the doctor establishes, maintains, terminates or denies the sick role to his patient.

References

[1] Cormack, J.J.C., Marinker, M. and Morrell, D.C. (eds) (1976) *Practice: A handbook of primary medical care.* London: Kluwer Publishing.
[2] Platt, R. (1968) *Lancet, 2,* 55.
[3] Pickering, G. (1968) *Hypertension.* London: Churchill.
[4] Butterfield, J. (1968) in *Screening in Medical Care.* Nuffield Provincial Hospitals Trust. London: Oxford University Press.

18

The doctor–patient relationship: confidentiality

Marshall Marinker

Introduction

Few aspects of general practice present so many challenges to the teacher because the term 'the doctor–patient relationship' is so much part of everyday speech, and has become such a key term in the rhetoric of medical politics that there are assumptions about meanings and significance which easily escape challenge. 'The doctor – patient relationship' has been used by medical politicians in debate about contracts, payment and confidentiality. It is used to refer to different concepts and concerns by clinicians, by sociologists, psychologists and many other behavioural scientists concerned with the medical transaction. This suggests that the teacher must have a grasp of the different meanings ascribed to the term by a variety of disciplines and writers.

Further, the term implies that the general practitioner teacher himself, in teaching about this subject, is both the teacher and at the same time also the object. His own behaviour is part of the syllabus that must be learned. As doctors who teach about the doctor–patient relationship, what we have to discuss and demonstrate is primarily our own interaction with the patient. We are denied that comfortable distancing between observer and the object of study which is usually demanded of the behavioural scientist. In few other areas of medical teaching must the teacher, therefore, demonstrate so much self-understanding. He must be able to develop and teach the habit of participating in a consultation, at the same time monitoring the quality, content and feeling of the encounter.

As though this were not difficult enough, the needs and preoccupations of the learner in this field will vary greatly. In general terms the experience of many teachers is that the medical student has a quite different orientation from the vocational trainee and the established principal. The medical student sees his own role in these clinical encounters as that of an observer: his first task is to learn, not to care for the patient. This is not to say that the medical student is not concerned with medical care, but simply that he is more interested in the question, 'What is going on?' than with the question which must concern the vocational trainee and practitioner, 'What shall I do?' These two perceptions, these two levels of involvement, have important implications for teaching about the doctor–patient relationship.

The doctor–patient relationship concerns not only stereotyped expectations and behaviour, but must also reflect intimately the personalities of the teacher and the learner. The authoritarian rigid highly-defended student will have problems with this subject very different from those of the empathic non-directive student whose emotional involvement may become overwhelming. Both may become casualties in the course of their medical education: both may damage both their patients and themselves.

Whatever methods may be selected, or content agreed upon, the medical student and trainee will learn about the doctor–patient relationship by modelling. This is to say there will be unconscious learning by the student, who will see the clinical teacher as a model or example to be emulated. It is in this way that we acquire attitudes to patients, strategies for dealing with particular situations, even mannerisms. To this day I can detect the influence of my great mentor Michael Balint not only in some of the phrases which I catch myself using, but even, occasionally, in the hint of a Hungarian accent. The styles of each of us are composed of such fragments from our own medical education.

The ethics of the relationship

The Declaration of Geneva (1948) states, 'I will respect the secrets that are confided in me'. Much of the received wisdom which we have about confidentiality gives us the illusion that there are rules of conduct which doctors simply have to learn and follow. But as in so much else in medicine, we proceed on the basis of custom, our 'facts' are often unproven or unreliable, and we have to tolerate a great deal of uncertainty. What constitutes a secret? What are the patient's expectations concerning the information that he gives? A young woman patient may have no sense of stigma concerning her homosexuality, but regards the psoriasis which she hides behind her long flowing dress as the most sensitive secret of her life.

Public and private information

There is no sure way of assessing the sensitivity or secrecy of a piece of information. The clinical teacher must be aware that there are a number of partial and complementary frames of reference.

1. *What sort of information is being given?*
    Common sense is always a useful touchstone — that is to say, the sensitivity of the information which the patient gives may be judged according to the perceived practices of our society. Metcalf suggests the following hierarchy of sensitivity of information:[1]

(a) Non-sensitive information which the patient would not mind the doctor sharing with all members of the practice team, e.g. data about the common cold.

(b) Information that the patient is prepared for the doctor to share with only staff members directly involved in his care, e.g. data about diabetes.

(c) Information which the patient is only prepared to let the doctor share with another doctor whom he may come in contact with in the practice (in an emergency, because the patient can always avoid delegation to an ancillary worker).

(d) Information which the patient is only willing to divulge to that particular doctor with the understanding that he will remember it for as long as he remains his doctor (e.g. a controlled alcoholic).

(e) Information which the patient is only prepared to divulge to the doctor to enable him to cope with an acute episode and which the patient would rather the doctor 'forgot' immediately afterwards (e.g. an extramarital affair resulting in venereal disease).

2. *What does the patient tell you about the information being given?*
Beyond any consideration of societal norms, the doctor must consider what the individual patient regards as sensitive and non-sensitive information. Certainly the patient cannot be expected to give a sensitivity rating to everything that he says. Sometimes the sensitivity rating is easy to assess: 'I don't want you to write this down, doctor', or 'Nobody knows about this apart from my wife'. But much more often a clue to the sensitivity of a piece of information comes from the patient's unconscious behaviour. The patient may have difficulty in finding words to express himself, may blush, may lower his voice to a whisper. When this happens the student or trainee must be shown how to respond. The response may be verbal and direct, 'You want to tell me something painful and confidential. That's all right'. The doctor's response may sometimes be appropriately non-verbal. He may put down or close his pen. Social psychologists have demonstrated a whole range of body language and facial expressions which indicate a change of mood or tempo in an interview, signifying the exchange of confidential or secret information (see Chapter 20).

3. *With whom is the information being shared?*
The Shorter Oxford English Dictionary makes it clear that inherent in the idea of a secret is the idea that it is information which is shared with someone. The status of a secret is therefore reflected in the status of the person or persons with whom it is shared.

Patients are aware that medical records are filed by clerks, that letters of referral are typed by secretaries and read by others, that many doctors, nurses, technicians and others may be involved in the solving of a particular problem, even though for the most part the meeting between doctor and patient is personal, intimate and exclusive.

Sensitive information in medicine is the exception rather than the rule. Illich does well to remind us of the patient's right to automony, but his analysis fails to recognize that persons do not always wish to be autonomous and that the act of becoming a patient is in its essence also a surrender of some autonomy.[2]

Secrets and the team

Much tension arises between members of adjacent professions, for example between doctors, social workers and health visitors, because issues of professional rivalry and distrust masquerade as issues of confidentiality and professional ethics. These have their roots in different educational traditions, different theoretical frameworks for looking at the problems of patients or clients, as well as baser rivalries concerned with territory, status and rewards. The confidentiality of the relationship with the patient/client can become not so much a matter of mutual professional concern as ammunition for interprofessional warfare.

Each professional group, and each professional individual, has beliefs about what sort of information is privileged. The social worker may claim that no one else has the right to know about the detailed financial status of a client. The doctor may feel that only doctors have the right to know that a patient has early multiple sclerosis. Quite often during interprofessional case discussions, the complaint is made that vital information was withheld by one professional so that the 'whole picture' was not available. In the end the whole picture is never available to one professional: indeed its possession would give that professional — doctor, social worker or nurse — such total control of the patient's problem that there would be no room for autonomy and no possibility of escape. The helper would easily become the controller.

The final integration of health care occurs within the patient, it cannot occur within the health care team. 'Need to know' is a useful principle. It may be important for a social worker to know that a diabetic client complies poorly with treatment and that his disease often becomes uncontrolled. It may be no part of the doctor's direct concern that this same patient habitually defaults on hire purchase agreements. Teaching about whole person medicine should be much concerned with the doctor's willingness to look at wide areas of the patient's life and not simply at the manifestations of his disease. Teaching should make it clear that a concern for the whole person does not confer on the doctor the right to invade the whole person. The sharing of information which is perceived to be sensitive, whether that sharing is direct and intended or simply the result of making a written record, must always be negotiated with the patient.

Professionals can become too 'delicate' about such secrets. There seems to me to be no gross invasion of the patient's privacy in such statements as, 'I think the social worker ought to know about the problems you are having with your diabetes' or, 'You tell me that you are getting a lot of help with your problems from the social worker. Do you think these problems are making it difficult to keep your diabetes under control?' The vast majority of patients are neither feeble-minded nor servile and can defend their own secrets.

Secrets and the family

Students and trainees must be encouraged to ask the question, 'What harm can come from sharing this patient's secrets?' There are two categories of possible harm. The first concerns the social and psychological damage that can ensue. For example a patient may lose a job or be socially embarrassed by the public knowledge of a private disability. The second concerns the doctor's capacity to help. If there is no confidence in the doctor's ability to guard secrets reasonably, the patient will not tell them and much information which is important in the solving of clinical problems will remain unknown.

Issues of secrecy and confidentiality are never more sensitive than when they apply to family secrets. In his 1967 Reith Lectures, Edmund Leach said, 'Today the domestic household is isolated. The family looks inward upon itself; there is intensification of emotional stress between husband and wife and parents and children. The strain is greater than most of us can bear. Far from being the basis of a good society, the family with its narrow privacy and tawdry secrets is a source of all our discontents'. One does not need to share Leach's profound pessimism to acknowledge that all small groups are rife with secrets. Within the small group of the family, the intensity of relationships and feelings is such that secrets are peculiarly sensitive and potentially destructive. For this reason, the so-called family doctor must remember that he is first and foremost a personal doctor. Information gained from one member of the family, or about one member, cannot be readily shared with all the others. In so many instances of patients with, say, venereal disease or cancer or mental illness, the general practitioner treads a minefield of family secrets. In this sense, the notion of the family as patient runs counter to the notion of a medicine of persons.

In few other areas of our professional work is there a greater need to respect secrets. Ill-conceived notions of a family orientation in general practice can be both confusing and misleading to the student and trainee, who may be led into making otherwise avoidable confidentiality gaffes.

Preaching ethics and learning skills

Issues of confidentiality will become important in tutorials, in small group case discussions and often in the management of student or trainee projects. There is a great temptation for the teacher to enunciate rules for good professional behaviour which will simply reinforce the learning by modelling described earlier. Sometimes the teacher's exhortations may seem to contradict his own behaviour, so that what may be learned is the disparity between what the doctor preaches and what he practices.

Much more potent is the reflection back to the learner of the questions that he asks. The daughter of an elderly patient may telephone to discuss her mother's condition, and in the course of the telephone conversation the doctor may refer not only to the mother's increasing dementia, but also to the fact that another daughter, living with her mother, has recently suffered an exacerbation of gallbladder disease. The trainee may want to question the propriety of this discussion. The doctor may instinctively wish to leap to his own defence, or escape into a generalized discussion of broad ethical issues. A much more powerful response might be, 'What confidential knowledge did I betray? How do you define a secret? What do you think are the consequences of sharing this information — consequences for the patient, for her family, or the other members of the team?' If the learner is obliged to think through these issues he becomes equipped not with ready answers, but with the faculty for the analysis of unpredictable problems of confidentiality which will be posed to him throughout the rest of his professional life. In this, although questions of confidentiality must in part reflect moral judgements, the teacher will do well to emphasize that the rhetoric of ethics sometimes obscures the need for a sharper examination of skill and competence in handling the doctor–patient relationship.

References

[1] Metcalf, D. (1977) Unpublished paper on 'Confidentiality and medical records'. London: Royal College of General Practitioners.
[2] Illich, I. (1974) *Medical Nemesis*. London: Calder and Boyars.

19

The sociology of the doctor–patient relationship
Marshall Marinker

Introduction

Under this broad title I refer to that view of the doctor–patient relationship which is concerned with such issues as authority, power and control. The literature of medical sociology on this subject is vast and many academics concerned with medical education have doubted the appropriateness of much of it to the training of doctors. In part this is because the analysis of the doctor–patient relationship in sociological terms is part and parcel of much wider concerns in academic sociology. Doctors may or may not learn something about their own behaviour from reading these studies, and what they learn may or may not change their behaviour and this in turn may or may not modify the quality of the care which they give to patients. The arguments put forward are often couched in a language difficult for the layman to understand (and in the world of the behavioural scientist the doctor is a layman). The research methodology is often unfamiliar to doctors, so that it may be difficult to judge the quality of a piece of work or to distinguish between the results of findings and the eloquent statement of a point of view.

Nonetheless there is a theme which runs through much of this work. Stated crudely it is that the nature of medical education, and the place which the doctor occupies in society, put great power in the hands of doctors and weaken the position of the patient. As a result, interaction between doctor and the patient becomes one-sided, the doctor is able to impose his own view on the patient, and the patient is denied that autonomy or reciprocity which he might expect in other relationships. While this may be true of all professional relationships, in the medical transaction the inequity of distribution of power is particularly great and the possibly harmful results of this inequity are particularly severe. What lie at the heart of this critique of the consultation in medicine are the facts which Friedson and other sociologists have pointed out: first, doctors do in fact possess special knowledge and skills which are unique to the profession and important in the care of patients; second, there is an implied need in the doctor–patient relationship that the doctor should be seen by the patient as someone of authority.[1] It is the misuse of this authority, or rather the dangers inherent in the use of this authority, which has often been the focus of attention of medical sociology.

Activity and passivity

Szasz and Hollander look at the relationship of the doctor and patient in terms of the amount of freedom and autonomy available to the patient.[2] The first model that they describe is that of activity–passivity. The doctor is active and the patient is passive. This is the sort of relationship which occurs in medical crises: the patient is severely injured, in great pain, delirious or comatose.

The second model is described as guidance–co-operation. Although the patient is relatively helpless, he understands what is happening to him and is able to take some part in the transaction. Examples might be a patient with pneumonia, or recovering from a coronary thrombosis, or presenting with a Colles's fracture.

The third model is that of mutual participation. Most of the patients seen in general practice, because of the sort of problems that they present, are able to participate in the relationship in a mutual way. Here the distribution of power between doctor and patient is more even.

Parent, adult and child

Eric Berne, the founding father of so-called transactional analysis, developed a theory of human behaviour in which he said that we take up one of three stances in our interactions with one another.[3] We can play the role of 'parent' which he characterizes as being authoritative, judgemental, appearing calm and aloof; we can play the role of 'child' which he characterizes as being dependent, wilful, uncontrolled, passionate and demanding; or we can play the role of 'adult' which is characterized by reciprocity, by openness, by an ability to express needs while at the same time recognizing the needs and rights of others.

In Berne's model, each of us is able to occupy these three roles and to switch between one role and another according to the situation, or according to the person with whom we are interacting. This is of course a gross over-simplification of his theories, and they are better studied in some depth from his own sharp and amusing writing. But on the basis of this view of human relationships, Berne has much to say about the doctor–patient relationship.

Intimacy and detachment

Parsons suggests that doctors have to have a certain view of their own feelings and behaviour in order to be able to perform their tasks.[4] First, doctors wish to base the practice of medicine on 'scientific truth'. That is to say that each clinical problem will be solved in terms of some universally accepted facts about the nature of the disease, and the way which this disease responds to certain remedies. For example, Mrs Potter is brassy, plump and flirtatious. Whenever she comes into the consulting room she draws her chair close to the doctor and sometimes puts her hand on his arm while she recounts her symptoms. On this occasion she gives of a history of polydipsia and polyuria and the urine sample which she produces is loaded with sugar. There will be 'scientific' truths about carbohydrate metabolism and the biochemistry of insulin which will underlie the doctor's diagnosis and his approach to her very individual situation.

Second, Parsons suggests that doctors like to think that their field of work is clearly defined. We in general practice know how uncomfortable we are made to feel when our clinical work seems to spill over into counselling about personal relationships, or making judgements about housing priority, and sometimes even about certification of absence from work. How much more comfortable most general practitioners are with Mrs Potter's diabetes than with her complaint that her husband is an unsatisfactory lover.

Third, Parsons asserts that doctors try not to become emotionally involved with their patients. In this sense Mrs Potter's flirtatiousness cannot be admitted into the frame of reference of the consultation. Still less that there is a mutual attraction between them:

Mrs Potter: Doctor, there's this irritation, you know, in the front passage. (Leaning forward), I feel there's nothing I couldn't tell you about myself doctor...

Doctor: This sometimes happens to women with diabetes. Now, there are some tests that I would like to perform.

The usefulness of Parsons's model is that it describes only partial truths; it is also a pastiche of everything that goes on in the doctor–patient transaction. Freidson and others have shown how far the reality departs from this model.

Nowhere are these large departures more clearly visible than in general practice. Again, these differences are not so much due to a different ethos of clinical medicine among general practitioners as to the different setting of general practice.

Authority

Goffman, in his analysis of power and autonomy in institutions, shows how in a closed institution the staff are able to impose conformity on the inmates.[5] In general practice, in sharp contrast, the patient has considerable independence. No matter what the constraints of the National Health Service there is a great deal of freedom of choice, for example, whether to consult or not, whether to take advice or reject it, whether to comply with medication or simply to stop taking the tablets and refuse a return visit.

In a study of physician authority in Great Britain, Marie Haug describes three modes of power which are exercised by doctors.[6] The first is traditional power, power vested in the role which doctors play in society. The second is charismatic power, power conferred on the doctor as an individual, quite separate from his social role. Most general practitioners are keenly aware of the way in which their patients ascribe special power to them: at the most simple level the trainee will have experience of a patient who has consulted him, been quite happy to accept his technical expertise, but has also required a subsequent consultation with 'his own doctor' because of a deeply held belief in his doctor's ability to heal him. Third there is bureaucratic power, the power of the doctor to manipulate the health care system. Haug comments in particular on the British general practitioner's key position in the Health Service, and the way in which his decisions can influence much of the patient's care in other places, for example in the hospital. Such power is almost unique to a health care system like our own.

Robert Strauss, in an article on 'Medical education and the doctor–patient relationship', writes

'Just as many marriages fail today over the inability of men and women to communicate with each other and to develop mutually supporting interpersonal relationships that extend beyond the physical aspects of sex, so many medical encounters fail because of the inability of physicians and patients to communicate effectively or to develop a relationship that extends beyond the biological or physical aspects of disease. The analogy between a medical and a sexual relationship has at least one more aspect. The doctor–patient relationship, like the sexual relationship, must be viewed as a two-way process. To physicians this means cultivating skills in learning about their patients: helping their patients to say "This is who I am", "This is why I am here", "This is what I fear", "This is what I hope you will do for me".'[7]

Here the concerns of the sociologist abut on those of the psychologist concerned with communcation, and with those of the physician who uses the relationship to widen his concept of diagnosis and to improve his effectiveness in treatment.

Conclusion

Many of these ways of looking at the role of the doctor and his relationship with his patient will have formed part of the background reading of the learner — both during the undergradute phase of clinical education, and often as part of the day release programme for vocational training. The clinical teacher should have some familiarity with the literature and the language, so that these issues may be highlighted in the course of teaching about the consultation.

Mr Jones is a 50-year-old schoolteacher in a private preparatory school. In the course of a consultation with the trainee, ostensibly concerned with a sore throat, he asks for a repeat prescription of some antacid medicine for his wife. 'She has been getting trouble with her gastritis, and is being a very naughty girl and not keeping to her diet.' Later in discussion the trainer points out that Mr Jones avoided mentioning that his wife was an alcoholic. In the course of a subsequent discussion of this consultation the trainer might reveal a long-running marital battle which preceded the wife's alcoholism, and the problems which Mr Jones had in keeping his wife's condition hidden from the board of governors of the school. Much about the husband–wife relationship might be explained in terms of the 'parent role' which Mr Jones revealed in his 'naughty girl' speech. The way in which his wife's underlying condition was omitted from the consultation may also be best understood in terms of what Goffman has to say about stigma. It is not the role of the clinical teacher to demonstrate aspects of medical sociology in the consulting room. But these perspectives can often deepen and enlarge the doctor's understanding of the transaction.

References

1 Freidson, E. (1970) *Professions of Medicine.* New York: Dodds Mead.
2 Szasz, T.S. and Hollander, M.H. (1956) 'A contribution to the philosophy of medicine: the basic models of the doctor–patient relationship'. *Archives of Internal Medicine, 97,* 585.
3 Berne, E. (1961) *Transactional Analysis in Psychotherapy.* London: Evergreen Books.
4 Parsons, T. (1951) *The Social System.* London: Routledge & Kegan Paul.
5 Goffman, E. (1968) *Asylums.* Harmondsworth: Penguin Books.
6 Haug, M.R. (1976) 'Issues of patient acceptance of physician authority in Great Britain' in Geographic Health Studies *The Doctor–Patient Relationship in the Changing Health Scene.* US Department of Health and Welfare.
7 Strauss, R. (1976) 'Medical education and the doctor–patient relationship' in Geographic Health Studies *The Doctor–Patient Relationship in the Changing Health Scene.* US Department of Health and Welfare.

Further reading

Magraw, R.M. (1966) *Ferment in Medicine.* London and Philadelphia: W.B. Saunders Co.
Tuckett, D. (1976) *An Introduction to Medical Sociology.* London: Tavistock Publications, pp. 190-221.

20
Communication between patient and doctor
Marshall Marinker

Introduction

There are many aspects of communication in medicine which are not central to the study of the doctor–patient relationship. These will be considered in Chapter 23. Here we are concerned largely with the structure and function of the clinical interview. How can the doctor put his patient at ease, create an appropriate 'social distance' between himself and his patient so that the patient is neither overwhelmed nor frightened by an inappropriate intimacy, nor intimidated by too great a distance from the doctor — spatial, verbal and emotional.

The setting

The structure of the consulting room, the way in which the furniture is arranged, the nature of the decorations, the absence or presence of medical apparatus (for example a tray full of syringes and needles on the desk), all have powerful predetermining effects on the nature of the communication between doctor and patient. In this sense, the way in which the clinical teacher sets out his consulting room conveys a message to the patient about what to expect and how to behave, and conveys a similar message to the trainee or the student.

If the doctor and the patient are seated facing one another across a large expanse of desk, the possibilities for intimacy, or at least for a particular sort of physical intimacy, are limited. The doctor will not be able to lean forward at one moment in the consultation and touch his patient's arm. By the same token if the positions of the doctor's and the patient's seats are fixed, say, very close to one another and side by side, the patient will not be able to withdraw his chair to indicate that he, the patient, wants to create some distance, spatial and perhaps emotional, from his doctor. This is not to suggest that there is necessarily a right or a wrong way to set out the consulting room. For that matter, doctors rarely have complete control over the layout of their consulting rooms, which may have been inherited from a previous doctor, and which may have architectural constraints which make change difficult. What is important for the teacher is to study the nature of his consulting and teaching environments, to allow the trainee to discuss the constraints imposed upon him by the structure of the rooms in which he consults, and to consider the implications of this for useful communication with the patient.

Language

In looking at communication the teacher may wish to employ a number of frames of reference. For example he may wish to consider the use of language. Doctors often lapse into professional jargon when talking to patients out of carelessness, out of a wish, conscious or unconscious, to control the situation, or as a means of escape from an emotionally difficult confrontation. 'They said at the hospital it was just an ulcer, doctor?' 'We hope it will prove to be an ulcer, Mr Brown. Actually, I am still waiting for the histology.'

Doctors may also use the language of bureaucracy or simply fail to realize that patients often use words which have a quite idiosyncratic meaning. The word diarrhoea, for example, may be used by the patient to indicate a copious frequent watery stool or the passage of one poorly-formed motion. Each locality will have its own special words for common symptoms and the need to learn and extend these vocabularies should be stressed by clinical teachers who will almost have forgotten how they came to learn them, and how easily and unselfconsciously they use them.

One of the most useful descriptions of verbal behaviour in the consultation is Byrne and Long's study *Doctors talking to Patients.*[1] Even though I might wish to quarrel with some of the categories and models suggested by these writers, their demonstration of preferred styles which sometimes amount to linguistic tics is masterly. These same patterns of behaviour may be demonstrated in both teacher and learner alike, and the study of a series of audiotapes of consultations, particularly during vocational training, may enhance the learner's sensitivity to his own problems of communication.

A study of the conscious use of language must be paralleled by a study of the unconscious use of words. Mrs Flanagan unconsciously addresses the doctor as 'Father' when she comes to ask for a repeat prescription. Both doctor and patient may make a joke of this slip of the tongue, but the thought might cross the doctor's mind that Mrs Flanagan has something to confess and the joke may become helpful and revealing.

Non-verbal communication

Parallel to a study of verbal communication the teacher should acquaint himself with the literature on the non-verbal aspects of doctor–patient communication. Again, the books suggested at the end of this chapter will make useful reading. Throughout their interaction, doctor and patient signal to each other by the way they dress, the posture they take up, the movement of eyes, hands, and even a range of sounds which are neither words nor meaningless and random utterances. These sounds, and the silences which surround them, may signal impatience, disapproval, acceptance and sharing.

It would seem unreasonable and perhaps even ridiculous to suggest that every consultation which is discussed should be analysed in this way. But time and again an issue of communication may turn the key for a clinical problem. 'She came to see me five times complaining of the pain in her back. I never thought once to examine her breasts.' The response, 'In a patient of this age the possibility of secondary deposits from carcinoma of the breasts should always be borne in mind' may ignore the powerful messages which this patient may have sent the trainee about what she feared, what she suspected, and how far she was prepared to let him find out.

Compliance

Finally, issues of remembering and compliance may be of vital importance to the learner, particularly when it comes to problems of management, including prescribing. Again the learner should familiarize himself with such findings as those of Philip Ley on how to increase patients' compliance with advice.[2] Not all the findings of experimental psychology can be easily incorporated into the natural dialogue of a consultation. Ley suggests that patients retain much more information if that information is given in 'explicit categories'. 'First, I am going to tell you what is wrong; what the treatment will be; what tests will be necessary; what you must do to help yourself...' Further, he suggests that repetition of information leads to better recall, and that specific instructions are better remembered than general ones. The example he gives is that the statement, 'You must lose weight', was considered less important by the patient than the statement, 'You must lose half a stone in weight'. The clarity of information given by doctors to patients and the implications of this for compliance, can often be well demonstrated in the analysis of tape recordings of the learner's consultations.

Conclusion

In addition to these frames of reference, the teacher who wishes to comment on a trainee's or student's clinical interview may want to take up such issues as, 'How did the consultation begin?'; 'How did you end the consultation?' Sometimes the question, 'How many times did this consultation begin again?' may alert the learner to all sorts of problems which the patient may have had with him in trying to state his problem. The learner should become sensitive to the ways in which he redirects the

145

patient, steers him away from areas which he, the learner, finds painful and so on. The teacher will not be able to facilitate such learning unless he himself becomes aware of his own strategies for defence.

References

[1] Byrne, P.S. and Long, B.E.L. (1976) *Doctors Talking to Patients*. London: HMSO.
[2] Ley, P. (1976) 'Towards better doctor–patient communications' in A.E. Bennett, (ed) *Communication between Doctors and Patients*. London: Oxford University Press.

Further reading

Bennett, A.E. (ed) (1976) *Communication between Doctors and Patients*. London: Oxford University Press.
Enelow, A.J. and Swisher, S.N. (1972) *Interviewing and Patient Care*. New York: Oxford University Press.

21

The doctor–patient relationship in diagnosis and treatment

Marshall Marinker

Introduction

Teachers, vocational trainees and medical students are primarily interested in the clinical uses of the doctor–patient relationship. These concern the ways in which the relationship illuminates the diagnosis and the ways in which the relationship facilitates, and often constitutes the treatment.

It is impossible in these pages to summarize the large variety of findings in the work of Michael Balint and his colleagues. But some key concepts will recur in clinical teaching.

First, Balint regarded the continuing relationship between general practitioner and patient as having considerable value for both. The relationship is rich in shared experiences: both doctor and patient have, over the years, given much to it. Information is shared, the intimacy is both physical and emotional, and a whole range of feelings may have been expressed: trust, love, fear, anxiety, relief, hate. Balint coined the term 'mutual investment company' for this relationship. Both doctor and patient have much invested and both draw interest.

The second key concept is that of the drug doctor. Long before Balint, doctors recognized that they themselves were the most potent drug that they prescribe. Balint introduced the idea that if doctors use a very potent drug, then they ought to understand its pharmacology. In this sense, the doctor should know the characteristics of his actions, his synergists and antagonists, the signs of underdose and overdose, the range of unwanted effects, the possibility of anaphylactic shock. Quite often a consultation which appears to be straightforward and self-explanatory to the doctor, completely mystifies the student. For example, a 50-year-old woman with long quiescent rheumatoid arthritis comes to see the doctor for a bi-monthly check. For years she has been taking a small dose of paracetamol. Almost nothing is said about joint pain, mobility or medication. The woman tells her doctor that she is still living alone in the flat where her mother died ten years ago. She mentions, as she has done so many times before, that her mother's room is as neat and tidy as it was when she was alive. Somehow the doctor's approval for this is elicited and then the patient goes.

To describe the problem that is being dealt with at this consultation as rheumatoid arthritis, or the treatment as paracetamol, is to misunderstand the reality of whole person medicine and the potency of the drug doctor.

But how the clinical teacher discusses these aspects of medicine with medical students who, despite all their sophistication in the behavioural sciences, are still grounded in a bio-engineering view of modern medicine, taxes the teaching skills of us all.

Another of Balint's key concepts is that the doctor–patient relationship is a mirror of other relationships in the patient's life. At first this seems to be an extravagant claim. After all, we ourselves have occasionally consulted our colleagues. Was our relationship then indicative of the intimacy which we share with our husbands or wives, or parents and children, or former teachers or present students? The answer to this must depend on the length of our relationship with the doctor and on the sort of problems which we brought to him.

Each of us has a particular style and particular strategies for dealing with others. Brassy, plump, flirtatious Mrs Potter, for example, may use her flirtatiousness not in order to permit more intimacy with another person but rather to limit that intimacy to a level which she finds bearable. In this sense her flirtatiousness in the consultation may be a way not of inviting a vaginal examination, but of trying to make sure that the doctor will not touch her. The patient who is deferential, who puts the doctor on a pedestal, may flatter him but at the same time ensures that while he remains perched on his pedestal he is out of harm's way.

The timid middle-aged man who does not like to bother the doctor, who is so sorry for taking up his precious time, may well employ similar strategies at work and at home. Much may be explained about his clinical history: for example, the fact that his duodenal ulcer which had been giving symptoms for years was only diagnosed when a change of boss resulted in a row at the office and a flare-up of his pain and vomiting.

Not all doctors are comfortable with these ideas, even though they may accord closely to their clinical experience. By the same token, not all medical students will be comfortable with these ideas. But they may be discussed and tested against the reality of the consultation or at least against its perceptions. One of Balint's most cryptic epigrams was, 'If you only ask questions, all you will get is answers'. By this he meant that the traditional questions of clinical medicine, or for that matter of clinical psychiatry, severely limit the response that patients can make, and hence limit the doctor's view of what is wrong with the patient. In the case of the timid man, questions about palpitations, sweating, or tearfulness, or early morning waking, may result in a diagnosis of anxiety or depression, but will take neither doctor nor patient further than a prescription for diazepam or amitriptyline.

The clinical teacher should be familiar with some of the basic literature of this school of thought, and a very short reading list is appended.

It may be important to enter one caveat about the work of Michael Balint and his 'school'. Despite the heated controversies which sometimes surround these ways of looking at medicine in general practice, it would be difficult to exaggerate the impact of Michael Balint's work on the way in which general practice has come to be seen as an academic subject and on the way in which it is taught. And yet, such is the nature of accelerating change in our society that many of the assumptions about social structures and the nature of the doctor–patient relationship which were fundamental to Balint's work, may no longer hold in the near future. Just to give one example, many predictions about geographical mobility in what has come to be called the post-industrial society suggest that in many locations the possiblity of large numbers of doctor–patient relationships extending over many years will be remote. When this happens, new techniques will have to be found to create the intimacy and trust which characterize Balint's mutual investment company, new ways of testing the efficacy of the drug doctor in much shorter and episodic relationships than Balint found when he first began to investigate the world of general practice.

Conclusion

Clearly a wide variety of teaching methods will be appropriate to the teaching and learning in this area. Much may be learned from observed consultations and their subsequent discussion. In learning about communication there is much to be said for a preliminary phase of reading, or even attending lectures and demonstrations. Subsequently the learning may be reinforced by the discussion of audiotapes of a learner's consultations, by role-play and the use of closed circuit television. Classically the established doctor developed his understanding of the doctor–patient relationship in Balint's seminars. This demanded of the learner that he became a participant in a research-oriented programme, and that he committed himself to weekly or twice-monthly attendance at small group sessions for a period of not less than three years. Such a commitment would usually be outside the possibility of a vocational training scheme. Elsewhere I have argued that Balint-type seminars may be inappropriate for both medical students and vocational trainees. Essentially Balint groups were concerned with an often painful exploration of the doctor–patient relationship over many years. Such groups of doctors often went through difficult periods, when negative aspects of the doctor–patient relationship, disappointed expectations and frustrations were often mirrored in similar feelings expressed by members of the group to each other and to the group leader. Two aspects of Balint made it possible to overcome these difficulties. The first was the continuing relationship between the doctor and the patient. The second was the continuing relationship between the group leader and the members of the group. Neither of these two conditions is possible for the medical student or the

149

vocational trainee during his one year in the teaching prctice. For these reasons I concluded that Balint groups were quite inappropriate during these early stages of medical education, and should be reserved for the postgraduate training of the established general practitioner.

But many of the concepts which came out of these Balint group researches will surface again and again in case discussion of all sorts — in the consulting room, the tutorial and the small group. What is required most of the teacher is a basic grasp of the vocabularies used by those who have written about the doctor–patient relationship, and a sensitivity to the learner's conflicts and his unspoken questions. A tutorial which begins with, 'I am having some difficulty in controlling this patient's diabetes' may contain a quite different and hidden statement about a problem in the doctor–patient relationship. In this, as in so much else, the parallels between the relationship between doctor and patient on the one hand and the teacher and learner on the other bear constant re-examination.

Further reading

Balint, M. (1957) *The Doctor, his Patient and the Illness*. London: Tavistock Publications.

Balint, E. and Norell, J.S. (1973) *Six Minutes for the Patient*. London: Tavistock Publications.

Berne, E. (1960) *Games People Play*. London: André Deutsch.

Byrne, P.S. and Long, B.E.L. (1976) *Doctors Talking to Patients*. London: HMSO.

Browne, K. and Freeling, P. (1976) *The Doctor–Patient Relationship*. Edinburgh: Churchill Livingstone.

Marinker, M. (1970) 'Balint seminars and vocational training in general practice'. *Journal of the Royal College of General Practitioners, 19,* 79.

22
The family
Marshall Marinker

Introduction

The term 'family medicine' has, in some countries, for example the USA and Canada, replaced 'general practice' as a description of our subject. Even in the UK the term 'family doctor' is used as an alternative to 'general practitioner'. Most practising doctors are aware that a family history, for example a knowledge of the diseases suffered by the parents and siblings of the patient, may be an important part of clinical problem-solving — not only in general practice but in internal medicine, gynaecology and almost every branch of the profession. Sometimes the significance of the family history is quite clear to the doctor, even though the mechanisms involved remain mysterious. A young man of 20 presents with a typical history of duodenal ulcer. The doctor discovers that his father and uncle have both had proven peptic ulcers, and that an elder brother has recently died. The family history gives one possible source of recent stress, and suggests a pattern of illness in the family which may reflect similar personalities, similar dietary habits or ways of reacting to anxiety, and perhaps also a similar (genetically determined) physical make-up. The diagnosis of the young man's condition is confirmed, and he makes a good response to cimetidine. How important was the family history?

What cannot be denied is that the idea of being a family doctor is of central importance to most general practitioners. Most of the declamatory literature of general pracice takes for granted that the relationship between the patient and the family, and the family and the doctor, is central to the function of the general practitioner. The expression of a contrary view is a solitary exception. [1]

The clinical teacher may wish to refer to the family of his patient for a number of reasons. First the family represents the biological and social setting of the individual. A 50-year-old man presents with severe but 'atypical' chest pain. Has the student elicited a strong family history of IHD? Or the problem may reflect a complicated inheritance whose transmission may be as much behavioural as genetic. A teenage girl is grossly obese and seeks help. The trainee may understand much more when he sees the girl's parents and her older sibling, all of whom are similarly overweight. Attempts in the past to prescribe diets for the parents have met with little compliance, and now the mother is diagnosed as suffering from maturity onset diabetes.

The clinical teacher may express anxiety about a child, which the trainee is at a loss to understand. John is three years old and remains quiet and passive throughout an examination for abdominal pain. The clinical teacher knows that there is a family tradition of physical aggression, and it is this knowledge of family behaviour together with the quietness of the child, which determines his search for other evidence of non-accidental injury.

Frameworks for teaching about the family will be discussed later in this chapter. The clinical teacher, although he is not concerned to teach the behavioural sciences, may nonetheless wish to share with his student the language which demographers, sociologists and others use in describing family structure.

Family structure

The *family of origin* is the one into which we are born. The *family of orientation* is the one into which we enter, usually by marriage or some similar arrangement. The tendency of people to marry within their own ethnic cultural and socio-economic group is called *assortive mating;* love may appear to threaten the likelihood that the young person will marry his or her 'own kind', but sociologists have demonstrated how selectively Cupid aims his arrows, and how likely they are to hit those of similar background.

The basic family unit of parents and children within one household is referred to as the *nuclear family,* and this is the most important social unit in our society. The larger group of relatives, often living at some distance in modern society, is called the *extended family.* Just how important the extended family has now become in terms of medical care is uncertain. The tendency for extended families to be geographically dispersed is increased in the higher social classes who may therefore have fewer immediately available close relatives, for example siblings, to rally round at times of medical crisis.

This dispersion of families, now greatly increased because modern industry and commerce require a more mobile labour force, is called *geographical mobility. Social mobility* describes the migration of one member of the family out of his own social class into another. The 'success' of a shop assistant's son in becoming a senior manager may disrupt family relationships and cause serious emotional disturbances in both the parents, who may feel betrayed and left behind, and in the son who feels guilty.

Doctors are aware that there are particular clinical problems associated with different phases of the family's life cycle. A period of *expansion* describes the mating, marriage, child bearing and child rearing years of family life. Here the student or trainee may meet a number of clinical problems concerned with the forming of relationships and the changing roles of young men and women. Clinical problems may arise from difficulties with sexual adjustment, separation from the family of origin, and the working out of househould duties and responsibilities between husband and wife, which behavioural scientists call *conjugal roles*. Classically, the working class family is said to exhibit highly differentiated conjugal roles. The father would not expect to bath or feed the children, and the wife would not expect to assume economic responsibility for the family, or dig the garden. The middle class family shows much less differentiation, and conjugal roles will more often be shared than divided. Nonetheless in most western societies the old social class variables are less and less in evidence. In particular the changing expectations of women, most powerfully brought about by the control of conception, has resulted in a much more complex pattern of roles and relationships than the foregoing simplistic description suggests.

The period of *dispersion* refers to the stage when children grow up and leave home. Again the clinical teacher is often aware that the mother's early menopausal symptoms may coincide with her daughter's puberty and the beginning of sexual activity. Here the student or trainee may meet something of the paradox and conflict implicit in the notion of the family doctor. The daughter's request for contraceptive advice, her wish to leave home and escape from her mother's dependency may well be part and parcel of her mother's deepening depression and attempted suicide. The immediate needs of mother and daughter are not easily reconciled, and the general practitioner as family doctor must also be an effective personal doctor to them both, and perhaps to the father who rarely consults his general practitioner, but may be a key figure in the drama which is brought into the doctor's consulting room.

The period of *independence* describes marriage after all the children have left home. It is at this stage that many of the major diseases begin to take their toll. The period of *replacement* describes old age, often with only one partner surviving. The problems of caring for an elderly, infirm and socially isolated woman will be among the most difficult problems facing the young doctor in training.

The tidiness of this classification obscures the fact that these descriptions apply only to models, almost abstracts of family life. In effect these periods overlap. In a family with many children born over most of the childbearing period, it may be impossible to distinguish between the periods of expansion and dispersion, and the period of independence may be curtailed to a very few years indeed.

The *nuclear family* is the basic unit of western society. This describes two parents and either two or three children. But with changes in social mores, easier divorce, liberalizing of attitudes towards extramarital intercourse and homosexuality, other forms of family configuration become increasingly common. The proportion of single parent families is increasing in our society. When illness occurs, the trainee should be asked to list the special problems which the one parent family presents. How will the conflict between the need to work and earn money on the one hand, and to stay at home and care for the sick child on the other hand, be resolved? What social resources are there to help the parent?

The single child family and the family with five or more children will present the doctor with important variants in relating family life to the clinical problems with which he must deal. The trainee may make simplistic assumptions about both these families, and for that matter about the childless couple. Not all of these states are accidental or involuntary. The childless couple may live in an unconsummated marriage, may have happily opted for a life of foolproof contraception, or may deeply mourn the babies they cannot have.

A particularly difficult problem for the clinical teacher is how to handle the relationship between the members of such families and the student or trainee. The temptation is to tell the learner beforehand what the clinical teacher already knows about the family, its predicament, the choices which have been made or the situations which have been predicted for them. Mr and Mrs Brown are both in their fifties. They lead busy and successful lives as schoolteachers. There is a practice policy to carry out cervical cytology every five years. Mrs Brown is due to see the trainee and it is more than likely that he will offer her an appointment at the practice's Well Woman Clinic. If the clinical teacher warns the trainee that Mrs Brown is still a virgin, that in the past she has indicated strongly that she does not wish to discuss this, the patient will certainly be protected from any embarrassment in the ensuing consultation. By the same token the trainee will be denied what may be a most important learning situation. Much must depend on the clinical teacher's estimation of his trainee's senstitivity and social skills.

Family records

There have been a number of attempts to produce a record system based on the family, or reflecting the family relationships of the individual patients. Kuenssberg and Sklaroff introduced a Family Register in 1961 for use as an epidemiological tool.[2] Here, using a loose-leaf file, each household for which the practice provided medical care was represented by a sheet in which the mother was recorded as the key figure, and other people living in the same household were indentified in relation to her. Where other relations lived in other households for which the practice provided care, there were cross references. The information was gathered by medical reception staff at the time when the patients attended surgery, and the information was gradually enriched over a period of years. Using this register it is possible to construct quite extended family trees within a practice, and to extract from the notes a great deal of clinical information. Using the so-called F Book it was possible to ask questions about the familial incidence of a number of diseases, to compare patterns of attendance over time, and so on. The setting up, and even more the maintenance of such a complex demographic register will not be undertaken lightly and the vast majority of teaching practices will have no use for the F Book. Nor does such a register allow the doctor to have immediate information about the family, when he has seen the patient.

Cormack has devised a notation for producing 'family portraits' in the individual patient's notes — though he has the advantage of using A4 size records.[3] Others have developed adaptations of his idea. A few practices actually file the patient's record in family groups, and this collection of records is available to the doctor whenever he consults. None of these methods is used in the vast majority of teaching practices. Much more common, however, is the inclusion of information about the patient's family on a Summary Card or Significant Information Sheet. Here, particularly strong family histories may be recorded — for example atopy or ischaemic heart disease. Important demographic data, for example divorce, the death of a spouse, and so on will also be recorded. Where a form of family records exists, the student or trainee may be able to mount a number of studies of 'family medicine'. The absence of such records, however, in no way prevents such project work in the practice.

Family function

The language to describe the structure of the family is common to most behavioural scientists. There is no such common language used to describe the function of family life. On the contrary, there is a wide variety of 'schools' and a number of intriguing and inventive models to describe family relationships. The clinical teacher would do best to stick to layman's language which he can share with his students and trainees without ambiguity.

The Jones family consult frequently. Robert Jones is 45. His wife Mary is 40. There are two children, Rose aged 18 and Diana aged 16. Robert is a machine operator and suffers from asthma. Mary used to complain bitterly about the side effects of the pill, and began to have very heavy periods after an IUCD was inserted. The symptoms persisted when this was removed, and a year later she had a hysterectomy. Rose has been suffering from anorexia nervosa for some years, but this is now improving. Diana alone remains relatively well and has asked the doctor to put her on the pill, but not to tell her parents. When Mary developed her menstrual problems and later had her hysterectomy, Robert's asthma considerably improved. Only now have the symptoms recurred, and when he comes for his bronchodilators he complains of Diana's behaviour and her 'wild' friends.

Such a constellation of individuals and their clinical problems may present at the consultation with any single member of the Jones family. In looking at the family aspect of the patient's problem, the clinical teacher may choose to talk about the family *atmosphere*. Is the Jones family permissive, or is there an expectation of conformity, of sticking to the rules? And what happens if the rules are broken? He may talk about their illnesses in terms of *role bargaining*. Either Robert or Mary 'agreed' to take on the sick role. Robert was asthmatic until Mary relieved him of the job by developing menstrual symptoms. The illnesses may well have served, among other things, to legitimate their sexual dilemmas, or perhaps their sexual indifference. Diana's relative health may have been purchased at the expense of Rose's illness. Again the situation may be probed in terms of the *tradition* of ill health in this family, or their myths about who is frail, who is strong, who is the real child in the family and who is allowed to be grown up. In this respect Eric Berne's notion of games and life scenarios may be useful (see Chapter 19).

One extreme view of family medicine is represented by Howells's notion of Family Psychiatry.[4] Howells holds that the psychiatric patient is almost never an individual. The patient is almost always the family and its relationships. He writes, 'The family is sick rather than the individual. Indeed the family is the patient. Family psychiatry has as its central idea that the family should replace the individual as a sick unit and that the family group psyche rather than the individual's psyche be the target for assessment and treatment.' He makes it clear that he is talking about something much more radical than an attention to the family history. In dealing with Rose Jones's anorexia nervosa, the general practitioner is enjoined to interview the family together, to watch them interacting, to interpret the interactions and in this way modify the behaviour and relationship of the whole group. This approach has a small following among general practitioners in the UK, but the literature on family medicine from the USA and Canada suggests that such an approach is seen as being fundamental to family practice. In a textbook on this subject, Williams and Leaman write, 'The family physician has chosen the family . . . as his basic interest. He recognizes that this group of people are interdependent emotionally and physically. His basic tool is the intimate doctor–patient relationship that the family and he develop together. . . the family is the logical unit on which he focuses his attention.'

The problem with this view of family medicine is that it glosses over the right of the individual patient to privacy and autonomy. Indeed the general practitioner as family doctor is often forced, because different members of the same family look to him for care, to face and resolve what lawyers call 'a conflict of interest'. In this sense the general practitioner at each consultation has to redefine the boundary between his function as a personal and a family doctor. Most often he will do so unconsciously, weighing what he knows about the individuals, their openness with one another and their conflicts. It may require a positive effort to bring these considerations into consciousness when teaching from the consultation.

Teaching about the family

Most teaching about the family in medicine will be opportunistic. That is to say that the issues discussed earlier in this chapter will appear in the discussion of many consultations. But issues of family structure and function will not appear at every consultation, nor should the confusion of terms between general practitioner and family doctor force upon the clinical teacher the necessity to mention the family in every clinical discussion. Often the family will not be an important issue, and to drag it in because of some belief about the importance of the family to general practice will be to weaken the impact of more relevant teaching.

In a few medical schools, early teaching in the behavioural sciences may be reinforced by placing the medical student with a family who have a particular medical problem. If the general practitioner who is responsible for the care of the family acts as course tutor, the teaching of the behavioural scientist can be greatly reinforced and enriched. In my own medical school, first and second year students are attached to a family over an 18-month period. They make a minimum of six half-day visits to the family and each of these visits is followed up by a small group discussion led by the general practitioner responsible for the family's care. At each of these small group discussions particular aspects of each family are discussed. To start off with, the clinical teacher may ask the students to talk about the problems they encountered in establishing their relationships with the family, and their own role as medical students. What was their perception of the relationship? Would they be interested to note how these perceptions change over time? The second seminar might be concerned with the culture of the family, social class determinants and the contrast between the patient's family and the student's. And so on.

The following is a detailed list of the objectives of this course. The student is told that on completion of the courses, 'You should be able. . .':

1. To identify the culture and social class of the family and relate these to accommodation, neighbourhood, schooling, work and leisure activities.
2. To describe the family structure and the stage(s) of family development.
3. To describe the family's support network, including the extended family.
4. To discuss the perception of the members of the family of parental and conjugal roles.
5. To list the family's definitions, traditions and myths of health.
6. To list and describe the experiences of unhealth (observed by and reported to you) in members of the family during the two observation years.

7. To describe the way in which individual members of the family came to occupy the sick role, the bargaining that took place and the effect of changes in the sick role on other roles and behaviours in the family.
8. To discuss the process of seeking medical care in relation to aims 6 and 7.
9. To list what you consider to be the social and medical needs of the family and its members.
10. To list the available medical and social resources in the community which might have been appropriate to the needs of the family during the observation period.
11. To estimate the degree to which the needs of the family were or were not met from available resources.
12. To identify the reasons why some needs remained unmet.
*13. To describe the effect on the family of your presence and interactions with it.
*14. To discuss your own feelings about the members of the family, any problems in communications or relationships and the possible causes of these problems.
*15. To describe your own role, difficulties and satisfactions in helping to organize the care of the family.

The last three objectives are asterisked because they involve the student in looking at his own feelings and behaviour, and for this reason may be the most difficult. The student is also told that these objectives are no more than a framework for his observations. In no way should they be taken as a sort of check list which the student takes in with him to his family visits. It is rather a check list against which he can later organize what has been learnt.

In the clinical years, and perhaps during vocational training, important aspects of family medicine can be taught by projects. The technique for these is described in Chaper 10. One group of students in their penultimate year, asked to devise a project on the topic 'are general practitioners family doctors?', devised a questionnaire for patients in waiting rooms of group practices. This questionnaire looked at the patient's perception of family doctoring, and collected information about the number of relatives in the same household who looked either to the same practice, or the same doctor, for care. Individual students can be asked to compose family portraits and to enlarge these with narratives about the health experiences of the family and their relationship in time and space.

In contrast to the opportunistic teaching about the family described earlier, a medical student may be asked to monitor family aspects of a series of consultations, perhaps during a part of his attachment to a practice. In how many of the consultations was the family background referred to by the doctor? How often were further data about the family elicited? How often were family factors important in understanding the cause of the illness, or the way in which it presented, or the way in which it was to be managed? A small group of ten students may quickly acquire a great deal of information about, say, 200 consultations. From this they may be asked to argue the case for and against the institution of a family record system.

Conclusion

This chapter has suggested a number of ways of looking at the relationship between the individual patient, his family and the illness. Most of the teaching will take place in the context of case discussions. Other methods, based on projects, may stretch the imagination of both teacher and learner. The enthusiasm for looking at the family dimension of general practice must always be tempered by a sense of the appropriate, the relevant and the realistic.

References

[1] Marinker, M. (1975) 'Family in medicine'. *Proceedings of the Royal Society of Medicine, 69*, 115.
[2] Kuenssberg, E.V. and Sklaroff, S.A. (1961) *Eugenics Review, 52*, 225.
[3] Cormack, J.J.C. (1975) 'Family portraits, a method of recording family history'. *Journal of the Royal College of General Practitioners, 25*, 520.
[4] Howells, J.G. (1970) 'Family psychiatry and family practice'. *The Practitioner, 205*, 280.

Further reading

Goode, W.J. (1964) *The Family*. New Jersey: Prentice Hall.
Huygens, F.J.A. (1978) *Family Medicine*. Nijmegan: Dekker and Van de Vegt.
Susser, M.W. and Watson, W. (1971) *Sociology in Medicine*. Oxford: University Press.

23
Communication with colleagues
J.J.C. Cormack

Communication with colleagues has assumed an increasing importance with the growth of group practice and primary care teams. The number of colleagues and the number of different types of colleagues with whom each general practitioner has to communicate have for most of us increased over the past decades. New patterns of practice organization have brought with them the need for a heightened awareness of the need for effective communication between colleagues.

Patterns of communcation are likely to vary between different practices and different localities. Teaching communication is better effected by example than by the exposition of theory.

For medical students and trainees exposure to the problems of communication between colleagues is probably best achieved by spending some time with particular groups doing their day-to-day work. It is valuable for students to spend a day observing the work of secretaries and receptionists in the office, or sitting in with the health visitor or going on rounds with the district nurse or helping in the practice treatment room.

Particular areas of communication with colleagues which should be considered include:
1. communication between doctors within a practice;
2. referral to consultants;
3. communication with nurses;
4. communication with secretaries and receptionists;
5. communication with members of outside agencies.

Communication between doctors within a practice

Much of the communication which goes on between partners is informal and relates to specific problems of individual patients. It might be thought that written communication between partners is rare, but on reflection it will be seen that such is in fact one of the major objectives of the medical record. Thus it is necessary to have some practice policy on the form and structure of the medical record (without stifling individual style or preferences).

Formal practice meetings, preferably on a regular basis, are usually needed to discuss administrative matters and proper minutes of decisions taken should be kept. Many practices find that additional meetings devoted entirely to clinical matters are helpful and stimulating. It is inappropriate for students to attend formal administrative meetings, though they should be welcome at clinical discussions. Trainees should be encouraged to attend both types of meetings.

Referral to consultants

Medical students, trainees and new entrants to practice should be acquainted with the local rules and customs with regard to out-patient referral, domiciliary consultations and emergency hospital admissions. The procedures vary from area to area, but many Health Authorities publish lists of out-patient clinics and the names of consultants who are available for domiciliary consultation. In some larger cities all emergency hospital admissions are arranged centrally through a Bed Bureau or some similar organization, while in other places requests have to be made directly to the hospital concerned.

There is no doubt that the more general practitioners and local consultants know one another on a face-to-face basis the better are the chances for optimal patient care and the less the scope for misunderstandings. Domiciliary consultations may help in this respect, and certainly postgraduate medical centres and local medical societies provide opportunities, perhaps not used as often as they should be, for consultants and general practitioners to meet on 'neutral ground' and get to know one another in an informal and social setting.

Referral letters, whether for out-patient appointments or emergency admissions, are important means of communication and deserve appropriate care and thought. It can be a helpful exercise to invite students to draft referral letters and then discuss the result, and in his early weeks in the practice a trainee may well find it useful to discuss with his trainer the contents of letters he prepares to send about patients.

It is useful to introduce the patient with some reference to his social details, e.g. 'retired railway porter, now widowed and living with a married daughter'. A succinct history of the presenting complaint and any positive physical findings and the results of any investigations undertaken will form the core of the letter. When relevant a summary of past medical history can be helpful (and for this purpose the presence of a completed summary sheet or card in the patient's medical record is invaluable). Current medication should always be indicated, along with a note of any known hypersensitivities and of immediate treatment given. Finally it is helpful to indicate just what help is requested: admission for further assessment, advice on management, consideration for surgery or physiotherapy, or whatever is appropriate.

162

Communication with nurses

There are, broadly, four categories of nurses with whom a general practitioner is likely to work. There are district or community nurses, practice or treatment room nurses, health visitors and midwives. Practice or treatment room nurses are often employees of a practice or group, while the other types of nurses are most usually employed by the Health Authority or Board and attached to individual practices.

There is, or should be, a good deal of individual contact and discussion between different members of the medical and nursing team to discuss the problems of individual patients. Decisions as to whether or not to have regular formal meetings or simply to organize such meetings on an *ad hoc* basis when particular issues arise which need to be aired will be dependent on local needs and views.

It is important to ensure that the opinions of the nurses immediately concerned are sought. Nursing tends to be a hierarchical profession (and of course nursing administrators have a vital role to play), but it is now recognized that nurses and midwives and health visitors are practitioners in their own right. It is not sufficient simply to state that nurses are valued as colleagues rather than ancillaries. The doctors must be able to work with them as genuine team members and acknowledge their own special expertise, knowledge and skills both as practitioners and teachers themselves. Not only do they have the right to be consulted, but the best interests of the patient may require the nurse's essential contribution.

It is sometimes difficult for nurses to appreciate fully the responsibilities and problems of the general practitioner's independent contractor status, but courteous communication by face-to-face meeting rather than written slips of paper, goes a long way to fostering a feeling of being part of a practice team, as well as part of a hierarchical nursing structure. General practitioners and nurses have managerial roles but they are basically 'workers' rather than 'management' and their common involvement in patients' problems forms the best basis for intercommunication.

Communicating with secretaries and receptionists

Secretaries and receptionists (and practice managers) are usually employees of the doctors with whom they work. Their responsibilities are considerable but it must be clear to all parties concerned that such responsibilities are delegated and must be exercised within policies established by the doctors.

The one universal policy should be that it is the primary role of secretaries and receptionists to serve the doctors' patients and not to protect the doctors. Of course efficient organization, the proper spacing of appointments, prompt passage of messages and dealing with telephone enquiries are all part of this policy of providing the best possible service to patients. But it is too easy for the doctor to feel (and sometimes show) irritation with the receptionist when the demanding Mrs Jones is slotted in (again) without having made an appointment or the ever complaining Mr Smith put through on the telephone in the middle of a busy surgery session.

Few of us can preserve ideal equanimity at all times, but we can all aim to achieve ideals. It is receptionists, now that appointment systems are almost universally operated, who have the very stressful task of being the members of the practice team in first contact with patients. It is the responsibility of the doctors to recognize this stress, to be sensitive to possible ways of alleviating the stress by improving working conditions (including providing adequate remuneration for their staff, in line with nationally agreed scales for employees in similar occupations) and by themselves trying to foster an atmosphere of calmness and cheerfulness.

Simple courtesy and consideration of others' viewpoints form the basis for successful communication, and teaching communication in this field, whether to students, trainees or new entrants to practice lies largely in encouraging an understanding and appreciation of job content. This may best be done by a short period of observation and possibly participation in some of the now quite complex and certainly varied tasks undertaken by these important members of the practice team. The key areas to be taught are the promotion of teamwork and the stressing of the interdependence of all in the task of serving the population of patients.

Communication outside the practice

Doctors often have to communicate with members of other groups and organizations on their patients' interests: with relations and employers, social workers and government and local authority officials, voluntary agencies and the clergy. To teach such communication it is first necessary to draw the attention of the student or trainee to the number and diversity of contacts involved.

Outside the immediate practice team and referral to professional colleagues it is of particular importance that issues of confidentiality are considered and that the patient's knowledge and permission are assured before information is divulged or conditions discussed. Generally, though not invariably, telephone communication should be avoided and either written reports or face-to-face consultation preferred.

Whenever possible it is helpful to get to know on an individual basis colleagues in other professions with whom one may have to deal frequently, and meetings with local social workers and local clergy on an informal and social basis can do a great deal to improve subsequent communication.

Teaching methods

Communication with colleagues can be taught by several different methods and in several different settings. Some examples have been given above and four suggestions follow for specific exercises which can help in covering aspects not already illustrated.

1. *The role exercise*

   This needs participants from different disciplines, such as doctor, nurse, health visitor, secretary, receptionist. A list of about 20 tasks is prepared and each participant is asked to mark on a questionnaire who they think should carry out the task. The answers are compared and form the basis for discussion. The tasks should be ones which may be undertaken by different workers, such as coping with a feeding problem in a child, a family in debt, a mother who visits the surgery with a child with a cold, a phone call for a home visit at 4pm, and so on. The exercise should reveal that different workers perceive their roles differently from their colleagues. Understanding this helps communication.

2. *Random records*

   If there is a secretary in the practice, a sample of copies of letters written by each doctor in the last week is taken by the secretary, without prior warning to the doctors. Alternatively, records can be drawn at random and the last letter written can form the sample. These letters are compared with the criteria suggested in the section 'Referral to consultants' above. A similar exercise can be devised of looking at the records themselves and testing them as a means of communication.

3. *The case conference*

   A case conference can be audio-taped or video-taped. This can then be replayed and the different members of staff can observe the way they communicate in a case conference.

4. *Problem solving*

   Problem-solving exercises concerned with communication breakdown or difficult areas of communication can be used, e.g. by role-playing practice meetings where the following problems have to be discussed:
   (a) How do you tell the trainee that he is lazy?
   (b) How do you deal with a partner who won't get out of bed at night?
   (c) What can you do about a receptionist with an abrupt manner?

Conclusion

Much of the essence of communication with colleagues should have been taught before the student even enters medical school, as it is based on good manners and sensitivity. On that foundation may be built an awareness of the needs of others and their roles in relation to oneself and one's patients. The methods of communication will vary according to the prevailing circumstances, the need for communication will be dictated by the perceived needs of the patient and the success of communication will depend on sensitivity to need and attention to detail.

24
Practice management
Michael Drury

General practice is one way, that adopted in the United Kingdom, of providing primary medical care. It is based on the concept that each primary care physician accepts responsibility for attempting to meet the medical needs of a defined population and each member of that population sees the general practitioner as his or her personal medical adviser. As a result of this arrangement, the general practitioner must accept that in addition to his clinical skills he needs the managerial skills to organize his time and resources in the most efficient way to provide the preventive care, first contact care and continuing care for the individuals in his practice. In carrying out this role, he works with nurses, health visitors, secretarial and reception staff. His ability to work with this team in an efficient way has an important effect on the quality of the care he delivers.

The trainer of young general practitioners and the teacher of medical students must determine how he can best convince his trainees and students that this is an important aspect of primary medical care.

'Mr Wheeler is found to have hypertension at an examination for life insurance. He later attends for a routine consultation at which his blood pressure is checked, perhaps his fundi examined, questions are asked about his medication and his prescription is renewed.'

For student and trainee such a consultation seems quite appropriate and is in the main line of his usual clinical teaching. But the questions that it should raise for him are seldom asked. Was it right that his hypertension should have been discovered in such a way? How many other unknown hypertensive patients are there who have entrusted themselves to this doctor when they registered with him? What sort of organization is required to identify and care for these and for many other patients? What is screening and what is case-finding? What is the effect of item-for-service payments? Will the patient keep his next appointment and how will we know if he does not? How do patients get to see a doctor? How will the patient renew his prescription and how will his doctor's partner know what drugs he is taking if he sees Mr Wheeler one weekend? What other people might be involved in his care?

Medical students and practice management

During his time in medical school the medical student may be taught in a didactic fashion about the pattern of organization of medical care. Freeling has shown that when general practitioners and students were asked to rank teaching about the organization of care for practice populations, students placed it at the lowest and general practitioners at the highest rank.[1] The part that general practice plays in the medical services for Great Britain was ranked for relevance half-way up a scale by both groups. Part of the discrepancy in ranking in the first topic may be due to the fact that this is more relevant to postgraduate education than to undergraduate education but it does, at any rate, reveal the conceptual gap that exists between thinking in terms of caring for individuals and caring for groups of people, between being a passive responder and an activator.

The general practitioner may be very skilled at managing illness but if he is not accessible to people with problems his skills are of little use. Accessibility to the doctor is then an important aspect of practice management.

The objectives set for the teaching of practice management will, of course, be very different for the undergraduate and postgraduate student. Objectives will usually be defined by the medical schools in broad terms such as:

'to describe the organization of care of a practice population', and
'to describe the role of general practice in the National Health Service'.

It is not easy for the teacher to decide within these broad terms what the concepts are that he hopes the students will have grasped by the end of the period of attachment. They must be defined and this will probably be helped by listing under the objectives topics such as:

1. The practice population — what it is in terms of numbers, age, sex, social structure and geographical distribution.
2. The range and incidence of major medical and social problems met within such a population.
3. The resources available to provide primary care for patients with these problems. These include workers such as receptionists, nurses (attached and employed), health visitors, midwives and social workers.
4. The relationships and communications between primary care and secondary and tertiary care, demonstrating an understanding of the way the referral system works.
5. How do patients obtain access to doctors? Appointment systems, out-of-hours cover and deputizing services.

From these it will be seen that the concepts the medical student should grasp are the managerial requirements for the care of groups of people as well as individual patients if effective and efficient care is to be achieved, and the role of the doctor in relation to other health care professionals.

Methods

It is much easier for medical students to move conceptually from the individual to the group and the teacher may find that starting with a particular consultation the student can be provoked to seek the answers to important questions covering the organization of primary care. Where the student discovers the answer himself he learns better. During the quest he will learn to develop a critical approach to the organization of primary care.

There is a wide range of different types of practice and different systems of management to be found. The student's experience must of necessity be limited to one or two practices. To overcome this difficulty different medical schools have devised a variety of strategies. Students are in most situations allowed to compare and contrast different practices and to share their experiences. It is necessary only for the teacher to allow the students to compare notes in the seminar setting and to evaluate critically the different patterns of organization they have observed.

Several strategies can be used to enable a student to meet the objectives. Starting from the consultation questions may be asked about the incidence and prevalence of a particular problem and this naturally leads him on to think about the practice organization. Many practices have an age/sex register. The student can be set some simple task which is useful to the practice. Let us say, for example, that a patient attends for a cervical smear. How many women in her age group have had cervical smears done? He can extract a list of names of patients in this age group and he may then tag the names in the age/sex register of those patients who have not had a cervical smear in the preceding five years. In the process the student should learn something about the logistics of anticipatory care, and the requirements of a record system. The relationship between this and the practice finances may be described. The fact that the student's activities in the practice are useful to the patients is an important motivating point. This is just one way in which particular groups of patients in a practice can be used to illustrate the relationship between organization and preventive care — examples include well-babies, immunization candidates, patients on oral contraceptives, hypertensive patients and the elderly.

Consultations often end with instructions for patients to return if not better within a given period. This may lead the tutor to discuss with his student the value of follow-up and how defaulters can be identified. The student may begin to think about the logistics of establishing a follow-up system — which patients? which diseases? what other registers are required and how are they established? About half the patients seen will leave a consultation with a prescription. Whether a prescription is necessary and what drugs are appropriate will frequently be discussed, but there are other important issues. If the prescription is to be repeated without a consultation what sort of system is required to exercise control? Would a structured 'drug sheet' be helpful in the records and how could this be introduced? If issues of this type are raised in the consulting room, the student will have plenty of material to contribute to a seminar on the relationship between the organization of primary medical care and the health of a population.

In teaching medical students about the role of paramedical professionals in the outcome of care and how they contribute to the resources of the primary physician, it is important that they should have personal experience of the roles of these workers. The student may be given personal experience of the role of the receptionist by working in the reception area under supervision.

The nurse and the health visitor have much to teach and attachment for a half-day can be very useful. The student should be not simply concerned with what these workers do, he should also consider the principles of delegation or substitution, the expanded role of these other professionals, their training and the way lines of communication are established and maintained.

About half the students passing through a practice will work eventually as general practitioners. They will learn about all these things later in much greater depth. It is the other half whose needs are really more important. This may be their only chance to grasp how important the organization and management of primary care is for the the care of individual patients.

Trainees and practice management

Area five of *The Future General Practitioner* lists in a succinct way the topics that need to be covered by the vocational trainee.[2] At the opening of the section on practice management comes the sentence: 'The best way to learn about management in general practice is to work in a practice where management knowledge and skills are successfully applied as a matter of course'. This must be true but we cannot assume that such practices are available for all, or that our way of running matters is the best, or that such knowledge and skills will be learned by the trainee without the use of specific techniques.

During his time as a trainee the young doctor will be taught in a fairly didactic way on his release course a number of subjects that are appropriate for this method of teaching. They will include:
— Practice premises
— Practice finance
— Partnership agreements
— The general practitioner and the law.

There are a number of other subjects that will be best covered by 'learning by doing' and once again it is important that teachers understand what they are trying to convey. It can be most easily summed up by saying that they are trying to show the *requirements of managing for change*. This implies that the steps in this process are thought out and can be acted upon. The management cycle must be familiar to most. The following diagram is one way of showing it:

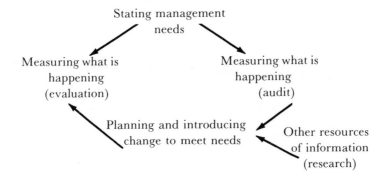

The most important part of this cycle is measuring what is happening. If the trainee practitioner is to be in a position to measure the effects of his care and to modify his organization accordingly, he must possess the skills necessary to look critically at the process and outcome of care. Teaching methods which may be used to cultivate this critical approach are described in Part IV of this book. In teaching about practice organization, trainees and students should be given group exercises in which they can examine critically such problems as the provision of cervical cytology to vulnerable groups in the community, the monitoring of repeat prescriptions, the completeness of immunization schedules, etc. One very effective way of making trainees aware of the importance of an efficient organization in the provision of such services is for him to undertake a small study in his training practice. In doing such a project the trainee will quickly recognize the importance of other members of the primary care team in providing comprehensive care. This should lead in turn to discussion of the relative roles of different members of the team.

Practice organization is concerned with defining the objectives of primary medical care, continually monitoring the process and outcome of care and continually supervising the doctor–patient relationship and communications. Many of the teaching methods described in Part IV are relevant to teaching about practice organization. Indeed, the care which the individual practitioner organizes reflects his knowledge, skills and attitudes in the use of finite resources to provide for the needs of a defined population.

References

[1] Freeling, P. (1980) 'General practitioners, students and the objectives of practice attachments'. *Medical Education, 14,* 273-276.
[2] Working party of the Royal College of General Practitioners (1972) *The Future General Practitioner: Learning and teaching.* London: British Medical Association.

Further reading

For undergraduates

Drury, M. and Hull, F.M. (1979) *An Introduction to General Practice.* London: Bailliere Tindall.

Morrell, D. (1976) *Introduction to Primary Medical Care.* London: Livingstone.

For postgraduates

Drury, M. (1981) *The Medical Secretaries Handbook.* 4th Edition. London: Bailliere Tindall.

Jones, R.V.H., Bolden, K.J., Pereira Gray, D.J. and Hall, M.S. (1978) *Running a Practice.* London: Croom Helm.

Pritchard, P. (1978) *Manual for Primary Health Care: Its nature and organization.* London: Oxford University Press.

25
Prescribing
J.J.C. Cormack

'From inability to let well alone; from too much zeal for the new and contempt for what is old; from putting knowledge before wisdom, science before art, and cleverness before common sense; from treating patients as cases, and from making the cure of disease more grievous than the endurance of the same, Good Lord, deliver us.'

Sir Robert Hutchison's prayer can fittingly guide our approach to the teaching of prescribing in general practice. Prescribing is the 'active' part of our work in the sense that this is one of the major activities we perform for our patients, once we have established some sort of diagnosis for their complaints.

Unlike the well-worn and accepted patterns of history-taking, examination and investigations, prescribing tends to be a highly personalized outcome of our activities and in teaching about prescribing we may need to be more than usually analytical and self-critical about the methods by which we arrive (or have arrived) at the decisions we take.

Throughout this chapter 'prescribing' is used in the rather circumscribed meaning of drug treatment (which is of course our most frequent active intervention) rather than synonymous with management which includes advice, counselling, referral, manipulation and surgery (the chapter in *Practice* on the 'Principles of management' provides a framework for the teaching of the wider aspects, and the section from that work on 'Principles of prescribing' is reprinted as an Appendix to this chapter). [1]

Teaching prescribing to the medical student

The medical student may well be more critical of the prescribing he sees in general practice than of any other facet of his introduction to the discipline. This reflects the influence of the teaching hospital and academic departments of pharmacology and therapeutics. In teaching prescribing to the student it is important to find out what he knows and has been taught (and in so finding out the general practitioner teacher himself stands to learn much). From this basis the student can be led to consider the problems of using data derived from experimental and institutional settings in the less structured setting of general practice where factors other than pathology and pharmacology may affect the decisions taken for the individual patient's best management.

The following areas can often be usefully explored with students during their general practice course:

1. The epidemiology of illnesses presenting in general practice, with its high incidence of self-limiting conditions suitable for self-medication, or needing no medication.
2. The problems of compliance where supervision is sporadic or absent (in general practice) rather than constant (in hospital).
3. The different patterns of antibiotic resistance in hospital and general practice.
4. The benefits and problems of self-medication.
5. The problems of polypharmacy in prescribing for the elderly.
6. The arguments for and against the use of combined preparations.
7. The use of generic as opposed to proprietary names in prescribing.

Opportunities will arise to discuss many or most of these topics in the course of practical work in the surgery or on home visits, and some of them at least can provide material for productive small group or seminar work.

It is important that by the end of his general practice course the student should be aware of the principles of prescribing in general practice, the social and psychological factors which may make prescribing in the community different from prescribing in the hospital and the need for a critical and analytical approach to the making of treatment decisions which affect the use of increasingly scarce resources.

Teaching prescribing to the trainee

The trainee is often bewildered by the freedom he acquires to prescribe from a vast range of drugs when previously he may have been constrained by hospital unit policies and the control of hospital pharmacies. Although practice customs, either in formal practice policies or more usually on an informal convention basis, will provide helpful guidelines, the trainee will need assistance to work out his own rational and economic approach to achieve a prescribing policy. The main objective in teaching the trainee about prescribing is to enable him to establish just such a framework by the end of his training.

It is important to avoid both over-enthusiasm and the natural desire to give each patient something tangible (usually a prescription) at the end of each consultation, and the progression of scientific scepticism into therapeutic nihilism.

During his course the trainee should consider the following aspects of prescribing:

1. Treatment aims.
2. Audit of prescribing.
3. Cost.
4. Drug interactions.
5. How to monitor long-term medication.

6. Assessment of new drugs: how to question drug firm representatives, how to assess published papers in the journals.
7. Reference sources.

1. *Treatment aims*

The trainee should be encouraged to consider for each consultation the questions of what the patient wants and what the patient needs (and whether these are necessarily the same thing). He should also be stimulated to reflect on the possible long-term implications of prescribing on the patient's subsequent behaviour and especially his perceptions of when and for what reasons it is appropriate to seek medical care and when and for how long is tolerance of discomfort and self-medication reasonable.

2. *Audit of prescribing*

Prescribing is a subject which lends itself to audit and the trainee should learn to challenge his own prescribing decisions, for instance in the course of random case analyses. He should be asked to demonstrate the scientific basis for his choice of drugs (e.g. he should know in terms of probabilities the organisms he is trying to eradicate when prescribing antibiotics, or in broad terms the pharmacological action of beta blockers). In addition he should be able to analyse the non-pathological factors which may influence his decision to prescribe or not to prescribe (e.g. when he gives an antibiotic to a girl with an upper respiratory infection who has to sing in public the next day, or when he declines to provide an antihistamine for a businessman with mild hay fever when it is known that the patient commutes long distances by car).

3. *Cost*

The financial implications of prescribing can be examined by a review of a batch of the trainer's scripts after return from the Pricing Bureau. This can be a salutory exercise for trainer and trainee alike and may be usefully conducted with the aim of answering for each set of prescriptions the question, 'Is there a cheaper and equally effective preparation which could have been used?' The fact that such a question can only rarely be answered unequivocally is itself of importance.

4. *Drug interactions*

The subject of drug interactions may produce a good deal of anxiety in the minds of trainees. It is a subject which is important, but which needs to be kept in perspective. The trainee should be guided to the various charts and books (one of the simplest and best of which is *Safer Prescribing*) which can be consulted on the subject. He should be aware of the various groups of drugs commonly involved in serious interactions — especially the barbiturates, anticoagulants and anti-convulsant drugs.

5. *Long-term medication*

The trainee as a prescribing doctor should be aware of the need for careful regulation of any procedures which may be in force in the practice for repeat prescribing. Aspects of this, impinging as they do on the area of continuity of care, can afford suitable subjects for short projects (see Chapter 10).

6. *Assessment of new drugs*

The trainee must learn to examine critically the claims of pharmaceutical firms and their representatives when new drugs are being promoted, and the results of drug trials reported in medical journals. The whole subject of pharmaceutical change and development is a complex one and the young doctor needs guidance in establishing his own criteria for evaluating the competing claims for attention with which all doctors are assailed. He needs for instance to know that 'higher blood levels' are less important than 'how does this product compare with its nearest rival in terms of outcome'. He should consider efficacy, reliability and cost. Teaching this topic can take place in the context of a journal club, in small groups or direct discussion.

7. *Reference sources*

Finally the trainee needs to establish the reference sources which he can consult when considering drug problems. The most easily accessible are the *British National Formulary* and *Monthly Index of Medical Specialties* (MIMS) and the Data Sheet Compendium. However, he also needs to be able to turn to more substantial and comprehensive works such as *Treatment,* Martindale's *Extra Pharmacopoeia* and a textbook on clinical pharmacology. From such sources and his own developing experience he should be encouraged to construct his own personal formulary having regard both to efficacy and economy and he should be guided into habits which will help him to revise and update this with the passage of time.

The established practitioner

Of all aspects of practice probably the fastest changing and therefore the most difficult with which to keep up to date are advances and changes in treatment. The practitioner, wishing to offer his patient the best that is available, needs convenient and regular access to information on the developing therapeutic scene. Refresher courses with lectures and discussions with specialists can be helpful, but the practitioner, like the student and the trainee, needs to be able to assess the claims of experts dealing in depth with a narrow field in the light of the broader realities and additional factors which influence treatment in the community.

Reading, if it is not to overwhelm the practising doctor, needs to be selective and critical. Original papers in the journals can be interesting and occasionally helpful, but in general review articles are more useful. In the specific field of prescribing both *Prescribers' Journal* and *Drug and Therapeutics Bulletin* are particularly helpful.

Practice clinical meetings, journal clubs and medical society meetings all provide useful forums for the discussion of prescribing problems. Increasingly general practitioners are coming to see the value of the sharing of experience and overcoming the tendency to defer to the opinion of 'experts' whose practical experience may be limited. A more mature attitude is becoming apparent which recognizes the particular problems of general practice and legitimate differences in approach and viewpoint between primary care and hospital clinicians, and the increasing confidence which such attitudes foster can and should be encouraged.

Habits once established are hard to change and patterns of treatment can easily become habitual. Continuing education with and by one's peers is one of the most effective means of examining, analysing and modifying prescribing patterns in response to changes in medicine, in society and in cultural perceptions.

The post-war pharmaceutical revolution has placed in our hands instruments for great good but also brings with it, in the form of biologically active drugs, potential for considerable harm. In no other aspect of practice is there more need to maintain an informed and critical approach to enable us to maximize the benefits which we can bring to our patients.

It is a truism that from the day he enters medical school until he retires from clinical practice the doctor needs to be a perpetual student. Prescribing is a subject where above all such continued learning and updating is of vital importance.

Reference

[1] Cormack, J.J.C., Marinker, M. and Morrell, D.C. (eds) (1976) *Practice: A handbook of primary medical care.* London: Kluwer Publishing.

Further reading

Beeley, L. (1976) *Safer Prescribing.* Oxford: Blackwell Scientific Publications.

Drury, V.W.M., Wade, O.L., Beeley, L. and Alesbury, P. (1978) *Treatment.* London: Kluwer Publishing.

Laurence, D.R. and Bennett, P.N. (1980) *Clinical Pharmacology,* 5th Edition. Edinburgh: Churchill Livingstone.

Martindale, W. (1977) *The Extra Pharmacopoeia,* 27th Edition. London: The Pharmaceutical Press.

Appendix

Eleven principles of prescribing

1. *The doctor should seek to prescribe from a limited number of useful drugs.* It is not important to know the characteristics of the majority of drugs in the pharmacopoeia. The doctor should familiarize himself well with one or two drugs in each of the major categories. He should resist the temptation to change frequently to newer preparations or variations of established drugs, on the grounds that small therapeutic benefits have been conferred on the new preparations. If he follows the policy of always changing to newer preparations, it is likely that the possible (often unproven) pharmacological benefits of the new drug will be more than offset by the fact that the doctor will never become familiar with the characteristics of the drugs that he uses.

2. *Where no drug is positively indicated, no drug should be prescribed.* A great deal of minor illness, for example acute viral infection of the respiratory tract, requires no prescribed drugs. It will take longer to explain this to the patient, and to educate the patient about his condition, than it will to write a prescription. In the long term the doctor will save himself and his patient the problem of treating the unwanted effects of the drugs he prescribed, and the patient will become more self reliant in the management of his own minor problems. Judicious use of aspirin, including aspirin gargles for upper respiratory infections, the use of hot lemon drinks and postural drainage and percussion of the chest by a relative in the management of chronic bronchitis, the tolerance of and even the creative use of the shortened sleep pattern of old age are all to be encouraged.

3. *The treatment of cause has priority over the treatment of symptoms.* Most treatment in general practice is (quite appropriately) symptomatic. Wherever possible, however, treatment should be directed at the cause (for example a bacterial infection) and not the presenting symptom (for example pain). Thus the earache of otitis media and the dysuria of cystitis should be treated with appropriate anti-infective agents: the symptoms will begin to diminish in 24 hours and self-medication with minor analgesics may be encouraged at this time.

4. *The fewer the drugs prescribed, the safer.* In the treatment of major and more chronic conditions, it is vital that whenever possible only one new drug should be introduced at a time. The patient seen initially with early congestive heart failure should not be treated at once with both digoxin and a diuretic. The patient whose benign hypertension is to be controlled should not be introduced to more than one drug at a time, and sufficient time should be given to observe the effect of this drug's action. For example, in the management of benign hypertension it would be quite

wrong to begin by exhibiting both a beta blocker and a diuretic, and for this reason most proprietary combined preparations should be avoided in initial treatment. The same principle applies to the management of depressive illnesses with manifestations of anxiety: if drug treatment is thought appropriate, and it may not always be so, then it would be wrong to exhibit both a tranquillizer and an antidepressant in the intitial trial of therapy.

5. *When a number of alternative treatments are available, choose the least toxic.* To quote the most obvious example, in terms of drug sensitivity, it might be argued that chloramphenicol is the drug of choice because of its effectiveness in controlling *H. influenzae*; the possibility that this drug may occasionally cause a fatal aplastic anaemia is sufficient to ban it from all use except one, where its specificity may be life saving (in the treatment of typhoid fever). Effectively, this means that chloramphenicol, except in the form of eye-drops, should not appear in the general practitioner's armamentarium. But there are other less dramatic examples. In the treatment of migraine-like headaches, simple analgesics or sedatives should precede the use of ergotamines, and the exhibition of methysergide, which is contraindicated in a large number of conditions and which may rarely cause retroperitoneal fibrosis, should be reserved for the most intractable and severe cases, in which other treatments have failed to bring relief.

6. *The cheapest effective medication should be preferred.* Whether, as in the vast majority of cases, the patient is being treated under the National Health Service, or whether the patient is being treated privately, the doctor should choose the cheapest possible effective medication. For the most part, though not always, this means that the doctor should prescribe a drug by using its approved name rather than a trade name. There are some exceptions to this rule: some proprietary preparations are cheaper, and in some instances the formulation or presentation of the proprietary drug may be superior.

In many cases the doctor is faced with a choice of drugs whose actions are pharmacologically related, but whose costs vary greatly. Treatment with talampicillin is approximately twice as costly as treatment with ampicillin, although in general practice the latter drug will usually be found to be quite as effective as the former in the treatment of *E. coli* urinary tract infection. Large disparities of cost exist in the choices available in other categories of drugs whose specificity and effectiveness are far less certain than the antibiotics: for example, the psychotropic drugs. It is worth noting that when a drug company produces a new preparation, its cost is greatest; indeed the relative cost of a preparation within a particular category is often in inverse proportion to its established utility in general practice. On the grounds of cost therefore, as well as on the grounds of safety and utility, a conservative approach to new preparations should be the rule.

7. *The patient should be given the fullest information about his drugs.* Once a decision has been taken to prescribe a drug, time should be spent in explaining what the drug is intended to do, what likely symptoms the patient may experience (for example drowsiness, dryness of the mouth, alteration in bowel habit, and so on) and the time sequences of the drug's action. These should all be carefully explained to the patient. It is of the utmost importance that the patient should understand that imipramine is unlikely to lift the feelings of depression for some ten days, although the unwanted side-effects of the drug may be experienced before then; that if the pain of otitis media has not receded after 24 hours' treatment with phenoxymethylpenicillin, the patient should return to the surgery in order to have the medication changed; that the five- or ten-day course of antibiotics must be completed even though the symptoms of the disease have receded; that the control of diabetes mellitus involves a fine balance between the ingestion of food and the injection of insulin, and that the patient must be aware of the dangers of missing a meal, or the effects of an intercurrent fever. Information about long-term steroids or insulin should be recorded on a Medic Alert bracelet.

8. *The cause of any new symptoms in an established illness should first be looked for in the drugs which have been prescribed for that illness.* In this way, the vast majority of drugs prescribed for drug-induced symptoms or signs can be avoided.

9. *The addition of any new drug in the treatment of an established illness should always be preceded by a review of the current drug regime.* When a new drug is added, the question should always be asked: 'Would it now be possible to withdraw some of the current therapy?' The problem of the multiplication of drugs is particularly acute in the case of the elderly, and geriatricians have stressed that the stopping of all medication often results in marked improvement in the health of the patient.

10. *Repeat prescriptions should be reviewed.* While being sensitive to the psychological contract implied by the repeat prescription, as already noted, there should be a policy of monitoring all repeat prescriptions and the doctor should be aware of instituting such repeat prescriptions, particularly of drugs of known or marked or cumulative toxicity. For those patients who require some form of continuing medication whose basis is psychological rather than pharmacological, inert or harmless substances should always be preferred. Small doses of ascorbic acid, simple linctus B.P.C., or a mild tranquillizer offered as an hypnotic may be acceptable.

11. *Frequent reference to the literature and a readiness to consult the hospital information pharmacist should be the rule.*

26
Counselling
Marshall Marinker

Introduction

Counselling is perhaps best described as 'listening and talking treatment'. As such it must be a part of every general practice consultation. But the extent of such counselling, its aims, its methods, and so on, must be subject to wide variation. There are perhaps three key elements which determine the part which counselling will play in the consultation. The first is the nature of the problem which the patient brings. A young woman comes to the general practitioner to be reassured that the oral contraceptive which she has been taking for two years is still regarded as relatively safe. She wants to know whether recent advances in treatment have produced a safer pill. What she appears to require is information and reassurance. A schoolteacher comes to complain angrily that her husband refuses to have a vasectomy. She says, 'It's always me. I have to take all the responsibility. I have to take all the risks'. Much more than information and reassurance seems to be called for.

The second key element concerns the personality and skills of the patient. How intelligent is she? How well does she communicate? Is she capable of becoming more aware of her problem and her own personality? How motivated is she to change her behaviour or to try to change the behaviour of others?

The third key element concerns the personality and skills of the doctor. How aware is he of the effect which his behaviour must have on the course of the consultation? What communication skills has he developed, and how motivated is he to explore further the problems which his patients bring, and the possibilities for therapy? One doctor, confronted with the young woman who asks if her pill is still safe, would be content to explain that there have been no recent advances in therapy, and that the risks to the patient remain acceptably low. A second doctor may see something much more complex behind the patient's question. His knowledge of the working of the unconscious, or his skills in asking open-ended questions and encouraging the patient to explore her own ideas, may uncover in the first patient, the anger and the dilemmas which the second patient expresses. In fact these are two different presentations of the same young woman with the same problem.

The name of the game

The term 'counselling' embraces a number of different activities, and sometimes gives rise to confusion on the part of the medical student or trainee. Is it counselling when the doctor says, 'You really must be sure to take this pill every day; make it a part of the routine of getting up in the morning, or going to bed at night'? How can this be the same sort of activity as that implied when the doctor says, 'Whenever we talk about your husband you seem to tense your body and clench your fists; perhaps we ought to talk about those feelings'? Scrupulous definitions of counselling probably do not take us very far in general practice. Terms like counselling and psychotherapy refer more to the status of the professional than to the techniques which he uses. When the psychiatrist is engaged in the 'listening and talking treatment', we call it psychotherapy and not counselling. When the social worker does it, we don't describe it as psychotherapy although the activities may be very similar. In general practice we tend to call it counselling, even though Balint tried to suggest that the word psychotherapy might be more appropriate. Psychotherapy, however, is often taken to be the 'listening and talking treatment' applied to a patient who has a psychiatric condition.

In general practice listening and talking have a much broader application. Four characteristics of the general practice consultation give a peculiar character to the general practitioner's counselling. First, the consultation in general practice is most often not a single event, but is made up of a number of clinical interviews sometimes spread over days, weeks or years. Second, the same doctor may be caring for a number of different members of the same family, and hence relating to a number of players in the drama for which a particular patient seeks counselling. Third, the general practitioner can never be a case worker like a social worker, or a psychotherapist like a clinical psychologist or psychiatrist. His 'contract' with the patient ensures that at one and the same time he must be concerned with the physical, psychological and social aspects of his patient's life. A number of writers have commented that in general practice psychotherapy must often be carried out simultaneously with a physical examination. Such a confusion of the physical and the psychological would be unthinkable, for example, to a psychoanalyst. Yet the general practitioner may talk to a young woman about her sexual feelings on the same occasion as he performs a vaginal examination. Lastly, although the counselling may have a beginning and an end, the doctor–patient relationship will often precede the beginning of couselling, and must continue when the period of counselling has come to an end. In this sense many of the major problems described in the literature on counselling concerned with beginning and ending counselling work, must be drastically reinterpreted.

The aims of counselling

In general the aims of counselling may be expressed as follows:
1. To identify the patient's problems.
2. To bring the patient to an understanding of his problems.
3. To explore with the patient the choices which are open to him.
4. To help the patient bring about some desired modification in his own behaviour.

This is a rather simplistic summary. Counselling proceeds on the basis of a number of theories of human behaviour, and is subject to the enthusiasms of a number of schools. But a consideration of these theoretical models, let alone a discussion of their relative merits and limitations, is outside the scope of this chapter. Basically, one set of theories is concerned with the psychodynamics of the individual and the counselling which stems from it is concerned with achieving a limited change in the personality of the patient. Another school is concerned with learning theory, and the counselling which derives from it aims at the unlearning of inappropriate behaviours and the acquisition of new and more useful ones. Some theorists and practitioners are concerned with the individual, others are concerned with relationships, for example, a marital relationship or the dynamics of the whole family unit.

Learning to counsel may involve the following three sorts of activities:
1. The development of the doctor's self-awareness, what Michael Balint called the achievement of a 'limited though considerable change of personality'.
2. The development of specific counselling skills. More will be said about this later.
3. The achievement of behaviour modification techniques. These skills are most commonly used today by clinical psychologists in primary care. It may be that there is a place for the acquisition of such techniques by general practitioners, but the constraints of time make it unlikely that general practitioners will in the future wish to take over responsibility for such treatment from clinical psychologists.

The range of counselling situtations

It would be fruitless to try to map the sort of consultations in general practice where counselling is appropriate. There is likely to be an element of counselling in almost all of the consultations which will be experienced by the medical student and the trainee.

A mother requests an antibiotic because her child has a cough and cold. After he has taken a history and made a physical examination, the doctor may give information, 'This is a virus illness; antibiotics are not useful here', and he may give advice, 'An aspirin may be helpful last thing at night'. But the competent general practitioner may already have picked up other clues in this consultation. The mother's anxiety may be disproportionate to the child's symptoms, and the doctor may find himself exploring the mother's fear of serious illness, or her feelings of guilt because she has a full-time job and has to share the care of the child with her husband's mother.

A 50-year-old man is due to have a hernia repair. He comes to ask how long he is likely to be kept in hospital. The doctor may simply give information, 'This particular surgeon will probably have you home again within five days'. Again the doctor who is sensitive to the whole range of his patient's communications may have picked up the patient's fears for his job. The patient is a storeman, and there have been many redundancies in the firm for which he works. Behind these fears of unemployment, there may be other darker fears about his health and even his mortality.

A 20-year-old man has recently been diagnosed as suffering from diabetes mellitus. The diabetes has been wildly out of control, and now the patient refuses to inject himself with insulin. Beyond the giving of information about the pathology of diabetes, and advice on compliance with medication, the doctor may need to explore the patient's anger and resentment at what is happening to him.

The range of situations is as large as the whole of general practice. It would be a travesty to suggest that counselling is a form of treatment reserved for the mentally ill, the bereaved and the sexually unhappy. Once the communication between patient and doctor moves beyond the exchange of information to an exploration of attitudes and feelings, the doctor becomes a counsellor.

Although the patients and the problems may be varied, whether the doctor is dealing with a mother who cannot feed her baby or with a chronic bronchitic who now faces the onset of heart failure and social isolation, the aims and methods of counselling are common to most situations.

The stages of counselling and the necessary skills

There is a large literature on counselling, much of it concerned with counselling outside the medical setting. Much of this literature may be valuable in extending the vocabulary of counselling responses which the doctor is capable of making. But in the end counselling cannot be learned from books. The reader is encouraged to consider this section in relation to two other chapters in the book: Chapter 20 (Communication between patient and doctor) and Chapter 21 (The doctor–patient relationship in diagnosis and treatment).

In considering the following five stages of counselling, the reader should be aware that they are not mutually exclusive, that they will not necessarily follow the order given here, and that components from each of these five stages may well be present in any one brief consultation.

1. *Acceptance of the patient and the problem*
Much has been written elsewhere in this book about the creation of an appropriate ambience for the consultation in general practice. Often, the doctor may come to the conclusion that the patient wishes to present a problem which is difficult to express, and which may require a level of counselling which goes beyond the sharing of information or advice. If he is to be effective in the early detection of his patient's wish to talk about such problems, the doctor will need to recognize clues from the whole range of verbal and non-verbal communications which his patient makes (see Chapter 20). The trainee may be at a loss to know how to move the consultation from a more superficial level of communication to a deeper one. What is he to say or do? The trainee may be shown how, at points like this in the consultation, the doctor may offer acceptance both of the patient and of the problem.

For example, the doctor may say, 'You are clearly worried about the risks of taking the pill. I have a note that we discussed this six months ago. I wasn't able to reassure you then — perhaps I got hold of the wrong end of the stick?' Whatever the words chosen, the intention is to accept both the patient and the problem; to make clear that whatever the patient now wants to say the doctor will regard it as a legitimate part of the consultation. If he is on the wrong track, and the patient does not wish to go further, the topic may end here. 'No, doctor, I was just checking that there were no new advances.' On the other hand if the patient says, 'I get so fed up . . .', the doctor now has the choice of deflecting the patient's feelings, or accepting and encouraging them. The trainee should be taught an awareness of his own body stance and expression. He should learn how the use of encouraging phrases, silences or even non-verbal encouraging sounds may make the patient feel safe enough to confide.

2. *Exploring the problem*
The trainee may have some difficulty in knowing how far to go in any one consultation. Most often in the hurly-burly of a busy morning surgery, the doctor may not go further than an acceptance that there is a problem which needs talking about, and an agreement to talk about it further. Doctors who were trained in Balint seminars would often see such patients for hour-long sessions at weekly intervals over many months. Eventually Balint and his co-workers came to the conclusion that such clinical work did not fit comfortably into the style and pace of modern general practice. But the trainee will certainly need longer than the 5–10 minutes normally allocated for consultations in general practice. Certainly in his training year, and in his early years in practice,

he may need to have a number of double or treble sessions (that is to say periods of time up to 30 minutes) when he can explore such problems further with his patients.

Here the trainee needs to learn the difference between close-ended questions and open-ended questions. For example, 'Do you want to come off the pill?' invites an answer of either 'yes' or 'no'. The question, 'What is it about your husband's attitude that upsets you?' demands much more from the patient. Often a short statement, which may be your summing up of what the patient has been trying to tell you, or perhaps even a reflection of your own feelings, may be even more powerful in encouraging the patient to explore further. 'You get very angry with your husband', or, 'Just now you seemed to feel so angry that it almost frightened you'. In the course of such exploration it is not only the patient's personality and feelings which come to the surface. The counsellor himself must often share in the feelings, and this requires of the young doctor an increasing degree of self-awareness. 'You keep wanting me to make the decisions for you. When I reflect this back on you, I feel you getting angry with me, so I feel angry with you in return.' Here the doctor–patient relationship begins to reflect other relationships in the patient's life, and the doctor may be able to throw light not only on the way in which the patient behaves, but on the way in which she makes other people feel.

Exploration of this kind may sometimes lead to an interpretation of what is going on. 'You say he never seems to give you what you want. I wonder if you are talking about having a child?' Sometimes interpretation gives way to confrontation. 'You say he is too weak to make up his own mind about anything. But isn't it you yourself who cannot decide whether or not to have a child?'

Without training and supervision, the trainee will be rightly apprehensive of a consultation which comes so close to the reality of the patient's feelings and his own. Two anxieties predominate. The first is that the doctor may go too far — he may blunder into personal areas of the patient's personality and life where he is not welcome. Here the concern is for the proper boundaries between professional and personal life. Such anxieties on the part of the trainee are to be accepted and valued until the trainee has acquired considerable counselling skills. The second anxiety concerns the potential destructiveness of counselling. The trainee will be anxious not to hurt his patient inadvertently, to give wrong advice or to precipitate or actually to cause a crisis in personal relations. Not least the trainee may be anxious not to disrupt the doctor–patient relationship itself. Again, in the absence of counselling skills, these anxieties are realistic. But effective training means that throughout his training year and for many years beyond this, the young doctor will constantly be enlarging the scope of his counselling, and this will involve him in taking small but definitive risks without which no counselling skill can be acquired.

3. *Formulating the problem*

Throughout the process of counselling, the counsellor will be reflecting his understanding of the patient's problem. He must always do this tentatively, making it clear that what he is expressing is his own understanding, that this is a temporary understanding, and that the counsellor accepts, even as he makes it, that his understanding may be wrong. 'It seems to me that what you feel...', or, 'Am I right in thinking...', or 'What you seem to be trying to say...' The pitfall here is that the counsellor will be anxious to make a neat and tidy package of the patient's untidy life problem. When the doctor formulates the problem for the patient, he must be scrupulous in observing his patient's reactions, commenting on any hint that the patient wishes to demur from what the doctor says. The formulation must, in the end, be made in a language which the patient can understand, and refer to feelings and dilemmas which are his, and not a clever invention of the doctor as a creative artist. It is at this stage of the counselling that the counsellor must be at his most tentative, 'Perhaps I have got it wrong, but we seem to be agreed that...'.

4. *Exploring choices*

The aim of counselling is to effect some change in behaviour. When the doctor prescribes a drug or recommends an operation, he is aware that the patient's motivation and co-operation are very important factors. But in changing the patient's behaviour, the motivation of the patient is overriding. That is to say for counselling to result in any sort of change, not only must the patient recognize the formulation of the problem as her own, she must want to change her behaviour in an agreed way. Here, what concerns the doctor is not only what changes may improve the patient's lot, but what changes are actually possible for the patient. This involves an exploration with the patient about what can be done, and also about what the consequences are likely to be. 'You say now that you are ready to tell your husband how much you want a baby. What will his reaction be?' If the doctor is to help the patient to make a choice, he must also help her to explore the likely consequences of what she chooses to do.

5. *Effecting changes*

The clinical psychologist who practises behaviour therapy has at his disposal a number of techniques for changing behaviour. A discussion of these is outside the scope of this chapter. The general practitioner will rarely be involved in such techniques as desensitization, relaxation

3. exercises, selective reinforcement, and so on. In the setting of general practice, the doctor's remit probably does not often go beyond the stage of discussing choices. The autonomy of the patient as a person is perhaps the most important ethical maxim in counselling. How the patient changes as a result of an exploration of her problems and an exploration of the choices open to her, is for her to decide and effect. It is for this reason that counsellors try to abjure directive counselling, as opposed to the non-directive counselling which has been outlined in this chapter. Even here there are pitfalls and dangers. The more skilled the counsellor becomes, the more easy it is to become highly directive of the patient, although appearing always to use non-directive methods. 'Only you can decide if you are independent enough (mature enough, feminine enough, and so on) to do it . . .' Counselling must be very different from persecution by insight, or effecting a change in behaviour by moral coercion.

Learning and teaching

William James wrote, 'We must philosophize well or ill, but philosophize we must'. The same holds true for counselling in general practice.

There are four methods which have been successfully used in the development of counselling skills. The first is supervised counselling. The trainee finds himself in a counselling situation with a patient or family which may involve him in work over a number of consultations. He discusses these consultations, perhaps he makes tape-recordings of them (see Chapter 12), and discusses these with his trainer. The purpose of the tutorials between trainee and trainer is not only to examine the counselling situation, or to discuss the development of counselling skills, but more important still to examine the challenges, strains and stresses of a developing doctor–patient relationship. Here the teacher needs to develop in his relationship with the trainee the same sort of skills in observing and communication that he uses with the patient (see Chapters 3, 4 and 5).

The second method is the Balint seminar. Although in Chapter 21 and elsewhere I have argued that this method is unsuitable for medical students and trainees, there have been a number of experiments with both sorts of groups which have produced encouraging results. In particular as far as the trainee is concerned, the group leader has to remain sensitive to two features of the trainee's relationship with his patient. First, because he is new to general practice, a trainee is likely to have major anxieties about clinical problem-solving. What sort of diagnostic criteria should he recognize? How far should his laboratory investigations go? How safe is it to tolerate uncertainty? Because the problems of physical diagnosis are so difficult and so important in the early years, the group leader cannot afford to discount this part of the young doctor's work, in the way that it may be safely ignored in a Balint seminar for established doctors. For the trainee, the Balint seminar must always be a seminar in whole person medicine, and this includes the physical aspects of diagnosis. Second, the doctor–patient relationship for the trainee has a short life-span — inevitably it must be terminated in months, sometimes in weeks. In the same way, the relationship between the group and the group leader is also relatively short. Unless the group leader is prepared to tackle the problems of both these separations — the impending separation of the doctor from his patient and of the group member from the group leader — the stresses within the group may make it difficult to keep to the task in hand (see Chapter 8).

The third method which may be used is role-play (see Chapter 11). Here the learners are personally involved in playing the part of counsellor and counsellee, and are able to examine and observe the development and effects of their own skills. Ideally these role-plays should be recorded on video-tape and examined in some detail afterwards. In this way the effect of the counsellor's behaviour on all of the components listed earlier in this chapter can be observed in relation to the way in which the counsellee reacts. Both actors in the drama can then be asked to 'talk through' the recording, and discuss their feelings and reactions.

The fourth method, a variant of the third, is the use of trios.[1] Here, the exercise is carried out by three people — one takes the role of counsellor, the second the role of counsellee and the third acts as an observer of the process. The counsellee is expected to present a real problem to the counsellor, and the interaction is observed by the third learner. There should be no shortage of real problems to be discussed. The medical student or trainee may have a problem either with a patient, with a colleague or with one of his teachers. In the first two sessions the counselling is taken to the point of elucidating the counsellee's problem. The third session is concerned with generating possible solutions and the fourth with identifying the solution which is most acceptable and appropriate to the counsellee. Between each of these sessions, the members of all the trios in the course meet together to discuss aspects of the work.

There are, of course, a number of variants of all of these methods, and there is much need for future experimentation. Good role models are essential. These may be available on film, but may perhaps be most persuasive when they are generated by audio or video recordings of the teacher's own practice. The model of the general practitioner as counsellor, the skills that he employs and the boundaries he observes, may influence, more than any other characteristic teaching from general practice, the style and scope of the future general practitioner.

Reference

[1] Long, B.E.L., Harris, C.M. and Byrne, P.S. (1976) 'A method of teaching counselling'. *Medical Education. 10,*(3), 198-204.

Further reading

Balint, M. (1964) *The Doctor, the Patient and the Illness,* 2nd Edition. London: Pitman.
Halmos, P. (1965) *The Faith of the Counsellors.* London: Constable.
Hopkins, P. (ed) (1972) *Patient-Centred Medicine.* The Balint Society and Regional Doctor Publications Ltd.
Marinker, M. (1970) 'Balint seminars and vocational training in general practice'. *Journal of the Royal College of General Practitioners, 19,* 79.
Munro, E.A., Manthei, R.J. and Small, J.J. (1979) *Counselling: A skills approach.* Menthuen N.Z. Ltd.
Storr, A. (1979) *The Art of Psychotherapy.* London: Secker, Warburg and Heinemann.

27
Anticipatory care
Nigel Stott

'Anticipatory care' is the term applied to planned intervention to achieve early diagnosis and/or treatment of a condition which may not yet be producing symptoms or be recognized as causing symptoms. The term was probably coined by Van den Dool following a large multiphasic screening programme of 4,000 patients in his own rural general practice in which he came to the conclusion that population screening was an inappropriate activity for the primary medical care team because it was wasteful and failed to make use of the natural advantages of the primary medical care setting.[1] He favoured the opportunistic use of every patient contact to achieve base-line observations on healthy patients and early diagnosis of reversible disease without resort to specific population screening; he called this anticipatory care. Van den Dool emphasized that the frequent spontaneous contacts between patients and their primary medical care workers provide the most efficient and acceptable of case finding methods. A similar view has been expressed by Tudor Hart[2] but opinions differ regarding how much the public should be educated to expect routine medical checks or procedures from their doctors. Public demand for numerous inappropriate examinations or procedures can absorb so much medical time that selective and appropriate case finding may not occur.

The concept of the periodic health overhaul was introduced in the Peckham experiment which aimed to promote family health through education for nutrition and healthy habits including a periodical family medical check.[3] With the advent of the National Health Service the experiment was unfortunately halted and the routine medical check-up alone was adopted by American private medicine; this led to heightened public expectations for routine medical checks from doctors and commercial surveillance clinics in a way which has been very foreign to the British public. The cost-effectiveness of routine medical examinations and many multiphasic screening programmes has been called in question in recent years[4] unless the programme fulfils the rigorous requirements shown in Table 1. However, even those conditions which qualify for early detection by the criteria in Table 1 do not always lead to successful outcomes for the patients because when the screening personnel differ from the providers of continuing care the programme may become diagnostic yet not therapeutic.

1. The condition should be important.
2. An accepted treatment must be available for the condition.
3. The facilities for diagnosis and treatment must be available.
4. A latent or early symptomatic stage in the condition must exist.
5. A suitable screening test must be available.
6. The test/examination must be acceptable to the population.
7. The natural history of the condition must be understood.
8. An agreed treatment policy on whom to treat must exist.
9. The cost of case finding must be acceptable.
10. Case finding must be a continuing process and not a once for all project.

Table 1. Criteria for pre-symptomatic screening (Abbreviated from Wilson[5])

Morrell has reported that the South London screening study in a large general practice population between 1967 and 1977 confirmed that screening in the middle age groups is unproductive, and that the cross sectional detection of disease does not ensure any therapeutic intervention or any change in the natural history of that disease in the population.[6] Furthermore 93 per cent of the patients in the practices studied had consulted their doctors in the previous five years, and all the patients who were screened and found to have diastolic blood pressures in excess of 115 mm of mercury had consulted their doctors during this period. Sackett and Holland thus coined the term 'case finding' to demonstrate the way in which general practitioners can easily identify the more vulnerable members of a practice population during day-to-day consultations, thereby co-ordinating the diagnosis, treatment and continuity of care of the patient in one person or source of medical care.[7] Such a policy is feasible in relation to hypertension case finding and is consistent with the opinion of Tudor Hart who said, 'Screening should be fully integrated with continuing personal care, so that the information it generates is fully and effectively available to the doctor responsible for first contact with the patient. Such integration will seldom be achieved by intensive short-term case-finding campaigns.'

What conditions should the doctor/nurse be looking for in an anticipatory manner?

In 1971 Professor G. Rose reviewed the evidence for effective and efficient early diagnosis in 14 chronic diseases and he concluded that only the following can be wholly recommended:[8]
1. Phenylketonuria;
2. Pulmonary tuberculous in high risk groups;

3. Urinary tract infection in pregnancy;
4. Hypertension in young/middle age groups;
5. Chorion carcinoma following hydatidiform mole.

By 1980 the situation had changed very little but generally accepted additions to this list would be glaucoma in the first degree relatives of sufferers and it is likely that cervical cytology in high risk groups is also becoming more widely accepted. In contrast with the chronic conditions, the acute and congenital disorders in infancy and childhood are sought for by increasing numbers of health workers whose aim is to diagnose deafness, visual problems, dislocations of hip and other deviations from normal development earlier. Routine antenatal care is another highly structured example of anticipatory care.

The general practitioner who sees a high proportion of his patients every year, including the high risks groups who often fail to attend local authority or hospital clinics[9], is placed in a powerful position to record base-line clinical information, to identify areas for anticipatory care in each age group and to work out with the health visitor, nurses and others in the primary care team how it can be done in a manner which is both effective and efficient. Failure of the doctors in the primary care sector to rise to the challenges of anticipatory care will simply encourage all that Hart and Morrell have warned about, viz: duplication of effort, unfortunate omissions and inappropriate follow-up of risk groups by other doctors with a fragmented primary care team directed in part by community physicians or the expensive secondary care sector. Anticipatory care is part of high quality primary care. It must be centred on a system which aims to achieve continuity and teaches the value of opportunistic case finding rather than prescriptive screening, yet maintains rigorous criticism and review of all the methods used and their outcomes.

Choice of life style

In recent years the rapidly accumulating knowledge about the relationship between life style and health has brought further pressures to bear on primary care workers because the consultation is seen as an opportunity to encourage patients to adopt improved life styles in the interests of future health. This emphasis on habits, diet, exercise, relationships, etc. is apparent in the consultative document *Prevention and Health: Everybody's business*[10] and it raises many questions for the professional working in the National Health Service because it assumes that the primary medical care worker may have to change his/her pattern of work towards more identification of risk groups for health education and primary prevention. Furthermore this philosophy assumes that the public will be willing to assume greater responsibility for health maintenance, and place fewer demands on the curative services to free medical staff for this preventive role.

The promotion of healthy life styles, like anticipatory care, is an activity which can be considered to be 'opportunistic' in the context of the consultation. The clinician can choose to widen the scope of his work and take the opportunity offered by the patient for prevention, or he can confine himself to new and continuing clinical problems alone.

The term 'opportunistic health care' has been used by Stott and Davis to embrace both anticipatory care and life style choices for health[11] but the same workers have emphasized that much more research is needed to clarify our understanding about the public's conceptions of health and illness before such a policy can be widely adopted. Furthermore Stott and Pill have provided preliminary evidence that current health education policies may be making assumptions about human behaviour which are not fully justified.[12] A shift from the traditional non-moralizing stance of the trusted clinician could lead to serious changes in the doctor–patient relationship by introducing notions of blame for illness which are normally eschewed by the medical profession.[13] For example, patients who feel that they are blamed for their ill health may need confidential clinics (as in venereal disease) and the simplistic labelling of lung cancer, ischaemic heart disease, peptic ulcer, etc. as 'diseases of life style' could be as unfair as it is untrue and lead to difficulties in the provision of care for sensitive patients with these conditions. The doctor who is normally a neutral provider of care may be perceived as one who feels judgemental about the style of life which his patient has led.

The challenge to primary care workers is to avoid the temptation to impose their own values on patients and to become skilled at helping them to make their own informed choices about life style. When a disease associated with life style does occur there is no place for censure and the fostering of guilt. Concern and humility about the limitations of our understanding in this evolving field of work are essential because to care enough to prevent ill health is as important as providing informed and compassionate care in the event of ill health. Yet we know very little about the barriers which exist to the adoption of more personal responsibility for health maintenance and further research is urgently needed to clarify these ethical and practical issues.

Conclusion

The question which should haunt every general practitioner in the future is, 'Do I take the opportunities my patients offer for early case finding and primary prevention and am I being sufficiently imaginative about the organization of my clinics and ancillary staff so this work can be achieved?' A flurry of activity which expends energy on computerized records, special recall systems and screening clinics will probably perpetuate the failures of the past whereas a professional attitude to every patient which looks beyond the presenting problem and into the opportunities for anticipatory care and encouragement for life style choices in the individual and his/her family may lead to real progress. Progress should come as more questions are asked about the ethics, the methods and the limitations of the suggested strategy. Task satisfaction for the doctor/nurse should come as the exceptional potential in every primary medical care consultation becomes apparent. The medical student can grasp the principles of opportunism in the consultation with relative ease, whereas the postgraduate will need to be encouraged to work through the theoretical, practical and organizational aspects of its application in the day-to-day clinical situations which differ according to local facilities, needs and customs. Our patients will gain from these new ideas provided we use them with humility and in a spirit of enquiry.

References

[1] Van den Dool, C.W.A. (1970) *Huisarts & Wetenschap, 13,* 3 and 59.
[2] Hart, J.T. (1975) in C.R. Hart (ed) *Screening in General Practice.* Edinburgh: Churchill Livingstone.
[3] Pearce, I.H. and Crocker, L.H. (1944) *The Peckham Experiment: A study on the living structure of society.* London: Allen & Unwin.
[4] McKeown, T. (1968) in *Screening in Medical Care.* Nuffield Provincial Hospitals Trust. Oxford: University Press, Chs. 1 and 13.
[5] Wilson, J.M.G. (1966) in J. Teeling Smith (ed) *Surveillance and Early Diagnosis in General Practice: Proceedings of colloquium* London: OHE, pp. 5–10.
[6] Morrell, D. (1978) 'Screening in general practice'. *Health Trends, 10,* 40–42.
[7] Sackett, D.L. and Holland, W.W. (1975) 'Controversy in the detection of disease'. *Lancet, 11,* 357.
[8] Rose, G. (1971) 'Early diagnosis of chronic disease'. *British Journal of Hospital Medicine, 6,* 647.
[9] Zinken, P.M. and Cox, C.A. (1976) 'Child health clinics and inverse care laws'. *British Medical Journal, 2,* 411.
[10] *Prevention and Health: Everybody's business* (1976). London: HMSO.
[11] Stott, N.C.H. and Davis, R.H. (1979) 'The exceptional potential in each primary care consultation'. *Journal of the Royal College of General Practitioners, 29,* 201–205.
[12] Stott, N.C.H. and Pill, R. (1980), *Health Beliefs in an Urban Community — A feasibility study to develop methods of measurement.* Report to DHSS.
[13] Davis, A.G. (1979) 'An unequivocal change of policy: prevention, health and medical sociology'. *Social Science and Medicine, 13A.* 129–137.

28
Continuing care
Nigel Stott

Introduction

'Continuing care' is the term applied to the care of patients with chronic problems which require regular monitoring and/or treatment in addition to those acute problems which need review on one or more occasions. Continuing care is therefore the antithesis of episodic acute medicine and the need for continuing care increases with the number of people with chronic or disabling problems in the population. The term must not be confused with 'continuity of care' which implies personal doctoring in the sense that a patient normally sees the same doctor who may or may not be skilled at continuing care. Familiarity can lead to carelessness or short cuts, particularly if consultation speed is more important to the doctor than the quality of the consultation and peer group pressure can result in a situation whereby 'the number of patients seen in an hour' becomes more important than the number of problems managed per patient. For example, it may be tempting to prescribe for a superficial skin infection in a patient with multiple problems and give a sigh of relief if she fails to mention any more of her complaints before leaving the consulting room or, even worse, to be unaware of her chronic problems because of inadequate records or history taking.

Videotape recordings of consultations confirm that many doctors deal mainly with the presenting complaints alone. In one large teaching practice only one patient in seven was likely to have more than one problem dealt with at a consultation, and even among the elderly fewer than half the patients seen had two or more problems reviewed at each consultation. Pressure of work, the size of the pool of chronic disease in our community, and the fact that medical education is geared more towards curing acute conditions have sometimes made doctors reluctant to expand the content of their consultations for problems which the patient is not actively complaining about.

How can continuing care be encouraged?

The traditional method to achieve continuing care of chronic conditions or the follow up of acute conditions is to bring the patient back to a special clinic for this purpose. Antenatal care is a well-organized example of structured continuing care involving several professional workers and active patient participation. Hypertension or diabetic control can be organized on an equally structured basis where there is enthusiasm for such methods. However the specialized follow-up clinic in surgery, health centre or clinic is not the only way to deal with problems requiring continuing care and the factors which will influence whether continuing care can be conducted well are:

1. Application of a professional discipline in primary care.
2. Use of methods which facilitate continuing care, for example, medical records, organization of care, and special recall methods.
3. Personal care and interpersonal skills.

Continuing care as an application of a professional discipline

Responsibility for the continuing care of patients in a defined population has been included as a task in *The Future General Practitioner*[1] and the place of continuing care is also illustrated in Figure 1 which summarizes the potential in every primary care consultation.

A Management of presenting problems	B Modification of help-seeking behaviour
C Management of continuing problems	D Opportunistic health promotion

Figure 1. The potential in each primary care consultation — an aide-memoire. (Reproduced by kind permission of the Editor of the *Journal of the Royal College of General Practitioners.*)

All consultations involve the patient presenting a problem or a request (Area A). Whether the doctor deals with the presenting problem alone or takes the opportunity to review any continuing problems (Area C) is the basic difference between the episodic doctor and the one who is prepared to consider the need for continuing care in every consultation.* The discipline of applying a conceptual framework to every consultation introduces numerous opportunities for continuing care which are most important for patients who are infrequent attenders at the doctor's surgery and yet have chronic or recurrent conditions.

*Area D is dealt with in Chapter 27 and Area B is an important and controversial component of the doctor's work which has been described by Stott and Davis.[2]

In the United Kingdom where over two-thirds of patients on a general practitioner's list are seen by him every year, the opportunities for unobtrusive attention to continuing care are enormous. For example, the request for a repeat prescription, the consultation for a sore throat, or the attendance for a minor injury, are all situations which may provide opportunities for continuing care if the patients also have other problems such as squint, developmental delay, hypertension, diabetes, recurrent otitis media, eczema, epilepsy, etc. Even the most informed patients often underestimate the need for periodic review of chronic or relapsing problems and it is incumbent on the clinician to use each contact with the patient for continuing care when this is appropriate.

Students have to be taught to apply the comprehensive principles as rigorously as a surgeon applies aseptic technique in his operating theatre. The practitioner must ask himself at every consultation, 'Are there any continuing problems which I should review while the patient is with me?' The answer to this question may be 'yes' or 'no' but if it is ever 'don't know', this indicates a serious need for examination of those skills and methods which promote continuing care in the practice.

Use of methods which facilitate continuing care

Medical records are the most important tool to ensure satisfactory continuing care because few doctors can remember enough about each of their patients and all doctors sometimes delegate their duties to locums, partners or trainees. The well-structured, legible and orderly record is an invaluable tool to ensure that important continuing problems are not overlooked. For example, the management of acute tonsillitis will often be modified if the patient is known to be a diabetic, and many patients on hypotensive therapy are seen by doctors for new problems but fail to take the opportunity for blood pressure review. A summary problem list will ensure that any doctor seeing the patient is in full possession of the basic facts, and use of simple flow-charts or well-structured records can help to ensure the best possible continuity of care under shared care circumstances.[3]

The General Practice Unit in Cardiff has used flow-charts for many years to encourage doctors to set therapeutic goals at the time of initial consultation so that nurses, health visitors or other doctors can be quite clear about the primary targets of the responsible physician. Another outstanding example of a flow-chart in general use is the co-operation card used in antenatal care and carried by the patient to enhance the co-ordination of care between the various hosptial and community based providers of care. Patient held systems have worked less satisfactorily for hypertension control, perhaps because supervision has to continue for so many years, and in the author's experience, flow-charts kept in the medical records which are fully understood by the patients are probably the most satisfactory compromise. Such arrangements can lead to tightly controlled and structured recording of clinical information, but they may fail to deal with multiple problems presented by many patients.

The use of special clinics for disease monitoring is only suitable for relatively common conditions and the arrangement may fragment primary medical care if the patient has to attend at a different time for a complaint which is incompatible with the special clinic's function. This discontinuity of care is most likely to occur if a clinic is run by a nurse or aide with specialized training though many practice nurses can become most effective nurse-generalists organizing follow-up clinics for 'patients' rather than 'diseases'.

Computer recall systems have been used to ensure appropriate follow-up of thyroid patients and to a lesser extent patients with malignancies. These elegant recall systems can be extremely helpful to the clinician who wishes to review his patients at infrequent intervals, but they suffer two disadvantages. First, the patients are required to pay a special visit for review rather than it being part of a routine surgery consultation for some other purpose. Secondly, computers are expensive and only appropriate for a minority of the conditions which require continuing care in an ageing society suffering from so many degenerative diseases. For these reasons the computer systems are likely to remain useful for a limited range of disorders but unlikely to replace the need for constant professional vigilance to work beyond the confines of episodic medicine in a high proportion of patients attending the doctor or nurse in primary care.

Personal care and interpersonal skills

Skilled and genuine communication between doctor and patient is an essential feature of every successful clinical consultation and primary medical care has become a laboratory of research into these processes in recent years.[4, 5, 6, 7] Undergraduate and postgraduate departments of primary medical care now provide opportunities for the teaching and learning of interpersonal interview skills for those who are willing to accept that interviewing is one of the most important of clinical skills. The fragmentation of continuing care by increasing specialization and team care does upset many patients[8] and this may be minimized if doctors and nurses are made more aware of the problems felt by patients and are then willing to modify their attitude appropriately. Skilled and active listening is essential for effective patient care, including continuing care (see Chapter 20).

Conclusions

Tools, methods and skills which help the doctor to conduct effective continuing care will obviously enhance professional judgement and performance, particularly when he feels stressed by limited time. In this chapter the advantages and disadvantages of the various strategies have been discussed but they can only operate optimally when applied together by a well-trained practitioner in a well-organized situation.

The teaching of continuing care is often conducted on the basis of a patient with a chronic or relapsing condition. This provides excellent opportunities for a student or trainee to learn about the natural history, functional and social implications of disease, but it differs very little from the teaching of a specialist in rehabilitation, or the physician with a broadly based training and concept of disease. The general practitioner must also teach on patients with chronic diseases but his professional role will force him to provide continuing care for patients with intermittent disorders which may require intervention (e.g. recurrent otitis media), or those problems of living which often present as physical complaints. The general practitioner should be able to review continuing problems other than those presented by the patient, either because he knows the patient well or because his records and staff help him to do so.

There is a danger that continuing care in the future may be left to the computer and/or the special clinic recall system instead of being based on professional vigilance and the kind of contractual arrangement between doctor and patient which ensures that both are aware of problems that need periodic review. Any system which helps the doctor identify patients who have greatly exceeded their review time will obviously be helpful, but it is inconceivable that review appointments can or should be sent out for more than a fraction of patients requiring review, first because patients are not good at responding to recall for routine review, and secondly because over the course of three years most general practitioners will see over 90 per cent of their patients at least once, and every contact is an opportunity to deal with continuing problems. The doctor must ask himself whether there are continuing problems to be dealt with every time he sees his patient and his records and staff should assist this professional discipline. Even where continuing care is delegated to aides or nurses the same principles should apply because the primary plan of management will be made by the responsible clinician. Continuing care demands of him an awareness of the discipline of primary medical care and the application of skills and methods which will improve the quality of the service he offers.

References

[1] Working party of the Royal College of General Practitioners (1972) *The Future*

General Practitioner: Learning and teaching. London: British Medical Association.

[2] Stott, N.C.H. and Davis, R.H. (1979) 'The exceptional potential in each primary care consultation'. *Journal of the Royal College of General Practitioners, 29*, 201-205.

[3] Weed, L.L. (1969) *Medical Records, Medical Education, and Patient Care: The problem oriented record as a basic tool*. Cleveland, Ohio: Case Western Reserve University Press.

[4] Browne, K. and Freeling, P. (1967) *The Doctor—Patient Relationship*. Edinburgh: Churchill Livingstone.

[5] Byrne, P.S. and Long, B.E.L. (1975) *Learning to Care*. Edinburgh: Churchill Livingstone.

[6] Verby, J., Holden, P. and Davis, R.H. (1979) 'Peer review of consultations in primary care — the use of audiovisual recordings'. *British Medical Journal, 1*, 1686-1688.

[7] Davis, R.H., Jenkins, M., Smail, S.A., Stott, N.C.H., Verby, J. and Wallace, B.B (1980) 'Teaching with audiovisual recordings of consultations'. *Journal of the Royal College of General Practitioners, 30*, 333-336.

[8] Cartwright, A. and Anderson, R. (1979). 'Patients and their doctors, 1977'. *Journal of the   Royal College of General Practitioners*, occasional paper 8.

Further reading

'Health and prevention in primary care'. Report from *General Practice 18*. London: Royal College of General Practitioners, February 1981.

'Prevention of arterial disease in general practice'. Report from *General Practice 19*. London: Royal College of General Practitioners, February 1981.

'Prevention of psychiatric disorders in general practice'. Report from *General Practice 20*. London: Royal College of General Practitoners, February 1981.

29
Medicine and society
James McCormick

This rather strange title requires some expansion and clarification. In the sense of the title medicine certainly does not refer to a dose of physic but rather to the organized services for health care, in particular care by doctors, which at the moment devour very large amounts of national resources, especially in the developed world. In the UK this amounts to almost £200 a year for every man, woman and child.

Notions of health, disease and sickness are quite various and have undergone dramatic changes. There are two current concepts of health which are popular. One is the World Health Organization's definition which speaks of health as 'not merely the absence of disease but a state of complete physical, mental and social well being'. The other, which may be gaining ground, rejects the optimism of WHO, and regards health as the achievement of maximum functional ability. This allows the possibility of health to the old, the halt and the blind.

Another notion which has been widely canvassed and promulgated by political parties and governments is the notion of health as a right. This carries the implication, never critically examined, that somebody, presumably mostly the medical profession, is in a position to dispense health. As we are only too aware health, rather than being in the hands of doctors is in the hands of the people. It depends, as McKeown has most persuasively argued,[1] on behaviour: the avoidance of cigarettes, motor bicycles, alcohol and promiscuous relationships.

In some sense health as a right refers to the right of access to health services, to doctors and to hospitals without crippling economic consequences. There is no doubt that despite vociferous, eloquent and sometimes justified criticism[2,3] people by and large have come to rely on doctors, nurses and hospitals as a force for good and capable of restoring those who are ill to health.

It is a normal part of the human condition to seek to avoid death, except in extreme old age, and to try to minimize the ill effects of disease. There are no cultures which do not respond to these needs by endowing certain individuals with power to heal and by recognizing certain rituals and medicines as beneficial to health. We still underestimate, at times seriously and expensively, the power of the placebo and the inability of patients, and doctors, to distinguish things which are associated and those which are causally related.

Doctors are still, *mirabile dictu*, accorded high status in western society. It is a status which varies and is, perhaps both understandably and rightly, greatest in the case of the surgeon who undertakes dramatic procedures and least, perhaps understandably but wrongly, in the case of the community physican. Doctors still exercise a great deal of political power, and despite cries of anguish, determine the vast bulk of health service spending. They have the privilege of a profession to regulate their own behaviours through the General Medical Council which can exercise considerable authority over an individual's right to practise his profession.

It can be argued without much difficulty that high status, income and privilege can only be justified by exceptional behaviours.[2] In so far as doctors derive their behaviours from the rest of society and from trade unions in particular they may diminish their right to a special place in society.

One of the most recurrent and persistent complaints about doctors is their failure to communicate. Part of this criticism is a plea for the demystification of medicine. The advance of science has encouraged a mechanistic view of disease which likens the human organism and its ills to disordered machinery. If this is indeed the case the patient no longer requires a father figure or priest but should demand a competent plumber.

As practising doctors with responsibility for teaching we cannot afford to ignore the perceptions our patients have of us. These will depend not only upon individual characteristics — our age, our sex, our sympathy or lack of it — but also upon their notions of the nature of health and disease and the limitations and potential of modern medicine. There is no single universally agreed view but rather a spectrum ranging from the doctor as magician to the doctor as servant. We need to be aware that we may be cast in different roles not only by different people but by the same people at different times. A single individual may easily require of us the right to abstain from work, a supply of drug upon which dependence has grown, a confessional ear or rescue from imminent and avoidable death.

A central issue, not much spoken of, not widely debated and of particular relevance to general practice, is the setting of legitimate bounds. There are two contrasting and perhaps extreme views which require serious consideration. One would hold that the content of general practice is the demands that patients bring. This catholic view would encourage and accept not only, 'I have pain in the chest' but also, 'my budgerigar has died' and 'I hate my mother-in-law'. The other extreme view would restrict general practice to the content of most undergraduate curricula — the diagnosis and management of predominately physical illness and a triage function to protect the hospital service.

As doctors we are part of society and derive many of our values and behaviours not from our special training and knowledge but from society at large, from our parents, our schools and our social class. In addition we represent, and this is particularly true of general practice, the interface between human anguish and the relief, either real or imagined, that medicine can bring.

There are opportunities in vocational training to explore the practical consequences of what may seem a philosophical and irrelevant approach. These are primarily of two sorts — an examination of our own perception of ourselves and an examination of the patient's perception and expectation of his doctor.

Much of our behaviour is determined by our self-image. If we behave in ways which are discordant with this image we feel unhappy and guilty. This is, if you like, a humanist account of conscience. It is an interesting and revealing exercise to write down some of the component parts of the self-image. It is easy to hope that the trainee and the trainer would include 'caring person, servant to my patients, scientist, mature, educated, broad minded, balanced, preferring prevention to cure, accepting death and impotence to cure'. What is the relationship of these to a self-image as 'labourer, wage-earner, pupil, deserving of high status, exploited and subservient, confident or uncertain'? It may also be useful to explore from whence this self-image derives. How much is determined by family, school and social class, how much by medical education, how much by the historical evolution of the profession?

Similarly teachers must encourage the exploration of patients' expectations. When consultations are unhappy it is usually a result or symptom of a discordance between the patient's expectations and the doctor's ability to respond by recognizing the patient's goal or alternatively because an appropriate response, from the patient's point of view, is in conflict with the doctor's self-image and is therefore at worst impossible or at best painful.

It must be important that not only should we see ourselves as others see us but that we should understand that we represent the hopes and expectations of society about medicine. We cannot afford to ignore the nature of those expectations because they carry the hope of happiness if not the promise of immortality.

References

[1] McKeown, T. (1976) *The Role of Medicine: Dream, mirage or nemesis?* The Rock Carling Fellowship. London: Nuffield Provincial Hospitals Trust.
[2] McCormick, J.S. (1979) *The Doctor — Father figure or plumber.* London: Croom Helm.
[3] Illich, I. (1976) *Limits to Medicine.* London: Marion Boyars.

30
Ethics
J.J.C. Cormack

'I will practise the art of medicine with care, with purity of conduct and with uprightness, and so far as in me lies, will faithfully attend to everything conducive to the welfare of the sick... Whatsoever things seen or heard in the course of medical practice which ought not to be spoken of, I will not, save for weighty reasons, divulge.'

This undertaking, clearly deriving from the Hippocratic Oath, is sworn by all graduates in medicine at Edinburgh University. It is still a relevant statement of the accepted basis of medical ethics, grounded as they are in the concepts of Greek humanism and Judeo-Christian morality.

Today life is more complex that it was in the previous century and the first half of this one; the basic principles of medical ethics remain, but their interpretation becomes more difficult, both in relation to changing social structures and philosophy, and to the problems posed by the technical advances of the science of medicine.

The teaching of ethics in the past consisted largely of the handing down of such rules as *primum non nocere* and the reconciling of the interests of individual patient care with concepts of the greatest good of the greatest number.

Ethics could, until the recent past, be considered to prescribe the rules of conduct governing the practice of medicine. Today it would be more accurate to define ethics in terms of a framework within which moral decisions may be taken and social problems analysed.

Many of the ethical rules of the late nineteenth and earlier part of the twentieth centuries were concerned with inter-professional relationships in the context of competitive private practice: questions of advertising, fee splitting and association with unqualified practitioners exercised the profession's elders. The apparent certainties of the ordered world of the Victorians and Edwardians have given way to a more open and more questioning society. What has now to be taught is not so much rules as attitudes.

All teaching in medicine involves in some degree the promotion of changes in knowledge, skills and attitudes. In the clinical disciplines and specialties it is perhaps natural that knowledge and skills are predominantly taught while it is assumed that attitudes are learnt, as it were, by a kind of osmosis. No doubt the example of individual teachers helps to mould attitudes but it is the responsibility of all medical teachers, not least general practitioner teachers, to ensure that objectives relating to the teaching of medical ethics are defined and pursued. These objectives will differ at least in emphasis during the three main stages of the general practitioner's development as the medical student, the trainee and the established doctor.

The medical student

During the student phase the aim should be to establish the fact that there is an ethical framework within which medicine is practised and to indicate areas of possible ethical dilemma in primary care.

Perhaps the most useful starting point is the question of confidentiality. The student coming into contact with patients outside the protected environment of the hospital can be treated not only as an observer but also as a junior colleague, already in a real sense a member of the medical profession with consequent duties and responsibilities. One of his prime responsibilities is to maintain confidentiality. While it is an ethical duty of the doctor/teacher to ensure that the patient is aware of and agrees to the presence of a third party during a consultation it is the responsibility of the student (and must be pointed out to him at the start of any attachment, and not simply assumed) to respect the confidentiality of that consultation.

The student may hold that the rule of confidentiality is absolute but it is often not difficult to find situations where such a stance may be questioned; for instance, the spouse of a patient gravely or terminally ill may legitimately seek and be given information which it would be quite improper to disclose to the same patient's employer, enquiring equally innocently.

Confidentiality must be mentioned, if not necessarily discussed in depth, right at the start of the student's introduction to practical general practice. Individual consultations or teaching in small groups can be used to widen the subject, perhaps in relation to some classical problem as that of the train driver who has an epileptic fit and refuses to disclose the fact to the authorities. What is the general practitioner's role in such a situation? Such discussions are of value not simply for their outcome in terms of decisions arrived at but for the realization that such terms as 'ought not to be spoken of' and 'weighty reason' are debatable rather than strictly definable.

Other ethical dilemmas which may occur quite commonly in the experience of students during their exposure to general practice concern the provision of contraceptive advice to under-age girls or the problems of termination of pregnancy. Again the importance of discussion of such issues lies in the demonstration that there are few, if any, ethical absolutes and that exploration of attitudes, including and perhaps especially the attitudes of patients, must precede decisions which should involve respect of different moral standpoints.

Many medical schools in the UK now have a Medical Group, modelled on the London Medical Group, where regular meetings are arranged to discuss moral, philosophical and ethical issues in medicine. The clinical teacher should make himself aware of the current programme and may then find ample opportunities to explore these issues in the teaching practice.

The trainee

Trainees have independent responsibilities as registered practitioners. The teaching of ethics to trainees should have the objective of demonstrating the use of discussion and consultation either one-to-one between trainee and trainer or in small groups for exploring and attempting to resolve problems raised by social, moral and legal issues. The aim is to enable independent responsibility to be discharged through the testing of individual conscience against the consensus opinion of peers. The guiding rule must be that the welfare of the individual patient comes first, but it should be tempered by an awareness of the needs and rights of the community as a whole.

Issues of confidentiality can be explored at greater depth than is usually possible with students, by discussing the whole question of communication with third parties: receptionist and secretarial staff, social workers, employers, police and other government and welfare agencies and, of course, relatives. The sharing of records by different members of the practice team and the use of the record as a means of communication also raise questions of confidentiality. The topic is covered in greater detail in Chapter 23.

Consideration of prescribing habits can be widened to introduce the subject of resource allocation and the responsibilities of the individual practitioner to the Health Service as a whole as well as the nature and implications of the practitioner's role as an independent contractor.

The discussion of ethical issues may be incorporated in small group teaching (Chapter 8), role-playing exercises (Chapter 11) or by means of videotaped consultations (Chapter 12), and teachers should look for clinical examples which can be used for stimulating such discussions. For instance:

1. A young woman, recently engaged to be married, becomes pregnant and requests termination because she does not want to give up her job. What are the legal and moral implications of responding to her request?
2. A depressed octogenarian patient with uncontrollable Parkinson's disease develops a severe chest infection at home. Is it ethical to withhold antibiotics — or is it ethical to consider giving antibiotics at all in these circumstances?
3. A middle-aged housewife who suffers from chronic anxiety asks you to visit her husband (who is a truck driver) because she thinks he is drinking too much; he does not know that she has told you about this. How do you respond to this request? What responsibilities do you have towards the husband, the wife, the community at large?

There is a considerable range of subjects which can be shown to have ethical implications that may be explored with trainees. These include:

1. Behaviour modification, including the use of tranquillizers in the treatment of anxiety.
2. Terminal care and communication with the dying.
3. Obstetrics, including choice of place of confinement.
4. Alcoholism — a disease or a social problem?
5. Management of the psychoses.
6. The care of the elderly — do health care workers have the right to intervene uninvited?
7. Contraception, sterilization and abortion.
8. Self-poisoning.

In addition to considering clinical problems and their wider implications, the trainee should also be aware of, even if not himself directly involved in, the ethical problems of research, especially clinical research.

The trainee should also be aware of the machinery for consultation which exists in relation to ethical problems. He should be clear about the role of District Ethical Committees (usually established to examine the ethical implications of proposed research projects), of the medical protection societies and of the British Medical Association as sources of advice, of the Royal Colleges as the guardians of standards and of the General Medical Council as final arbiter.

Etiquette

Professional etiquette may be considered as a sub-division of ethics. Etiquette has been defined as 'the unwritten code of professional conduct' and is concerned with the relationship of members of the professions with one another.

Demonstration of issues of etiquette to trainees is most effectively achieved by discussion within the teaching practice of such questions as:

1. What is the practice policy about patients who wish to change their doctor from a neighbouring practitioner?
2. How does a general practitioner cope with a patient who is dissatisfied with the consultant he is seeing at the hospital and demands a second opinion?
3. What is the relationship between the doctors in the practice and a local osteopath?
4. What are the proper boundaries in a relationship between the general practitioner and the local pharmacist?

Customs in matters of etiquette are largely governed by local circumstances. The trainee should be aware of the need for such customs as a framework for harmonious relationships but should also appreciate that they are neither immutable nor universal.

The established practitioner

The objective for the established practitioner must be to maintain an awareness of issues where his actions have social or moral implications and to be prepared to re-examine received or established opinions.

Changes both in technology and society challenge us to review our ethical attitudes in relation to such subjects as oral contraception, termination of pregnancy, the definition of death or the computerized record. There are no ethical absolutes, but many ethical issues.

It may be that dramatists and novelists and, indeed, poets have more to teach us about ethics at this stage than we can learn by 'keeping up with the literature'. Of course we can, and should, learn from our colleagues and even more we can, and should, learn from our patients. At the same time we need to be continually sensitized and refreshed by disciplined, if necessarily sporadic, contact with our cultural roots and the changing patterns of society to enable our ethical approach to be part of a dynamic development which can continue throughout working life.

Further reading

British Medical Association (1980) *The Handbook of Medical Ethics.* London: British Medical Association.

Duncan, A.S., Dunstan, G.R. and Welbourn, R.B. (1977) *Dictionary of Medical Ethics.* London: Darton, Longman and Todd.

Part IV
The search for standards

Providing medical care for defined populations of patients is concerned with relating the resources available to the needs of the population. In setting and deciding the standard of the care provided, it is necessary to apply skills based on epidemiological concepts. Ideally, the education of undergraduates should encompass the acquisition of these skills. They are relevant not only to setting standards in primary care, but also in evaluating published papers and indeed looking critically at all forms of care. If this aspect of undergradute medical education has not been completed, it is necessary to introduce it during the period of postgraduate education.

This section of the book looks at some of the problems presented by the ideas implicit in the concept of 'medical audit'. It goes on to describe a series of teaching exercises designed to provide the knowledge and skills required to look critically at medical care. Having acquired these skills, it is likely that the group members will wish to test them out by carrying out a simple study. The last chapter of this section describes how such a project may be launched. Carrying out a project helps to round off the education of doctors who wish to be able to look critically at the care they provide in their own practices and to read critically published material, on the basis of which their care may be improved.

31
Effectiveness and efficiency
David Morrell

When a doctor enters general practice, he possesses knowledge and skills concerned with the diagnosis and management of disease. Much of this has been acquired in hospital practice. The undergradute during his course in general practice, the trainee practitioner, or the new young principal in practice is faced with modifying the approach he has properly learned as appropriate for the hospital doctor to the situation he encounters in providing primary care. If he accepts this challenge, he will be forced to look critically at the demands for his care in general practice, relate these to his patients' needs for care and develop a system of providing care which makes the best use of his resources in satisfying his patients' needs.

Measuring the effectiveness of his care involves him in relating the care he provides to the outcome of care which he wishes to achieve. Efficiency of care introduces questions of costs and benefits. These two terms, 'effectiveness' and 'efficiency', are frequently combined and confused in the term 'medical audit'.

An audit is described in *The Concise Oxford Dictionary* as 'an official examination of accounts'. In commerce, the accounts normally reflect the efficiency of a business enterprise. If this term is applied to medical care, it is expected to reflect the same.

This is an over-simplification of the situation. In commerce, the ultimate measure of efficiency is the financial profit made by the company, although such factors as the value of the company to society and the job satisfaction of the employees may be important, and in some instances society may agree to subsidize a non-profit making company because of the contribution it makes to the community. In medicine, it is not always easy to describe or measure the desired outcome of care. In some cases, this may be the cure of a particular disease, but in many instances it is concerned with care rather than cure. In setting objectives for medical care it is, in addition, often difficult at the outset to identify the main problems which must be solved even if the value of the service to society appears self evident. Two examples may help to clarify this difficulty.

A patient presents to the general practitioner with headache. As part of his investigation of this problem, the doctor notes that the patient's blood pressure is 160/100. The doctor carries out certain investigations and prescribes treatment. The patient's blood pressure falls, but his headache persists. In auditing the care of this patient, questions might be asked about the investigations conducted and the treatment prescribed. The accounts to be audited are the practitioner's records on which he may or may not have recorded his findings or feelings.

The auditor will wish to know what investigations would be appropriate in a case of this type, but there is no certainty about this, and whether or not treatment is indicated; there is no certainty about this either. At the end of the day, the patient still has his headache and the auditor may ask whether the doctor has indeed identified his patient's real problem. Suppose the real problem is, in fact, depression. Then, of course, a totally different plan of audit would be appropriate concerning investigations, treatment and outcome. The difficulty is that audit starts from a diagnosis and, particularly in general practice, it is often not possible to put an accurate label on the patient's problems. The real problem may only become apparent with the passage of time, and even when it becomes apparent, the appropriate response often varies from individual to individual. The question, 'What is the patient's real problem?' may be difficult to answer. It may be the presenting symptom, it may be the disability produced by disease or it may sometimes be asymptomatic disease uncovered in the course of routine examination.

The second example concerns an elderly man with congestive cardiac failure due to ischaemic heart disease. The auditor may wish to know if the right tests have been carried out, the right observations recorded and the right treatment prescribed. The doctor may obtain full marks in all these respects. The patient may, however, be miserable, dejected and isolated and so disabled by his osteoarthritis and chronic bronchitis that his cardiac failure and its management may be largely irrelevant. He may be looking for a doctor who cares, who will visit him at home and listen to him. Audit of care for the elderly is particularly difficult because multiple pathology is often present and the patient's needs are often in the form of caring rather than investigation or cure.

Measurements of effectiveness and efficiency may not, of course, deal only with the management of specific diseases. It is equally possible to examine the performance of a practice. Such questions may be asked as:
1. How long do the patients have to wait for an appointment?
2. How long do they spend in the waiting room?
3. What proportion of children under five has been immunized against measles?
4. What proportion of the over 75s has been seen in the last year?

Each of these questions assumes that there is an ideal at which the doctor should be aiming. This is more or less true, depending on the particular questions asked. It is related to the population for whom the doctor is providing care, the geographical situation of the practice, and the priorities which the doctor holds in relation to the time he gives to preventive and curative medicine. Recognizing these difficulties does not mean that measuring the effectiveness of care is not possible and should never be attempted, but to base such measurements on a concept of normative behaviour in response to particular diseases or situations and apply them from outside a practice is often inappropriate and sometimes dangerous.

The alternative is to develop methods of measuring the effectiveness of care from within a practice and to build them into the day-to-day operations of the practice. The success of such a venture depends essentially on the general practitioners themselves. Unless they are motivated to look critically at the care they are providing they are very unlikely to improve their performance. Many of the methods currently proposed are so inappropriate that doctors are unlikely to see them as credible. What is urgently required, therefore, is the facility for general practitioners themselves to develop methods of measuring the care they are providing in their own practices.

Medical education in this country is not on the whole conducive to this approach. Undergraduates tend to be filled with knowledge about medicine. In solving clinical problems, they tend to be taught facts and skills rather than encouraged to develop the critical faculties which will lead them to seek for and to evaluate evidence. The following chapters are concerned with describing ways of teaching general practitioners to learn how to look critically at their own practices and how to look critically at new information.

Many doctors, and in particular general practitioners, are resistant to the idea of carrying out research. They see this as the prerogative of the academic, whom they often wrongly assume is out of touch with reality. Yet general practitioners who meet socially, and their spouses will testify to this, are notorious for their propensity to talk shop. Individual case histories are exchanged and ideas about the causes and management of illness are explored. These gatherings should be a rich breeding ground for research ideas. Unfortunately, they are rarely cultivated and the many questions raised remain unanswered. Somehow the day-to-day experiences of general practitioners, often richly garnished with new ideas, must be used to explore and expand the knowledge about primary medical care. Research has been defined as organized curiosity. This section of this book is concerned with training general practitioners to organize their curiosity so that they can not only look critically at their own work but also let the whole profession benefit from the ideas which flow from their continuing commitment to patient care.

While the teaching exercises described are particularly appropriate to general practitioners, either in training or established, they may be modified for use in undergraduate teaching. Each exercise will be presented in a common format starting with the learning objectives and followed by a description of the teaching method. The method is designed for use in small groups of six to ten students.

32
Looking at a practice
David Morrell

Introduction

Each of the chapters in this section of the book is concerned with describing teaching methods which have been used successfully by the authors in introducing general practitioners to the knowledge and skills which they should possess if they are to look critically at their own practices. The examples can be modified to satisfy local needs and, clearly, an approach which is appropriate to young principals in general practice may need to be modified for use with undergraduates.

The overall objective of these chapters is to illustrate ways to teach a critical approach to collecting data which can be used to describe the activities within a practice. Collecting inaccurate or incomplete data can be counterproductive by leading to erroneous conclusions. As the objective of the exercise is to reach valid conclusions which can be used to modify the care provided by the practice, inaccuracy must be avoided at all costs. The discipline demanded to ensure that the information collected is accurate and that the conclusions reached are valid may at times appear too rigorous, but it is hoped that the exercises once experienced will demonstrate that this is not so.

This chapter takes a broad look at the sort of information which can be collected in the consulting room. It is designed to bring to light some of the very basic problems which must be solved if this information is to be of value to the general practitioner in planning the services he wants to provide. Many of the issues raised in this session are described in much more detail in subsequent chapters. The session is planned to whet the learner's appetite for further enquiry.

Objectives

At the end of this session, the learners should be able:
1. To describe the limitations of information collected at random in the consulting room.
2. To describe the importance of a denominator, clear definitions and accurate and complete records in even simple studies in general practice.

Method

Each member of the group should be asked to collect information from three surgery sessions in one week as follows:
— Age and sex of each patient consulting
— The presenting symptom at each consultation
— The diagnosis recorded
He should be requested to analyse these data as follows:
— Into five age groups — 0–4, 5–14, 15–24, 25–64 and 65 or over
— Into two sex groups — male and female
— Into six disease groups — cardiovascular disease
         — respiratory disease
         — alimentary disease
         — genito-urinary disease
         — musculo-skeletal disease
         — all other diseases
The analysis should be presented to the tutor one week before the meeting. The tutor should then tabulate the results on a single sheet of paper under each doctor's or student's name with a separate column used to calculate mean values.

| Groups | Percentage of consultations | | | | | | |
Age group	Dr A	Dr B	Dr C	Dr D	Dr E	Dr F	Means
0 – 4							
5 – 14							
15 – 24							
25 – 64							
65 or over							

Sex

Male
Female

Disease groups

Cardiovascular
Respiratory
Alimentary
Genito-urinary
Musculo-skeletal
Others

At the meeting each participant should be presented with the results, which may also be written on a blackboard or projected.

Each course member should then be asked to comment on the results and to say what they tell him about the different recording doctors and their practices.

The correct answer is that the results tell nothing about the doctors because nothing is known about the denominator, the definitions used in collecting the information or the classification of diseases used. This answer is rarely forthcoming in the first round of discussion, but should ultimately be reached. There should then be further discussion about ways of making this exercise meaningful by calculating a denominator, agreeing definitions and developing classifications.

All these issues will be discussed in detail at later sessions. This session should be directed to identifying some of the questions which must be answered before studies of consultations in general practice can produce useful information.

33
How to describe the practice population
Michael Courtenay

Introduction

The concept of the practice population is intrinsic to the idea of a general practitioner's 'list' of patients in the National Health Service. Although there may be certain disadvantages for patients in that it makes it perhaps more difficult to change one's doctor than it should be, there is no doubt that having a relatively 'captive' number of people to look after has led to great possibilities for preventive care and research in general practice.

For many GPs, the actual shape of their practice population is probably obscure, partly because a small percentage (less than ten) may not be seen professionally in any given four-year period, and partly because 25 per cent of the population is likely to generate 60 per cent of the GP's workload. There is an unsubstantiated impression among some doctors that ten per cent of the population gives them 90 per cent of their work.

While GPs often pride themselves on their knowledge of their patients, this is limited, in fact, by at least two factors. First, patients tell doctors what they want to tell them, and omit all sorts of information they consider the doctor doesn't need to know, and, secondly, in many parts of the country, especially in cities, the mobility of the population has enormously increased, so that about 20 per cent of an urban practice may be relatively new (registered for less than a year) to the doctor.

In addition, many dates of birth are not recorded on the NHS record envelopes, especially in the case of older patients, and it is often humiliating to find one is not certain whether a patient is married or not. When it comes to social class categorization in terms of occupation, the amount of readily available information in the records is often derisory.

The construction of practice registers of one sort or another is the only way to delineate the shape and flavour of a practice population, but it is essential to help learners to overcome what may appear as the dryness of registers by making it clear that the drudgery can usually be delegated, and to stress the fascination of the emergence of a more vivid picture of the people for whom the doctor is responsible. What is more, the information can be of practical use to the doctor in planning how to spend his time most effectively.

Objectives

At the end of this exercise the members of the group should be able:

1. To construct an age/sex register.
2. To begin to construct registers showing social class and family structure.
3. To plan some kind of morbidity register.

Method

Before the session each group member is asked to bring either ten patient records selected at random or alternatively the following information from ten record envelopes:
1. All the information on the front of the envelope.
2. Diagnostic information about major pathology the patient has suffered.
3. The number of consultations in the previous year.
4. Any information about the family.
Assuming there are about ten students in the group, this means that they have created an artificial practice population sample of 100 people, and this is used to illustrate the various kinds of registers which can be compiled in general practice.

Age/sex register

The year of birth of each patient is recorded on a sheet and then, separating the male from the female patients, the patients born in each year are entered in alphabetical order under a given year. The years of birth are then grouped into the customary age ranges (0–4, 5–14, 15–44, 45–54, 55–64, 65 and over), and a simple histogram drawn showing the age distribution for each sex.

The limitations of a book-entry system for an age/sex register are demonstrated by using an old register of this type, showing how multiple deletions, occasioned by moving or death, make the register very untidy and difficult to read, and at the same time destroy the possibility of keeping the names in alphabetical order. A card index of more or less complexity is then demonstrated, showing how the defects of the book are obviated.

Histograms of patients' attendance rates in an actual practice are then produced to show that certain differences in demand in terms of age and sex are readily definable; males and females under 5 and over 65 are relatively high consumers of the GP's time, as are women between 15 and 44 in comparison with men, and the implications for the workload of the GP can be discussed.

This general information can be tested in a crude way by counting the number of attendances of each of the 100 patients in the group's sample records during the previous year and comparing the information from the figures from a whole, actual practice.

Marital and social class register and family structure

Again, all the information about civil state and occupation is gleaned from the 100 records brought by the students. The main object of this is to demonstrate how incomplete the information often is, especially with regard to occupation which, even if it is recorded at all, is often vague. An entry of 'engineer' for instance, is virtually meaningless because it may cover occupations in every social class from I to IV.

The fact that the constitution of the family of the patients is not shown on the record at all unless there has been special provision by the doctor is the next essential lesson. The diagrammatic method of recording family and social structure using a family tree as described by Cormack[1], is then introduced. The alternative or additional method of using 'family folders'[2] is also demonstrated, showing the added advantages of having clinical information about all members of the family available at the same time, even when only one member is currently receiving attention from the doctor. (See Chapter 22.)

Morbidity register

Again, using the 100 patient records, a count is made of major pathological conditions (e.g. hypertension, diabetes, renal disease, severe chronic respiratory disease and chronic cardiac conditions) and these are recorded on a sheet of paper, collated with age, sex and any other information already elicited in the exercise. It can then be shown that a simple morbidity register can be constructed in association with the age/sex register already prepared by fixing coded labels on the appropriate card. The way that this contributes to clinical care is by making possible the planned follow-up of certain conditions and the institution of some preventive activities, e.g. influenza immunization of patients at special risk.

The consultations of the year preceding the survey can be studied in more detail in diagnostic terms, consultations without a diagnosis being noted as a feature of general practice, but more specifically to illustrate the construction of a more detailed diagnostic index. This leads on to the consideration of the various classifications of diseases, contrasting the unidimensional 'International Classification of Diseases' with the classification produced by the Royal College of General Practitioners. This is a much shorter list with a limit of 500 items, and includes diagnoses involving symptoms as well as conditions, and having blanket headings for the rarer conditions in each section. Immediate cross reference with the ICD is, however, possible since the revision of the Diagnostic Classification in 1971.[3]

At this stage the group may be introduced to some of the diagnostic registers which have been evolved by members of the Royal College of General Practitioners over the last two decades, e.g. the 'E' Book.

The 'E' Book was developed by Eimerl, using a loose-leaf ledger of a size sufficiently small to enable it to be carried about, and each diagnosis could be entered on an appropriate page. This has evolved into a larger ledger designed for desk use, carrying larger data recording sheets separated by card interleaf sheets on which the College classification was printed in full. The principle of the 'E' Book has been maintained through a number of evolutionary changes; the contemporary version (the Diagnostic Index) has a modified data recording sheet which permits the recording of every item of service relating to the illness diagnosed. At the same time it is possible to record details of certain events in connection with the illness, such as admission to hospital or reference for clinical investigation. These modifications were incorporated in such a way as not to interfere with the comparability with material previously recorded in the older versions.

At the end of the session, some time should be set aside to discuss some of the limitations of morbidity registers and the group should be reminded of some of the problems identified in Chapter 32 concerned with definitions of morbid conditions in general practice.

Finally, the limitations of the method of sampling used to construct the artificial practice in this exercise should be reiterated and the group reminded that a later session (Chapter 36) will be devoted to methods of sampling.

References

[1] Cormack, J.J.C. (1975) 'Family portraits — A method of recording family history'. *Journal of the Royal College of General Practitioners, 25,* 520-526.
[2] Backett, E.M. and Maybin, R.P. (1956) 'The general practitioner and his records — experience with the family record folder'. *British Medical Journal, 1,* 17 March.
[3] 'The Diagnostic Index' (1971) Report, *Journal of the Royal College of General Practitioners, 21,* 609.

34
Defining what you are studying
David Morrell

Introduction

In the exercise described in Chapter 32, the students will have learnt the importance of defining the characteristics they wish to study. The teaching described in this chapter is designed to reinforce this fact and to encourage critical thinking about making and testing definitions.

Objectives

At the end of this exercise the students should be able:
1. To describe some of the common problems encountered in defining events in general practice.
2. To prepare a simple protocol to study a common symptom in general practice.
3. To know where to obtain information about the definitions commonly used in general practice research.

Method

At the start of each session, each member of the group is provided with an encounter sheet on which he can record information about eight consultations. The facts to be recorded are the type of consultation, i.e. whether the consultation was initiated by the patient or by the doctor, the presenting symptom, the diagnosis, the drugs prescribed and the duration of certified sickness absence. The encounter sheet is illustrated in Figure 1.

The consultations take the form of fictional case histories and each member is provided with a set of eight identical cases. The members working alone are then given 15 minutes to read through the histories and make a record which they consider appropriate on the encounter sheet. They then discuss their records as a group and compare notes. The eight case histories used by the author are appended to this chapter. They are designed to illustrate the sort of clinical situations which occur in general practice and generate the sort of problems encountered by a general practitioner undertaking simple recording. These include the difficulties of identifying the presenting symptom and diagnosis and relating the action taken to these, in the presence of multiple symptoms or multiple pathology. As a result of the exercise, the group should become aware of the need for clear definitions in carrying out work of this sort.

Consul-tations	Type of consultation	Presenting symptom	Diagnosis	Prescription	Certified sickness
1					
2					
3					
4					
5					
6					
7					
8					

Figure 1

The second part of the exercise challenges the students to define the information which may be collected in studying a particular symptom as it presents in general practice. The symptom selected should be a common one, such as backache, headache or pain in the chest.

The objective of the study should first be defined, such as, 'To describe the diagnosis recorded in response to patients presenting the symptom of backache in a group general practice of five doctors and the treatment and sickness absence prescribed'.

The group should then attempt to define the information to be collected. The following examples may be used:

1. Which patients are to be included in the study in terms of
   (a) age and sex,
   (b) type of consultation. Should it be confined to new episodes of backache or all patients presenting with backache. If the former, how is a new episode to be defined?
2. What is the presenting symptom? How should it be defined to ensure that all the doctors are describing the same thing?
3. Should there be any exclusions from the study, e.g. pregnant patients, patients with backache plus fever suffering from 'flu-like illnesses, etc.
4. How is the symptom to be described and recorded? Mode of onset, duration, site of pain, radiation of pain.
5. How is the diagnosis to be recorded? Should such imprecise terms as lumbago, fibrositis, etc. be included? If so, how should they be defined?
6. How is treatment to be described? Should it include such things as bed rest, manipulation, drug therapy and referral and, if so, how should these be defined?
7. How is certified sickness absence to be recorded? For how long should the patients be followed up and how will the end of an episode be

defined? What should be done about those who fail to keep follow-up appointments?

This exercise may occupy more than one session and it may be desirable after a preliminary discussion for each member to prepare a brief protocol as 'homework' and to discuss these at the next session. In doing this, they may be recommended to read *Research in General Practice* by J.G.R. Howie and *A Handbook for Research in General Practice* by T.S. Eimerl and A.J. Laidlaw.

Appendix

Case 1

Mr X, aged 24, complained that while knocking a nail in the wall he had hit his thumb. This, he explained, was now painful. Examination revealed that the skin was intact but some bruising was present. The doctor did not think an X-ray was necessary, applied some strapping and gave him a certificate for four days' sickness absence.

Case 2

Mrs A complained that she had been feeling unwell for three weeks. She could not describe her illness clearly but it transpired that she had been depressed and weepy. Her husband had walked out on her four weeks ago and she was unable to trace him. She had not previously suffered any mental illness. Without further examination, the doctor prescribed nitrazepam and told her to come back next week.

Case 3

Mrs B consulted with baby B complaining that baby B was off his food and that on three occasions in the last 24 hours he had vomited. The doctor examined the baby's chest, ears and abdomen and discovered during the subsequent conversation that the mother's feeding methods were completely unsuitable. His examination was entirely negative and he gave her a short talk on infant feeding.

Case 4

Mrs C consulted saying that the arthritis in her left knee was no better and what was the doctor going to do about it. The treatment she had received from the hospital was no good and she was not going back there for another three months. The doctor examined Mrs C's knee and could find no abnormality. This was Mrs C's fortieth consultation in the last year and although she had complained before of her knee, she had also complained of 28 other symptoms during that time. The doctor recorded his diagnosis, gave Mrs C a prescription and wished Mrs C 'good day'.

Case 5

Mrs D brought her baby aged 18 months to the doctor complaining that it was teething and was keeping her awake at night by screaming. The doctor confirmed that the baby was teething but also noticed that it had a running right ear. He treated this with penicillin. During the examination, he also noticed that the baby had a severe squint. He therefore referred it to hospital for an out-patient appointment with the ophthalmologist. Before the baby left he swabbed out the ear and instructed the mother on carrying this out when necessary.

Case 6

Mrs E consulted the doctor because she had been off work for four days and needed a certificate. She said she had a cold and in answer to his question said that this took the form of a blocked and discharging nose. The doctor gave her a certificate and as she was leaving she mentioned that she had had slight intermenstrual bleeding; 'This wasn't anything serious, was it doctor?'. Mrs E was brought back and examination revealed a carcinoma of the cervix. She was referred to hospital for a gynaecological opinion.

Case 7

Mr C attended the doctor for a renewal of his monthly certificate. He said he was still short of breath and his spit was now green. The doctor prescribed tetracycline and gave him a certificate.

Case 8

Mrs F said she was anaemic again. She knew this because her symptoms were just the same as last time. This was 14 months previously when she had pains in the head and spots before the eyes. The doctor weighed her and found she was five stone overweight as she had been when he had seen her three months before. He took a specimen of blood for haemoglobin estimation and gave her dietetic advice. She then began to cry and said she couldn't stop eating, that she felt so depressed that food was her only comfort. The doctor prescribed an antidepressant and told her to return in one week.

35
The accuracy of information collected
Chris Watkins

Introduction

In learning to examine critically his own work or the work of others, the practitioner needs to be able to assess the accuracy of the data which have been collected. The exercise described in this chapter is designed to develop these skills.

Objectives

At the end of this teaching exercise each member of the group should be able:
1. To understand the importance of identifying the causes of missing data.
2. To describe how data may be lost in a research project.
3. To make recommendations to overcome this problem.

Method

In undertaking this exercise the members of the group are presented with a problem which they are likely to encounter in their own practices. In attempting to solve this problem they will encounter many of the difficulties experienced in general practice in obtaining accurate information. The group members are provided with the following information in a handout two weeks before the teaching sessions.

The accuracy of your information

Background

You are the junior partner in an urban group practice of four general practitioners who care for a total population of 10,000 patients. Your practice is housed in purpose-built premises into which you moved 18 months ago. There is a practice sister, two district nurses and one health visitor attached to the practice. There are two full-time receptionists and a records clerk.

The problem

Before moving into your new premises there was no appointment system and one was started at the time of the move. It was expected that there would initially be a high proportion of patients who would attend the surgery without an appointment, expecting to see the doctor. The practice staff hoped that this number would decrease over time. However, for the last six months, 20 per cent of all patients seen still arrive without having made a prior appointment with the doctor. These are called 'casual attenders'. This is a cause of concern among all the partners and they have asked you to look into it on their behalf.

The questions
1. Do 'casual attenders' possess characteristics which distinguish them from patients who make appointments to see the doctor?
2. Do the types and duration of symptoms presented by 'casual attenders' differ from those of a control group who make appointments?

Study design

Using the form in Figure 1 information will be collected on all 'casual attenders' and a one in three sample of those making new appointments to see the doctor. The form is of a suitable size to be inserted in a medical record envelope (FP5 or 6) with the top section protruding.

Describe the way in which you will organize data collection to ensure that it is accurate and complete.

The discussion during the teaching session can concentrate on the following topics:

1. Definitions
What are the definitions of an appointment attender and of a casual attender?
What are the definitions of the presenting symptom and of the diagnosis?
What is meant by the patient's occupation? Is this information sufficient to determine social class?

2. Training of doctors and practice staff
How are the doctors, receptionists and secretaries to be trained in the application of your definitions?
Are your definitions simple enough to be understood by everyone who is involved in the study?

3. The feasibility of data collection
Is the paper on which the data collection form is printed thick enough to prevent it being lost in the medical record envelope?
Can those who are given the responsibility of identifying the study and control groups do their jobs adequately in the time available?

Appointment attender

Surname _____

Forenames(s) _____

Sex

Date of birth

Date registration

Address _____ Address

_____

Date consultation

_____ Morning (1) or

_____ Evening (2)

Telephone _____

Occupation _____

Was the appointment made by:

the patient   1

some other person   2

Symptom		
Diagnosis		
Action	Prescription	
	No prescription	
	Nurse/GP referral	
	Hospital referral	

Duration of symptoms: Hour(s)

Less than 1

Between 1 – 6

Between 6 – 12

Between 12 – 24

Over 24

0

Doctor

Figure 1

Is it feasible for the doctor to elicit the required information during the course of a consultation?

4. *Checking for missing data*

What checks can be used to make sure that information is collected on *all* casual attenders and on a correct proportion of all patients making new appointments?

How can the forms be checked to see that all the information needed has been recorded?

5. *Coding and extracting data*

What coding systems are available for coding the data?

What are the relative advantages and disadvantages of different systems of coding of

(a) social class?

(b) symptoms?

(c) diagnosis?

How are the numerical data to be extracted and checked?

This exercise is based on a project which was conducted by the author. It was never completed because of his failure to identify major problems in data collection before the study started. The course members should be able to identify the reasons why the inadequate data which were collected could not answer the original questions. The following suggestions are made by the author to overcome the problems of inadequate data collection.

1. At an early stage, involve all the doctors who are going to record answers to the questions and allow them to assist in designing the questionnaires that they will have to administer. It must be clear to the doctors involved that the research they are undertaking will be of direct benefit either to them or to their patients. For this reason the best person to design a research project in general practice is a GP within that particular practice.

2. Before the study starts, train the doctors and the staff with test situations so that they are aware of the implications of the study, and that the answers recorded are answers to the questions.

3. Do not ask any of the practice staff to take on responsibilities which they are unable to fulfil. In particular, do not ask the general practitioner to record anything which is outside the normal consultation process. Replies to additional questions will probably be worthless.

4. Code *all* the data within 48 hours of recording. If this is done missing information can be recovered before it is irretrievably lost.

5. Continually check throughout the study that data are being recorded on all the patients in the sample of the population that is being studied.

36
Choosing a sample
Charles du V. Florey

Introduction

It is not expected that every general practitioner who tries to look critically at his practice should have a sound understanding of sampling techniques; this is the province of the statistician who should always be called in to help at the design stage of a project. However, there should be no doubt in the practitioner's mind that sampling properly done provides unbiased results and is thus important in any evaluation of medical care. This exercise shows in a series of sampling games, using as little in the way of contrived situations as possible, what happens with grab sampling, sampling from a hat and simple random sampling. There is no attempt to consider more sophisticated techniques which must come later when the practitioner is reasonably conversant with statistical methods.

Objective

At the end of this exercise the group members should be able:
1. To explain the rationale for random sampling.
2. To explain how to use random number tables for sampling.
3. To use simple random sampling in a research project.

Method

The teacher plays a large part in this exercise as he must ensure that all the course members thoroughly understand what they have done at each stage. The teacher must therefore have a good background in simple sampling methods and the use of basic statistics.

In the introduction, the teacher should explain the reason why sampling is necessary — for example, that in many cases there are too many people to measure in a whole population (such as all the people on a practice list) so a representative proportion of them needs to be selected. The smaller number examined reduces the length of time needed for a study and may allow more time to examine each individual. It will also permit more attention to be paid to data checking and preparation, so increasing the amount of data on each individual that can be collected. This discussion should be extended until all the students accept that sampling may have advantages over measuring whole populations. So far no mention of bias in sampling has been made because this should be illustrated by the first part of the exercise.

Materials

The sampling material is made up of 1,000 identically shaped paper or cardboard squares with sides of about 4 cm or circles of 4 cm diameter. It is essential that the squares or discs are identical so that their shape will not influence or bias selection from the heap. The squares should have numbers 0 to 9 written on one side, in the following frequencies:

Digit	0	1	2	3	4	5	6	7	8	9
Frequency	8	28	79	159	226	226	159	79	28	8

(i.e. eight squares should bear the number 0, 28 squares the number 1, 79 squares the number 2 and so on).

Tell the students that the squares can be thought of as practice patients. The value of some attribute such as height, weight or blood pressure is given in coded form by the number on the square. Variables of this sort are either normally or nearly normally distributed in the population, i.e. the individual values are symmetrically distributed about their mean and the characteristics of the distribution obey certain rules. The true value of the mean of the population in the table is 4.5 but the students should not be told this as the aim of the exercises is to let them estimate the mean of the population from small samples.

The preparation of 1,000 squares in the proportions shown in the table is time consuming. They can be printed by computer but they still require cutting out. If fewer squares are desired it is very important that the distribution of numbers on the squares remains proportionately the same so that a normal distribution of numbers is maintained.

The games described below are for ten players. If you have only five then twice as many samples per player should be taken. The teacher can take part if the numbers are low. Apart from the set of squares, you will require a hat or waste basket to hold them while they are sampled. You will also need forms as shown in Figure 1, squared paper for drawing histograms, random number tables (a different page for each player) and a calculator with the four basic functions.

The games

Game 1 demonstrates the limitations of a grab sample. It may be explained as a sample of people interviewed on a busy street corner or those people who use a public weighing machine or consult a general practitioner. A grab sample is opportunistic and therefore is liable to be affected by unknown biases. Results cannot be generalized to the rest of the population.

Place all the squares with only the numbers 0, 1, 2 or 3 on them in an otherwise empty waste basket, hat or convenient receptacle and mix thoroughly. These squares represent people out shopping, weighing themselves or consulting a GP. Each player in turn grabs ten squares, records the numbers and calculates the average. After recording the average, the player should replace his squares and the 'population' should be mixed again before the next player selects his sample. All the means using this method will be below 4.5, but they will be close together and give the impression to the students that a reasonable estimate of the true mean might be obtained by pooling the results. The usefulness of the result as an estimate of the population mean might be discussed provided the students have not been told the true value of 4.5. It should be apparent that the sample comes from a highly selected section of the population since it contains only values from 0 to 3, or, in real life, only those out shopping, weighing themselves or consulting.

In game 2 more samples of ten squares are taken in the same way, but from the whole population of squares. The first player should take a sample and add up the numbers on the ten squares. The mean value should be written on the blackboard. He should replace the squares, mix the whole set of squares thoroughly and draw another sample. When he has drawn three samples in this way and the means have been recorded on the board, the turn passes to the next player. At the end of the game the mean values might be displayed as a histogram to show their tendency to cluster around the true value of 4.5.

Game 3 requires the experience of the first two games so should not be played out of turn. The squares are no longer required. Sampling in this game is based on the use of tables of random numbers. The group should be told that random number tables contain digits which have no systematic ordering or, in other words, every digit has an equal chance of appearing.

They should now be taught how to use the tables. Each player should have his own unique random number table with at least 625 digits. This number of digits occurs, for example, in a table with 25 rows and 25 columns. To find which row to start in, the player closes his eyes and places the tip of his pencil somewhere on the table (a random gesture). He reads the digit nearest the pencil and the one to its right and adds one to this two digit number (to avoid the value 00). If the number is not in the range 01–25 (the number of the rows in our table), the value 25 should be subtracted as many times (up to 3) as required to reduce the size of the number to within the desired range. For example, the number obtained may be 72. This becomes 73 on the addition of one, 48 on subtracting one 25 and 23 a second 25. As 23 is in the required range this is the number of the row to start in. The column number is obtained in the same way by using the next two digits on the table following the two used for determining the row. The digit on which the sampling starts is at the intersection of the column and row whose numbers have been obtained.

A sample of ten three digit numbers is then taken by each player, going either along the rows or down the columns and continuing on to the next row or column as required. These three digit numbers are selected at random so each has the same chance of being chosen. However, by converting the selected numbers to the values 0 to 9 according to the key at the bottom of Figure 1, it is possible to simulate drawing a sample from a normal distribution identical to that given in the text table and that used on the squares. The players should be asked to write the random numbers they have drawn on their form (Figure 1) and to code them. For example, if the three digit random number has the value of 327, this is coded as four because it lies between 274 and 499 (see key). In this way the random numbers are used to create truly random samples from a normal distribution of values 0-9. Examples of five selections are given in Figure 2.

1		2		3		4		5	
Rand. no.	code	Rand. no.	code	Rand. no.	code	Rand. no.	code	Rand. no.	code
Mean		Mean		Mean		Mean		Mean	

Grand mean =

Key to coding random numbers
000 – 007 = 0
008 – 035 = 1
036 – 114 = 2
115 – 273 = 3
274 – 499 = 4
500 – 725 = 5
726 – 884 = 6
885 – 963 = 7
964 – 991 = 8
992 – 999 = 9

Figure 1. Form for game 3

1		2		3		4		5	
Rand. no.	code	Rand. no.	code	Rand. no.	code	Rand. no.	code	Rand. no.	code
347	4	655	5	677	5	458	4	348	4
547	5	826	6	614	5	550	5	873	6
583	5	517	5	554	5	517	5	617	5
324	4	696	5	488	4	413	4	371	4
784	6	593	5	016	1	393	4	981	8
320	4	872	6	212	3	522	5	604	5
926	7	865	6	396	4	305	4	291	4
313	4	745	6	536	5	336	4	894	7
474	4	714	5	637	5	029	1	512	5
845	6	644	5	077	2	549	5	376	4
Mean 4.9		Mean 5.4		Mean 3.9		Mean 4.1		Mean 5.2	

Grand mean = 4.7

Key to coding random numbers
000 – 007 = 0
008 – 035 = 1
036 – 114 = 2
115 – 273 = 3
274 – 499 = 4
500 – 725 = 5
726 – 884 = 6
885 – 963 = 7
964 – 991 = 8
992 – 999 = 9

Figure 2. Game 3 form completed with an example of random numbers coded into values 0–9.

Five samples should be selected by each player if there are ten players in all (i.e. 50 samples are drawn by the whole class). Each sample should be totalled and the mean recorded. The mean of the five samples on each form should also be recorded. The mean values of the 50 samples obtained in this way should be plotted by the players on graph paper as a histogram (a half unit interval might be tried). This should show the tendency of the averages to cluster around the centre of the distribution and will give some idea of how frequently specified sample mean values occur when samples of ten are taken. These are only one per cent samples of the whole population. The samples may be added together to form samples of 100 observations (a 10 per cent sample) and their mean values plotted. These will be much closer to the true mean and should, unless your luck is out, demonstrate to the players that measuring only 10 per cent of a population can give a very reasonable estimate of the mean.

The session may be continued to show how the standard deviation and standard error of the mean describe the distribution and the variability in the estimation of the population mean. However, this extension requires a little knowledge of statistics before it can be adequately understood.

37
How to ask the questions
Michael D'Souza

In seeking effectiveness and efficiency in general practice, it is necessary to ask and answer questions about the care we are providing. In doing this, we must define clearly the questions we wish to answer because if we do not, our efforts are likely to end in failure and frustration.

The objective of this chapter is to describe how a group of students may be taught how to develop a clear and answerable question from a problem which they encounter in their practice.

It is a common experience that doctors and students have a great propensity to talk 'shop' when they meet either professionally or socially. They share their experiences and their difficulties and regale each other with 'interesting cases' they have encountered. These discussions should be a rich source of new ideas for study in general practice. Unfortunately, they rarely lead to new advances in knowledge because most general practitioners find it difficult to turn these ideas into questions which can be answered by carrying out studies in their practices.

Objective

As a result of this teaching session, the group members should be able to translate a problem which they have encountered in their work into a question which may be answered by simple research.

Method

The members of the group are each asked to bring to the meeting on a single sheet of paper the description of a problem which they have encountered in their practice, or if they have not yet entered practice, a problem which they perceive as being important in providing primary medical care.

When the group assembles, each member is invited to describe his particular problem. By consensus, the group agrees to discuss in detail one or two of the problems presented. The role of the group leader is to tease out from the problem presented a question which is answerable within the constraints of the resources available to the member presenting the problem. All the members of the group should be involved in defining this question. The following example illustrates the way the group leader may achieve his objectives.

Let us assume that the following statement is made by one member of the group. 'I seem to spend a lot of my time advising the parents of children in my practice on how to manage symptoms of minor illness. These parents should be able to manage these illnesses without consulting a doctor. This sort of consultation is a waste of my time, which I could use in providing care for those who really need a doctor. There should be more education for these parents so that they can learn to look after their children without running to the doctor with every cough and cold.'

Each member of the group is now invited to compose one question arising from this statement. Some possible questions which may be raised are as follows:

—What are symptoms of minor illness?

—How much time does the doctor spend in consultation for minor symptoms?

—Can patients manage these symptoms without consultation with a doctor?

—If the doctor did not spend time on these consultations, would he use that time to provide for those who really need a doctor?

—How do you define patients who really need a doctor?

—Would more education of patients about treating minor illness really alter the consultation pattern in the practice?

—In trying to educate patients to consult less for symptoms of minor illness, would they be deterred from consulting when this is really necessary?

The group are then asked to discuss which of these questions they would like to select and then further refine in order to form the basis of a research project. Let us assume that the question selected is: 'Would more education of patients about treating minor illness really alter the consultation pattern in the practice?' One way to proceed from here is for the group leader to suggest a number of questions which it is helpful for a researcher to ask himself in clarifying the work which he wishes to undertake. The following list of questions has been found helpful in the past:

—Why am *I* doing it?

—What am I doing?

—Which patients should be studied?

—What do I expect to find?

—How do I interpret what I find?

—What changes may result from what I find?

The group may now proceed with the discussion under these headings. The first question, *'Why am I doing it?'*, leads to some discussion about the motives of the member for undertaking this particular piece of research and the resources which are available to him. Is he, for instance, particularly well placed to obtain an answer to this question and will this fill an important gap in knowledge? This leads on almost inevitably to some discussion about what other research in this field has been carried out and

246

to the need to seek from the literature the present state of play in this area of research.

The question, *'What am I doing?'*, may lead on to discussion about the definition of minor illness and an attempt to clarify the particular symptoms which the member is interested in for carrying out his study. The group may then go on to discuss the type of educational intervention which may be suitable in order to try to modify demand. They might for instance decide that some sort of an educational booklet would be best.

The next question, *'Which patients should be studied?'*, challenges the group to decide which patients should be studied. As a result of their experience or background reading, they will realize that minor illness is usually presented in children. The sample to study will therefore have to include the young families in the practice. Ways of identifying these may be discussed, such as the use of an age/sex register or an attached health visitor's records.

'What do I expect to find?' The group is here asked to identify the common symptoms of minor illness, to discuss how frequently they present and to question how this demand may be modified by an educational intervention. They will also try to decide what they would regard as success in terms of the reduction in demand for care.

'How do I interpret what I find?' The group may discuss under this how they will interpret a fall in consultation rates as a result of an educational intervention. Does this mean that patients acquire more knowledge about the management of minor illness or are they simply deterred from seeking care for fear of the doctor? This may influence the design of the study in that it may be desirable at some stage to incorporate a questionnaire which tries to measure patients' attitudes to the educational booklet. The researcher should become aware of the need to seek help from a statistician at an early stage in the design of the study.

The last question, *'What changes may result from what I find?'*, encourages the group to consider how important a positive finding as a result of this piece of research would be, how it might alter doctors' methods of working and how widely it would be applicable outside the individual practice where the study takes place. This, in turn, may influence the design of the study which is undertaken.

By the time the group has covered this ground they will have teased out a researchable question from a general statement and be in a position to state the objective of their study, e.g.

> To measure by randomized controlled trial the effect of an educational booklet describing the home management of six common symptoms of illness on the consultation rates of children under the age of 16 years for the symptoms described in the booklet.

This is just one example of the way a group may work together to clarify how they can answer some of the problems they encounter in their clinical work. Many of these problems are organizational and a similar method can be adopted to unravel these.

Appointment systems are, for instance, a common cause of unrest among both patients and doctors. If the system does not seem to work smoothly, a series of questions may be asked, e.g.

—Is the demand for appointments excessive compared with the national consultation rates?

—Is enough consulting time provided each week in the light of the practice size and in relation to the mean national consultation rates?

—Are there particular days in the week when the system breaks down?

—Could this breakdown be avoided by a better distribution of doctor initiated consultations through the week?

—Are patients being recalled unnecessarily?

—Is there a practice policy about the frequency with which patients with defined chronic diseases are seen?

The number of questions which may be asked is almost unlimited. The group then have to decide how many of these they wish to try to answer in the context of the problems being encountered in a particular practice.

The role of the group leader is to help to frame questions in such a way that the issues being discussed are clarified. It is a task which is best undertaken by someone with research experience. In the 'real life' situation, as opposed to the classroom, it is often helpful to have present a specialist in the particular field of research being undertaken to contribute at this stage in developing a hypothesis. In the classroom, the leader's role is concerned more with demonstrating the value of this approach than providing answers to all the questions raised by the group.

38
Getting down to brass tacks
Chris Watkins

The purpose of this series of chapters has been to show how groups of practitioners can learn the skills required to examine their own work critically. Each chapter has described how an individual skill can be learnt, in the same way as the aspiring carpenter is shown how to use saw, hammer and chisel. By the end of the final session the participants in the group will need to try out the skills that they have learned on a project of their own. This final chapter describes in outline, for the course organizer, the help that the members of the group may need when they are setting up and running their project.

Choosing a project

Having a good idea is often the most difficult part of doing a project. For a project to be successful the idea behind it must concern a subject in which the practitioner is genuinely interested. He will have to live with his project for several months or more and will need to have the conviction to overcome the obstacles, both human and otherwise which cross his path. So a keen desire to see his question answered is of paramount importance to the success of the practitioner's project.

How do good ideas for projects develop? They can arise from personal doubt, or discussions between doctors on the effectiveness of management regimes, or the efficiency with which the service is delivered. It is frequently found in the course of examining the arguments used to support a particular point of view that there is little or no evidence to support many management decisions in general practice. Such evidence that is used to support a course of action is often derived from studies conducted in specialist practice on highly selected populations. Results from these studies can only be applied with caution to the patients that the general practitioner encounters. Projects concerning the management of particular conditions can improve the effectiveness with which patients are cared for. Examples of successful projects in this area include the choice of antibiotic for acute bacterial skin infections[1] and the duration of treatment of urinary tract infections with antimicrobials.[2] Good projects may also be stimulated by the desire to improve the efficiency with which the service is provided. This may involve examining the reasons why patients come to general practitioners,[3] extending our understanding of how general practitioners make their management decisions,[4] or training patients to use the service more appropriately.[5] The force of local feeling or argument may not only influence the practitioner's choice of a project but may provide the impetus to sustain his enthusiasm and those who work with him through all its stages.

After motivation, the second most important factor in determining a project's success is the scale of the project. It is very important that the first project which is done is small enough in scale and short enough in duration to allow the practitioner to understand each separate stage of the study from study design, through data collection to successful conclusion of the analysis. If the first study adopted is too large in scale, or involves more than a year of data collection, it may fail through loss of interest by the participants.

Finally, the question which the project concerns must be an important one. The project leader has to convince those who collect the data, those who extract them and those who help him with the analysis, that all the effort that they put into the project is going to be worthwhile. Lack of a personal conviction in the usefulness of a project is a more potent cause of failure than any other.

Choosing one's adviser

For his first project the practitioner needs someone who will provide sustained advice throughout the course of the study. This adviser needs to be someone who has some experience of conducting projects, but does not necessarily need to be a general practitioner. It is the job of the adviser to offer advice to the practitioner at all stages of the study. Probably the adviser is most valuable to the practitioner when he is trying to frame the question that he wants his project to answer. The final question decided upon should not lack the immediacy of the original concept but should be tempered by the constraints of practicality. The adviser should be able to give guidance on such issues as the size of sample to be used, the frequency of the events to be studied in the sample selected and the adequacy of the study design to test the hypotheses generated. He will need to look carefully at the techniques of data collection used, the definitions which are applied, the way the data are stored and the way they are to be analysed. However, more important than the practical advice which is given is the personal support which is needed by the practitioner. This is particularly necessary when the practitioner's morale is low after he has explored lines of enquiry which have proved fruitless. The personal adviser's role is thus to help the practitioner to sustain a sense of perspective and direction throughout the conduct of his project.

In addition to a personal adviser, the practitioner may need specialist sources of advice. The first of these is the library. It is crucial for the practitioner to be able to find out the work which has already been done in his field of interest and to be able to read about the techniques which may be useful to him in his project. A well-stocked library and a helpful librarian are invaluable. The use of the library is described in detail in Chapter 13.

The second specialist source of advice is the statistician. Many projects do not achieve their full potential because of failure to consult a statistician early in the design stage. The statistician can give advice on sampling techniques, sample sizes and data collection as well as on the analysis of results. If the advice of a statistician is taken at an early stage, the job of analysing the data at the end of the study can be made considerably easier.

The third specialist source of advice is the epidemiologist. His advice is useful in choosing an appropriate design for a survey or an experimental project. His advice will be especially valuable in choosing appropriate techniques of data collection and in particular the use of questionnaires. He will point out the limitations of questionnaires and the usefulness of other sources of data not immediately apparent to the general practitioner doing his first project.

Writing a protocol

However small in scale or short in duration it is vitally important that a protocol is written which describes the study in detail. To the general practitioner who is doing his first small project it may seem to be unnecessarily pedantic to write down every detail about sampling techniques, the definitions applied and the method of data collection and processing. Nevertheless, if this is not done, vital mistakes can be made which will invalidate the whole project. A guide to writing a protocol used by the Department of Community Medicine at St Thomas' Hospital is given here in full as it provides a series of useful headings to those engaged in writing protocols for studies (see Appendix).

Obtaining the support of the practice

One of the more difficult aspects of doing projects in general practice is to obtain the support of all members of the practice staff who will be involved and this will probably need several meetings with them. Each individual needs to appreciate how important is his individual contribution to the success of the whole study and that a successful conclusion of the project will be to find an answer to a question which is important. At these meetings each member of the practice needs to learn how his contribution fits into those of others. If the doctors are required to complete records at the time of consultation with a patient, it is important for them to understand clearly what is required of them and to feel comfortable that they are able to acquire the information within the constraints of a busy surgery. The definitions which the practitioner needs to apply to the events which are to be recorded must be clearly understood. To make sure there are no ambiguities in interpretation it is worthwhile presenting the doctors with hypothetical situations and to ask them to complete the data collection form for these. These exercises can identify faults in the design of data collection systems. They can also be used to measure the inter- and intra-observer variation of the same events. These can provide important measures of the reliability of the methods used for data collection.

Doing a pilot project

Before starting the study proper it is worthwhile to do a pilot project. This should be conducted over a short period of time in exactly the same way as the main study but it allows any last minute problems which were not previously identified to be discovered. It enables the feasibility of the whole study design to be tested and to be altered if necessary. By the time the pilot study has been completed, everyone who is taking part in the study should have a clear understanding of their contribution and be happy that they can fulfil it. A pilot study should test every aspect of the study design — from sampling, administration of the instruments used to collect information, checking the accuracy of the data to the extraction and analysis of the data. Failure to do a pilot study is a most important reason for difficulties encountered in projects in general practice.

Analysis and presentation of the results

Once the data have been collected, their accuracy checked and filed, there follows the job of analysing and presenting the results. The length of time and amount of thought needed to do this are considerable and are often underestimated by those doing a first project. However, the more thought that has been given at the time when the protocol is written to the way the data are to be analysed and presented, the more time will be saved at this stage. The simpler the method of presentation the more effectively are the results grasped by the reader. Histograms and figures are particularly useful in this respect. If tables are presented, they should be small in size. Few doctors are particularly numerate and lists of figures and percentages can be both boring and tiring to the medical reader. If statistical tests of association are used they should be as simple as possible and should support the written report rather than obtrude by their elaborate sophistication. Further useful advice on the presentation of results can be obtained from *Facts from Figures*[6] and *Research in General Practice*.[7]

By this stage the practitioner may be contemplating trying to get a report of his work published. Both the *British Medical Journal* and the *Journal of the Royal College of General Practitioners* are interested in receiving papers which examine the effectiveness and the efficiency of general practitioner care. A paper for publication needs to be succinct in style while getting a clear message across to the reader. To help him prepare a paper for publication, the general practitioner is advised to read the excellent book on the subject by the editor of the *British Medical Journal*.[8]

References

1 Everett, M.T. (1974) 'Staphylococcal resistance in general practice: A study of skin infections'. *Journal of the Royal College of General Practitioners, 24,* 85–91.
2 Charlton, C.A.C., Crowther, A., Davies, J.G., Dynes, J., Harvard, M.W.A., Mann, P.G. and Rye, S. (1976) 'Three-day and ten-day chemotherapy for urinary tract infections in general practice'. *British Medical Journal, 1,* 124–126.
3 Banks, M.H., Beresford, S.A.A., Morrell, D.C., Waller, J.J. and Watkins, C.J. (1975) 'Factors influencing demand for primary medical care in women aged 20–44 years — a preliminary report'. *International Journal of Epidemiology, 4,* 189–195.
4 Howie, J.G.R. (1976) 'Clinical judgement and antibiotic use in general practice'. *British Medical Journal, 2,* 1061–1064.
5 Morrell, D.C., Avery, A.J. and Watkins, C.J. (1980) 'Management of minor illness'. *British Medical Journal, 1,* 769–771.
6 Moroney, M.J. (1971) *Facts from Figures*. London: Penguin Books.
7 Howie, J.G.R. (1979) *Research in General Practice*. London: Croom Helm.
8 Lock, S. (1977) *Thorne's Better Medical Writing*, 2nd Edition. London: Pitman Medical.

Appendix

Points to consider when writing a protocol

The following list of general headings has been made to give guidance about what should appear in a protocol. Some headings may be inappropriate for your investigation and these should be omitted. A flow chart of the basic structure of a research project follows.

Title page. This should have an explanatory title for your project and the names of the principal and associated investigators.

Introduction. This should describe the need for the study and may contain references to other work to show the relevance of your project.

Aim of the study. Make this short and very clear. One sentence may suffice.

Statement of the problem and overall plan of study. Enlarge on your introduction, taking local aspects into consideration. Then describe what you plan to do, omitting the fine detail. This section will be read by someone who doesn't want to read the rest: it is a summary.

Details of method. The exact procedure should be described here in every detail. In this section you show that your proposal is practical and that you have thought of and coped with all the likely obstacles to obtaining the data. The population, your sample, laboratory methods and questionnaires as well as the organization of the field work should be described. When discussing the population and the sample you should justify them both, including the particular sample size you choose. Tables and figures may be helpful to get your points over clearly.

Procedures during survey. Make a list of the different phases of the study and what is to be achieved in each.

Evaluation and interpretation. Describe in detail how you intend to analyse the data to answer your main question. By the time you have completed this section there should be no doubt that your data and analysis will combine to give an answer.

Application of findings. What do you expect to be the practical results of your project?

Proposed schedule. Give a detailed accounting of the time you expect to spend on each phase of the study, and why.

254

Facilities available. Describe briefly what facilities are already available for the research, e.g. computing facilities.

Budget. Draw up the expected costs for each year of the study. These should include staff, travel, durable and non-durable equipment, etc.

Appendices. Include here:
- (a) criteria for diagnosis, etc.;
- (b) questionnaires;
- (c) coding methods;
- (d) data processing method. Give a start to finish account of how your data will move from the field to being punched, cleaned and stored.

Basic structure of a research project
(Protocol)

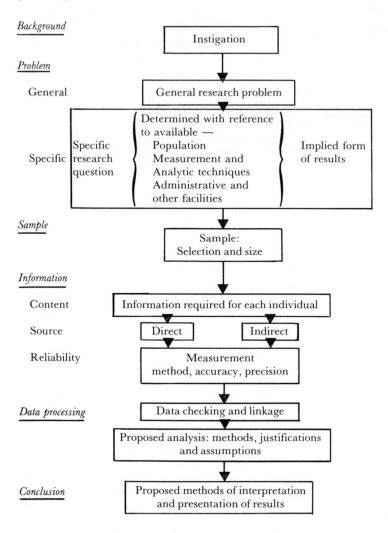

Acknowledgements

'Points to consider when writing a protocol' is extracted from Dr Charles du V. Florey's paper of the same name and reproduced with his permission; the flow diagram, 'Basic structure of a research project' is reproduced with permission of Mr Tony Swan.

Part V
Assessment

39
Continuous assessment
Michael McKendrick

Assessment, at least in any formal sense, does not seem to come easily to general practitioners. While criticism of the scientific work of colleagues comes easily to doctors involved in research, criticism of the clinical performance of colleagues is fraught with difficulties and taboos. Habits of professional etiquette and the imagined dangers of becoming involved in litigation with patients have conspired to erect a psychological barrier to honest and mutual criticism of clinical work.

The trainer's reluctance to comment on the clinical performance of his trainee, although perhaps understandable in these terms, is in fact based on a misconception about the purposes of continuous assessment. These may be expressed as follows:

1. An attempt to assess the trainee's strengths.
2. An attempt to identify deficiencies in the trainee's knowledge, skills and attitudes.
3. An agreement about how to make good these discovered deficiencies so that further learning can take place.
4. Follow-up, to see what has been achieved.

Experience over several years has shown that there is a surprising variance in the knowledge base of trainees who start their training year. For this reason a number of scheme organizers have developed initial tests of knowledge. Examples are Oxford Form TR20 and the North West Region's preacceptance test. Such validity as these tests have is based on the local knowledge of trainers, and what they have perceived to be the deficiencies in clinical knowledge which trainees have exhibited at the end of their initial junior hospital appointments. Many of these tests are self-administered by the trainee, who is thus able to see for himself the size and direction of the learning tasks before him. If the trainee and trainer discuss together results of such tests, there can be a mutual exchange of information and informed criticism which may do much to forge a robust teacher–learner relationship.

Much more difficult than the assessment of knowledge, is the assessment of skills and attitudes. Yet in practice, those trainees most valued by their trainers are those who score highly in the area of cognitive skills and attitudes. The most important work published in this field is that of Freeman and Byrne.[1] Building on the pioneering investigation of Maguire, Freeman and Byrne experimented with groups of trainees in Ipswich, Newcastle and Manchester some ten years ago, and developed a collection of rating scales applicable to a number of complementary criteria by which the trainee's performance might be judged. These are the Manchester Rating Scales and although they remain controversial, they still provide the only nationally comparable and experimentally researched method for making such assessments (see Appendix).

Detractors argue that these judgements are highly subjective and contaminated by the attitudes of the individual assessor. It has also been said that the expression of opinions in numerical form gives a false impression of precision and objectivity to what remain highly personal points of view. But others were enthusiastic about the collaborative completion of the scales by trainer and trainee. In this way the act of thinking about what the scales mean, how judgements may be formed in detail about satisfactory and unsatisfactory performance, itself constitutes a most important part of the trainee's learning. Explanatory notes are invited in order to amplify the numerical ratings, and this provides an important release from the unacceptable confines of the scales themselves. Many trainers have found it useful to repeat an examination of these scales as often as three times in a 12-month training period. It is interesting that these ratings correlate well with subsequent performance in the MRCGP examination.

The Manchester Rating Scales have also been widely used in an attempt to assess the hospital component of vocational training. Hospital doctors have, however, experienced some difficulty in applying some of the scales' criteria. For example, continuity of care is hardly a valid criterion on which to judge a doctor's performance in the accident and emergency department, and there are other examples which stem from the sometimes subtle and sometimes major differences between hospital medicine and the medicine of general practice. However, most scheme organizers have found the accumulation of profiles of trainee performance from a number of different sources a most useful way of building up a profile of the individual trainee.

Much work remains to be done on the development of continuous assessment in relation to the accreditation of a doctor on completion of training. In the UK, almost all three-year vocational training schemes have a modular structure, usually consisting of four six-month hospital appointments, and one year, often divided into two periods of six months or three months and nine months, in a training practice. Thus each trainee may accumulate up to six assessments from separate clinical teachers, and these provide evidence of the trainee's developing performance over three years. Sometimes performance in one particular post clearly deviates from an overall pattern, and this requires an examination not only of the trainee's performance in that post, but also the quality of the post and the judgement of the teachers. Most importantly, the trainee is not dependent on the assessment of any one assessor: an invaluable protection against biased marking. Also, over a period of time, the ratings given by a particular clinical teacher may be seen to be consistently high or low, and therefore these ratings may need to be discussed and sometimes corrected.

Of course all good teaching involves an element of continuous assessment. The trainer and trainee should form the habit of discussing the quality of audio-tapes, video recordings and directly observed consultations. It is the process of deciding what constitutes 'good' and 'poor' quality which provides one of the most important lessons which the trainee will learn.

Finally, a word of warning. Too much formal assessment can stultify learning and teaching, because it may become an end in itself. This is particularly destructive if the assessment concentrates only on the negative qualities of the learner, and fails to note his strengths or the ways in which he is successfully applying new knowledge and skills. In some medical school courses the over-zealous application of repeated tests and miniature examinations in the name of continuous assessment, increases anxiety to the point where learning is diminished. In particular, if the form of the assessment does not intimately reflect the tasks of patient care, the learner will be deflected from his development as a general practitioner, while he learns how to pass examinations. Much remains to be done in the development of appropriate techniques for formal continuous assessment. Most important, it should always be borne in mind that the purpose of continuous assessment is not that the trainee shall either pass or fail, but that he shall learn better how to learn further.

Reference

[1] Freeman, J. and Byrne, P.S. (1976) *The Assessment of Postgraduate Training in General Practice*. Guildford: The Society for Research into Higher Education, Ch. 6, pp. 112–115.

Further reading

Beard, Ruth (1976) *Teaching and Learning in Higher Education*. London: Penguin, Ch. 9, pp. 211–212.

Johnson, P.C. and Abrahamson, S. (1968) 'The effects of grades and examinations on self-directed learning'. *Journal of Medical Education, 43,* 360–366.

Learning and Teaching General Practice (1978) Scottish Council for Postgraduate Medical Education, Introduction, p. 8.

Working party of the Royal College of General Practitioners (1972) *The Future General Practitioner: Learning and teaching*. London: British Medical Association, Ch. 1, pp. 8–10.

Appendix

Vocational training: trainee evaluation form

(Prepared by the Department of General Practice,
University of Manchester)

Name of trainee ....
  (Surname)   Christian names)
Identification no. (if any) ....
Date form filled in ....

The Manchester Scales

The trainee is taking part in a programme of vocational training for general practice. The varied training situations require that the opinions of each of his teachers in hospital and general practice be solicited. A description of some salient and desirable qualities of an acceptable prospective general practitioner has been prepared. Please indicate where you believe this trainee fits by drawing a vertical line across your selected point on the horizontal line below each description of a criterion.

If a trainee scores a low mark on any one criterion please indicate to which of the suggested facets of the criterion the low scoring applies.

Please complete the following information about yourself:

Name of teacher ....
   (Surname)   (Christian names)
Teacher's code no. (if any) ....
Teacher's address or hospital ....
....
....
Teacher's specialty   ....

Your relationship to trainee (tick off as many as apply)

☐ Clinical tutor at hospital group where he* is training
☐ Consultant at hospital(s) where he is training
       if so, name the specialty ....
☐ Senior registrar at hospital where he is training
☐ General practitioner teacher to whom trainee was/is attached for one year
☐ General practitioner teacher to whom trainee was/is attached for short periods
☐ Community physician to whom trainee was/is attached for short periods
☐ Other (please specify)...

262

Period of teaching relationship with trainee

☐ 0 – 6 months   ☐ 6 – 12 months   ☐ over 12 months

Experience of trainee's work

☐ Unfamiliar   ☐ Slightly familiar
☐ Moderately familiar   ☐ Very familiar

* or she throughout

Criterion 1: information gathering

This criterion is concerned with the trainee's willingness, ability and skill in gathering information necessary for diagnosis and/or decisions.

The unacceptable trainee
follows no routine of history taking. He fails to identify or does not bother to develop salient leads. He will not pursue alternative hypotheses. He does not seek information on clinical, psychological and social factors. His recording is sketchy and not systematic. He tends to use investigations in a 'blunderbuss' fashion.

The acceptable trainee
takes a comprehensive history, when appropriate, including clinical, psychological and social factors. He examines patients thoroughly using local, regional, systematic or complete examination as appropriate. His investigations are intelligently and economically planned. He records his information carefully and uses previous and continuing records intelligently. He plans investigations and uses diagnostic services intelligently.

01	02	03	04	05	06	07	08	09	10	11	12
Poor			Marginal			Good			Excellent		

Criterion 2: problem solving

This criterion is concerned with the trainee's ability and skill in using information gained to develop a diagnosis and support clinical activity.

The unacceptable trainee
does not fully realize the implications of the data which he collects. He is unable to interpret the unex-

The acceptable trainee
realizes the importance of unexpected findings and seeks to interpret them. He understands the

263

pected result which he may often ignore and his thinking tends to be rigid and unimaginative and impedes his recognition of associated problems. His general shortcomings — rigidity of thought and lack of capacity to range round flexibly, i.e. 'diverge' when thinking over a particular problem — have an inhibiting effect on his effectiveness.

nature of probability and uses this to assist his diagnosis and decision making. He takes all data into account before making a decision and routinely tests alternative hypotheses. He thinks effectively — he has the capacity to range flexibly, or 'diverge', in search for relevant factors in connection with the particular problem in hand and he has also the capacity to focus, or 'converge', his thinking on whatever factors have been decided upon as relevant.

01	02	03	04	05	06	07	08	09	10	11	12
Poor			Marginal			Good			Excellent		

Criterion 3: clinical judgement

This criterion is concerned with the trainee's ability to use sound judgement in planning for and carrying out treatment and conveying his advice and opinion to patients.

The unacceptable trainee
is concerned more with treatment than the overall welfare of his patients. He plans treatment when not familiar with the procedures or therapy selected. His choice of treatment is rigid. He tends to use set routines or 'favourite' prescriptions, whether appropriate or not. He does not explain his proposals in terms understood by his patient.

The acceptable trainee
is familiar with the uses and limitations of the treatment he selects. He recognizes his own limitations. He considers simple therapy or expectant measures first. He shows regard for the individual patient's needs, wishes and total circumstances. He is flexible and will modify treatment or decisions immediately the clinical situation requires he should do so. He takes his patient into his confidence and explains his proposals in terms appropriate to the individual patient.

01	02	03	04	05	06	07	08	09	10	11	12
Poor			Marginal			Good			Excellent		

Criterion 4: relationship to patients

This criterion is concerned with the trainee's effectiveness in working with patients.

The unacceptable trainee
does not relate well to patients either through aloofness, discourtesy, indifference or pressure of work. He has difficulty in understanding his patients' needs. He is unable to give patients confidence and may even unnecessarily alarm them. He reacts poorly to a patient's hostile or emotional behaviour. He does not exhibit sympathy or compassion in dealing with patients.

The acceptable trainee
gives patients confidence, affords co-operation and relieves their anxiety. While patients appreciate his interest in their well-being he himself does not become emotionally involved. He is honest with the patient and his family. Patients like him and feel he is an easy person of whom to ask questions, or with whom they may discuss problems.

01	02	03	04	05	06	07	08	09	10	11	12
Poor			Marginal			Good			Excellent		

Criterion 5: continuing responsibility

This criterion is concerned with the trainee's willingness to accept and fulfil the responsibility for long-term patient care.

The unacceptable trainee
either loses interest after initial treatment or does not spend time on follow-up care. He becomes discouraged with slow progress and cannot cope with a poor prognosis. He is unable to communicate hard facts to a patient or his relatives. He uses ancillary personnel inadequately or demands greater assistance than they are competent to give him. He fails to review a patient's case at suitable intervals.

The acceptable trainee
encourages a patient to work for his own rehabilitation and shows that he too has the same objective. He observes his patient's progress and alters management and therapy as required. He understands the roles of ancillary personnel and makes maximum effective use of their help. He maintains a positive and persistent attitude to health and under proper circumstances to recovery.

265

01	02	03	04	05	06	07	08	09	10	11	12
	Poor			Marginal			Good			Excellent	

Criterion 6: emergency care

This criterion is concerned with the trainee's ability to act effectively in emergency situations.

The unacceptable trainee
panics easily and loses valuable time by ineffective action. He becomes confused under pressure and has difficulty in establishing priorities. He is unable to delegate appropriate aspects of care to others. He is unable or unwilling to make and sustain decisions alone.

The acceptable trainee
quickly assesses a situation and establishes priorities with full regard to life-saving procedures. He is aware of the consequences of delay. He is able to obtain and organize the assistance of others. He is able and willing to make and sustain decisions alone if necessary.

01	02	03	04	05	06	07	08	09	10	11	12
	Poor			Marginal			Good			Excellent	

Criterion 7: relationship with colleagues

This criterion is concerned with the trainee's ability to work effectively with his colleagues and members of the health team.

The unacceptable trainee
has difficulty in personal relationships and lacks the ability to give and take instruction gracefully. He tends to be tactless or inconsiderate. He is unable to inspire the confidence or co-operation of those with whom he works. He is unwilling to make referrals or seek consultation. He does not support colleagues in their contacts with patients.

The acceptable trainee
gets on well with other people. He is conscious of the need for teamwork and fits in well himself as a member or on occasion as leader of a team. He seeks consultation when appropriate and respects the views of others. He acknowledges the contributions of others. He creates an atmosphere of 'working with' not 'working for' in other people. He demonstrates self-control.

01	02	03	04	05	06	07	08	09	10	11	12
	Poor			Marginal			Good			Excellent	

Criterion 8: professional values

This criterion is concerned with the trainee's attitudes and standards as an individual member of the medical profession.

The unacceptable trainee
attempts to cover up his errors from his colleagues. He is difficult to locate in emergencies and absent when required without making deputizing arrangements. He discusses medical mismanagement with patients.

The acceptable trainee
is kind, courteous, honest and humble. He reports accurately, including his own errors. He respects the confidence of colleagues and patients. He places patient care above personal considerations. He recognizes his own professional capabilities and limitations.

01	02	03	04	05	06	07	08	09	10	11	12
	Poor			Marginal			Good			Excellent	

Criterion 9: overall competence

This criterion is concerned with your judgement of the trainee's overall competence as a potential general practitioner, taking into account criteria 1 to 8 inclusive.

01	02	03	04	05	06	07	08	09	10	11	12
	Poor			Marginal			Good			Excellent	

Published by The Council for Postgraduate Medical Education in England & Wales, 7, Marylebone Road, LONDON NW1 5HH

40
Sampling medical records
David Morrell

The medical record in general practice serves a variety of functions. In addition to containing the individual patient's identification data, it is used as an aide-memoire, as a record of the medical care delivered and as a place to record clinical or laboratory data over a period of time. It is often used as a place to store letters between the general practitioner and specialist, and in group practice as a means of communication between different members of the primary care team. The extent to which any or all these functions are achieved may be judged by examining medical records. They may also be used as a starting point for discussion of any of the details contained in them in relation to patient care or communications.

In using medical records for assessment, it is important to define in advance the objectives. They are most frequently used as a basis for continuous assessment. This is primarily an educational activity in that it helps both the learner and teacher to find out areas of defective knowledge or application, which they can then work together to correct. The secondary purpose of continuous assessment may be to award a mark to the learner which will contribute to some final pass or fail mark. While theoretically records might be used for summative assessment as part of a qualifying examination, this has rarely been done in the past and would require much closer agreement on what constitutes a 'good record' than exists at present in general practice.

Most experience in the use of medical records for continuous assessment has been obtained in vocational training for general practice, although it is a method of mutual assessment of doctors' performance which is becoming increasingly popular in group practices.

This method of assessment may perhaps best be illustrated by some examples:

Assessment of trainer and trainee

Method. All the records relating to a particular surgery session are retained by the trainee. The trainer then selects every third record. He examines these and rejects all those in which the consultation relates to continuing care. This leaves him three or four records relating to new episodes of illness. He proceeds to discuss each of these with his trainee.

Objective. To relate the symptom presented at the consultation to the problem identified by the trainee.

Example. The record describes a consultation at which a two-year-old child with a cough was brought to the doctor.

1. The trainer explores with his trainee the diagnostic probabilities when a child at this age with a cough is presented to the general practitioner.
2. They consider other possible reasons why a coughing child may be brought to the doctor and how the previous record of the child's illness may help to explain this.
3. They discuss the physical examination which may be undertaken.
4. They discuss the importance of understanding family relationships in identifying the patient's problem.
5. They relate the problem identified by the trainee to these facts.

Assessment of trainer and trainee

Method. Records are sampled as in Example I.

Objective. To relate the drugs prescribed to the patient's needs in the context of a National Health Service.

Example. An 18-year-old female patient presents to the doctor with dysuria and frequency of micturition. The trainee has prescribed a five-day course of Septrin.

1. The trainer explores in terms of probabilities the causes of dysuria and frequency in an 18-year-old female.
2. Details of the history taken, physical examination and investigations are discussed in terms of the patient's needs.
3. The organisms causing urinary tract infection in general practice and their sensitivity to different antibiotics are considered.
4. The cost and side effects of the drugs available to treat the condition are discussed.
5. The patient's needs in terms of counselling are explored.

Assessment in a group practice

Method. The practice secretary is asked to produce one record for each doctor in the practice where the patient has been referred to hospital in the preceding week.

Objective. To examine the reasons for hospital referral in the group of doctors.

Example. Doctor X has referred a patient who is suffering from asthma to hospital.

1. What does Doctor X expect to gain for his patient by hospital referral?

2. What investigations will the hospital carry out which could not be carried out in the practice?
3. What other factors provoked the referral, e.g. pressure from the patient, rejection by the doctor?
4. What therapeutic advantages is the patient likely to get from this referral?
5. What implications does this referral have for the continuing care of this patient?

Assessment in a group practice

Method. One record is taken at random from the consulting session of each doctor in the group.

Objective. To study the quality of the information recorded in terms of communication to other members of the group.
1. Is the entry legible?
2. Does the record reflect the doctor's identification of a patient's problem?
3. Does the record reflect the doctor's plan of action in the management of this patient?
4. Does the record contain information about the current therapy prescribed, and the follow up programme which is planned?

The use of medical records for summative assessment

Method. A sample of records is withdrawn at random from the practice files. Records which do not contain any entry in the previous year are rejected. The remainder are examined.

Objective. To evaluate the quality of the records. In order to do this, it will be necessary to establish what criteria will be used to judge the quality of the records. The following might be considered:
1. Is the presenting symptom recorded at each consultation for a new episode of illness?
2. Is the problem identified clearly recorded?
3. Are drugs prescribed legibly recorded?

Marking

A mark may be allotted for each item recorded and other items may be included if desired. More sophisticated techniques could include, for example, examining a sample of records of children under the age of five years to confirm their immunization status, or a sample of patients aged 40 to 50 years to confirm a record of the arterial blood pressure.

In the example given, each record is marked out of three and if ten records are examined the sum of these marks is awarded out of a possible total of 30.

There is no evidence that good medical records can be equated with good general practice. However, records which contain entries for each consultation and include the presenting symptom, the problem identified, and the drugs prescribed do at least ensure that the doctor has obtained and recorded information without which he would have some difficulty in providing adequate primary medical care. It is sometimes asserted that general practitioners retain this sort of information in their heads and do not therefore need to maintain good records. Such evidence as is available does not support this assertion. Examining the contents of the medical record on the assumption that they represent the medical care provided therefore seems reasonable, and when used for continuous assessment raises many important issues of concern to trainees and trainers.

41
Setting and marking essays and case histories
David Morrell

Introduction

The medical essay has been used as a method of examining candidates in medicine for many years. It may be employed to test knowledge, attitudes, or simply the ability of the candidate to express himself in a critical and comprehensible manner. The case history as a test of medical competence is a more recent addition to examination techniques and is concerned with assessing the candidate's ability to assemble and interpret information.

Method

In using the essay or case history as a method of assessment, it is important to determine in advance the objectives of the examination. The objectives selected will determine both the content of the question asked and the method of marking.

The essay question

Setting the question. The essay question may be designed simply to the test the candidate's knowledge, e.g. 'Describe the training of the health visitor', or 'What common side effects may result from the use of methyldopa in treating hypertension?' Pure knowledge is probably more easily and accurately tested by using multiple choice questions or the short essay question and so essay questions are usually designed to seek, in addition, information about the candidate's attitudes. The above questions might then be rephrased, 'What is the role of the health visitor in the primary health care team?' or 'A 55-year-old male is found to have a blood pressure of 170/100. Discuss the possible costs and benefits to this patient of treatment with methyldopa'. Finally, the question may be designed not only to test knowledge and attitudes but also the candidate's ability to make a critical appraisal of a problem. The question might then be rephrased, 'Discuss critically the role of the health visitor in geriatric screening in patients aged 75 years and over in a general practice', or 'A male aged 50 has a blood pressure of 170/100. What evidence would convince you that treatment of this patient with hypotensive drugs is justified?'

Marking the question. It has been observed that there is considerable inter-examiner variation in marking essay questions. It is, therefore, essential that the examiner should be provided with some guidance in the way in which the question should be marked. This is often provided in the form of a marking schedule. Framing questions to test different attitudes of the candidate is difficult. Preparing appropriate marking schedules is much more complicated.

Tests of knowledge

In these cases, a marking schedule may be prepared in such a way that the candidate is awarded a set mark for each item of knowledge which appears in the answer. A number of problems immediately emerge. An example will illustrate this. The first knowledge question asked was, 'Describe the training of a health visitor'. The following items might be considered important in the answer:
1. The health visitor is a trained nurse.
2. The health visitor undertakes a further year's training in health visiting.
3. The health visitor's course includes
    (a) health education,
    (b) infant feeding,
    (c) well baby care,
    (d) identifying vulnerable groups in the community,
    (e) identifying the medical and social needs of the elderly,
    (f) knowledge of the social services available.
If ten marks were available for this question, how would they be allotted? Statement 1 is extremely important, but all candidates should be expected to know this. Because it is important, should it be awarded, say, two marks out of ten, or should the candidate who fails to state this fact lose two marks? Similar considerations apply to the second statement. The statements included in 3 detail the health visitor's training. Some are more obvious than others. Should the more difficult statements be awarded more or fewer marks than the less difficult? And what about statements not included in the marking schedule but which clearly indicate that the candidate has a close knowledge of the training of a health visitor?
In preparing a marking schedule a number of decisions must be made:
1. Should marks be deducted if important statements are not included in the answer? Attractive as this may be, it presents serious problems in applying a marking schedule and may lead to some unfairness if the candidate considers that some statements are such common knowledge as to be unnecessary, e.g. that a health visitor is a trained nurse.
2. The alternative is to award high marks for knowledge which should be possessed by all candidates so that those who do not express it are penalized. The difficulty here is that the candidates may easily achieve a

pass mark on the basis of minimal knowledge while receiving few extra marks for more detailed knowledge. Such a method will fail the totally incompetent but will not discriminate between the good and the very good.

3. How many marks should be left to be awarded at the discretion of the examiner on the basis of the candidate's overall performance? If a large number of marks are allotted for this, the marking may reward presentation rather than content. If a small number of marks are allotted, it may detract from the really bright student's performance.

Tests of attitude and critical evaluation

Constructing marking schedules for tests of knowledge is not easy. Testing attitudes and critical evaluation is even harder. The examiners must decide in advance the particular attitudes they wish to assess. In the question concerning the role of the health visitor in the primary health care team, is the examiner interested in role definitions, communications, administrative considerations, etc? Each of these must be defined and allotted a number of marks. In the question about the critical evaluation of the health visitor's role in geriatric screening, the examiners must decide in advance what sort of information they are looking for. Is it the candidate's attitude to screening, is it evidence that the candidate can look critically at the administrative consequences of such a scheme, or is it the candidate's ability to discuss the relative costs and benefits in the particular age group described?

One way of approaching the problem of preparing marking schedules is to invite a group of experienced general practitioners to answer the question which has been set. The results of these answers are then analysed and those points most frequently raised by the group are regarded as having a high priority and are appropriately rewarded. The less frequently raised issues are given a lower priority. The number of general practitioners consulted in preparing the schedule need not be very large, and usually answers by five doctors will cover the main issues and having further referees only increases the amount of work in preparing the schedule.

Having prepared the marking schedule, the next problem is to ensure that the examiners adhere to it. This can be achieved only if examiners are prepared to practise together, for instance by asking pairs of examiners to mark a standard paper against a schedule and then to compare notes between themselves and between other pairs of examiners carrying out the same exercise. Frequently this is not possible, and the best that can be achieved is for each answer to be marked by two examiners and if there is a gross disparity in the marks awarded, for an independent examiner to adjudicate on the marking. In most large examinations certain examiners will very quickly be recognized to be either hard or soft markers. This problem may to some extent be overcome by pairing a hard marker with a soft marker or, alternatively, it may be necessary to counsel the examiners concerned in an attempt to bring about a more representative mark.

Timing essay questions

It is usual to allow 30 minutes for candidates to answer essay questions. Such rigidity is unrealistic and it is probably wise to try to determine more precisely how long a particular question should occupy the candidate and introduce more elasticity in to the preparation of examination papers.

Case histories

Marking recorded case histories depends, as in the essay question, on determining in advance the purpose of the exercise. The case history is traditionally made up of a number of elements, e.g.
— A description of the onset of the illness
— A description of the development of the illness from onset to the present time
— A description of the physical findings both normal and abnormal
— A catalogue of the investigations undertaken and the results obtained
— A past medical history
— A family history
— A social history
— Identification of the patient's problems in physical, social and psychological terms
— The problems of management in physical, social and psychological terms
— Detailed therapeutic considerations
— The prognosis for the individual and his family
    The value of the case history as a method of assessing competence in general practice is concerned with obtaining evidence of the candidate's ability to handle clinical information. The history should therefore demonstrate the ability to identify from a wide variety of facts those which are important. From these, the candidate should establish the patient's immediate and long-term problems and formulate a plan of action which is explicitly derived from the problems so identified.
    If such an assessment is to be fair, the candidates must be instructed in advance of the objectives of the exercise. They must be warned that the mere cataloguing of facts concerning the present, past, family and social history will not of itself obtain marks, and that the examiner is looking for the way these are synthesized into a coherent picture which describes the patient's problems and how they may be solved. The candidate may be

further advised that reporting irrelevant examinations and investigations may be penalized.

On this basis, a marking schedule can be prepared which might include the following:

1. Has the candidate responded appropriately as a primary physician to the presenting symptoms? Does he reveal knowledge of the probabilities of disease in respect of common presenting symptoms in general practice? Is he prepared when appropriate to use time as a diagnostic tool?
2. Does the candidate correctly interpret the clinical findings he describes? Has he looked for physical signs which confirm his original hypothesis?
3. Does the candidate display knowledge of the patient's past medical history and behaviour in response to illness in a way which indicates that he appreciates the relevance of this to the patient's current complaint?
4. Has the candidate interpreted the illness in terms of the patient's social and personal characteristics and identified the problems the patient is experiencing?
5. Does the candidate display an appreciation of the needs of the patient in terms of management and drug therapy?

Short essay question

This type of question is usually introduced with such words as, 'write brief notes on'. It is valuable in testing a candidate's knowledge, and it is easy to prepare a marking schedule for the examiners. In the context of the questions considered in this chapter it would be a useful way of identifying the candidate's knowledge of the side effects of methyldopa or the details of the training of a health visitor. It is more open than the multiple choice question and allows for marks to be awarded for a particularly good answer. It can be used to cover a wide field of knowledge because each question can encompass five or six fields of knowledge and the candidate is expected to spend perhaps five minutes on each section of the question, e.g. write brief notes on:

1. The common side effects of methyldopa.
2. The problems of screening for hypertension.
3. Compliance with drug therapy in the management of hypertension.
4. The training of a health visitor.
5. The statutory obligations of a health visitor.
6. Screening patients aged 75 years and over.

Conclusion

Essays, case histories and short essay questions may be used as a method of assessment for examinations in general practice. Some of the problems which examiners will encounter have been described in this chapter. The essay and the case history may, however, also be used as a method of continuous assessment when the object is to identify weaknesses in the learner in order to counsel him rather than as in the examination to pass or fail him. It may well be that use of the essay question and case history are particularly important in this type of assessment, as well as in the more conventional setting of formal examinations.

42

The patient management questionnaire
Eric Gambrill

Introduction

The simplest form of patient management questionnaire (PMQ) takes place orally when the trainer and the trainee discuss a case together following a surgery consultation or visit. What is the situation? What information do you have? What more do you need to know? What should you do next? What did you tell the patient? Are the family involved? Are any other agencies involved? Should they be? What did you prescribe? Why? What arrangements have you made for follow-up? What problems might arise in this family in the future?

This familiar litany gives us some idea of the essential features of the patient management questionnaire.

The questions need to be formalized and circumscribed in order that they should focus accurately on the important points of decision making: the range of possible answers needs to be validated, evaluated and weighted accordingly; and the whole package would need to be checked, rechecked and polished if it were to be used for formal teaching or examination purposes. Nevertheless, the essential core is already present. The very process of constructing and validating a PMQ provides an excellent educational opportunity for the participants and may be used as a basis for small group work in continuing education or vocational training for general practice. Established PMQs may be used in conjunction with a lecture or tutorial presentation, as a basis for individual self-assessment, or as a precise tool of evaluation in an examination such as the MRCGP.

Value of the PMQ

Why is the PMQ such a useful educational tool? Traditionally, most medical education, both undergraduate and postgraduate, has concentrated on teaching students 'the facts' and expecting them to be regurgitated on the appropriate occasions. While a broad base of factual knowlege is indeed essential for the practice of medicine it is an inescapable fact that other skills are at least as important, if not more so. The ability to reason as opposed to the ability to memorize; the skills of gathering information; choosing the type and degree of examination and investigation within the appropriate diagnostic range; making optimum use of the restricted time and unique time-scale in primary care; synthesizing the data and forming a working hypothesis on the inevitably limited information available are all skills of a high order appropriate to general practice. Similarly, the application of mature judgement to the clinical situation, taking into account the unique mixture of physical, psychological and social factors operating in primary care, and then developing a plan of management which encompasses all these features also requires skills of a high order in addition to the exhibition of appropriate attitudes towards patients and their problems.

The great strength of the PMQ is that it can be used to develop and foster these problem-solving and management skills and also to test them in the context of real clinical problems.

Types of PMQ

There are many types and variations of PMQ and it is important to consider for whom a given PMQ is intended when it is in the process of development. A PMQ intended for pre-clinical students, health visitors or social workers, perhaps on a behavioural topic, should not include clinical questions more appropriate to final-year medical students. Similarly, a PMQ designed for trainers or established general practitioners is likely to include proportionately more questions involving clinical judgement and management skills than would be appropriate for the medical student. More detailed discussion on this topic can be found in Hodgkin and Knox.[1]

McGuire has described the various types of PMQ in detail.[2,3] In some instances a section of a developing problem is distributed to a group of students. The answers are then collected before further information is given so that there is no possibility of changing the initial response in the light of subsequent development of the case. Alternatively, a very complex format may be used in which the student is presented with a variety of investigative options. When he makes his choice he may be required to interpret an X-ray, an electrocardiogram or a laboratory report. When a management choice is made information as to the effect which this had on the patient is fed back to him, up to and including the fact that the patient would have died had he proceeded with his chosen management option.

Murray and his colleagues devised an interesting experiment in computer-assisted learning using the PMQ format.[4,5] This technique involved giving the participant instant feedback, including explanation and justification for the preferred answers, either via the computer, when available, or by using a latent image technique, when the PMQ was completed by doctors at home after receiving it through the post. Further information on the case was also available by post or telephone and this service proved to be extremely popular. Marshall, in Australia, developed the 'Check' programme, which includes PMQs as well as other types of self-assessment material. This useful series is now available in the UK from Update Publications Limited.

The most open-ended form of PMQ, and the format which is most familiar to us in the UK, is the modified essay question (MEQ). In this type of PMQ the developing clinical situation is presented in the form of a booklet and each page must be completed before turning over. However, it is possible to turn back or look forward unless very close supervision is maintained, and care must be taken to avoid cueing the participant into an appropriate response and thus distorting his normal management of the case.

The MEQ as an assessment tool

This format was devised in the UK by Hodgkin and Knox as one of the forms of written assessment in the MRCGP examination. The other two forms in current use are the multiple choice question paper (MCQ) and the traditional essay question paper (TEQ). The MEQ has established a firm base in the written examination since it is used to measure, with a considerable degree of success, skills and attitudes which no other part of the written examination can assess.[6, 7]

Individual examiners construct possible MEQs for use in the examination from a case experienced in their own practice. The original outline is then examined and modified by a small group in order to define and clarify the key points in the story and lay appropriate emphasis on those aspects of management which are best tested in the MEQ format. The paper is then circulated to the 40 examiners who have responsibility for this part of the examinaion. These examiners are grouped into cells of four members who meet to discuss their views on the balance of the paper and the precise wording of the questions. One representative from each cell attends the first MEQ group meeting where the questions are finalized, and then the latest version of the paper is circulated to the whole panel of examiners. These experienced GPs all answer the paper and make their comments and thus the validity of the paper, i.e. its relevance to the real work of general practice, is established.

The MEQ group cells then meet to construct a marking schedule for their allotted question using the consensus of answers from the panel of examiners supplemented by reference to outside authorities, text books and original papers, where relevant. These marking schedules, which are finalized at the next MEQ group meeting, are used by the cells responsible for their construction in marking that same question for each candidate. Each question is marked by at least two examiners so that, in a nine question MEQ, a total of 18 marks are aggregated to arrive at a final score. This complex process helps to improve the reliability of the paper, i.e. the same paper completed by the same examinee and marked by different examiners should produce a very similar score. Reliability may be improved even more by re-marking exercises and by computer tabulation of individual examiners' marks. In this way each examiner can see how well his performance correlates with those of his colleagues.

Sample examination-type MEQs are available from a variety of sources listed at the end of this chapter. Suggested answers are available with most of them, but not for previous MRCGP MEQs.

The MEQ in learning and teaching

The MEQ may be used with profit as a self-assessment exercise by GPs or trainees, followed by discussion with the trainer or another colleague. However, it is probably most effective when used as a resource in small group learning, since changes in attitude and behaviour seem to occur most readily in this format. Initially, members of the group may work through some examples individually and then meet to discuss their suggested answers. The course organizer or tutor may or may not elect to inform the group of the 'correct' answers provided by the instigator of the paper. Inevitably there is a good deal of dissension and discussion and an active, participative group process is established.

Subsequently, group members can be encouraged to create MEQs based on their own cases and then develop them as a group activity. Creation of marking schedules involves experience, judgement and logical thought and is an excellent educational exercise. The tutor must insist on rigorous efforts to validate the schedules if a collusion of mediocrity is to be avoided.

The ultimate test is to offer an MEQ created by one group as an evaluation tool to a rival group and vice versa. Such activities are expensive in terms of time if not in material costs, but are worthwhile in view of the real educational advantages which may be obtained.

Conclusion

The PMQ is an excellent tool both for learning and evaluation in medical education. The MEQ is a relatively simple type of PMQ which can be used to great advantage in undergraduate, vocational and continuing education by and for general practitioners.

Sample MEQ papers

— 'Clinical Challenge' Series, *Update*, London.
— 'Self-assessment in General Practice' Series, *Update*, London.
— in *The MRCGP Examination*, 1978, MTP Press Ltd. Lancaster.
— in *MRCGP Study Book*, 1981, Update Books, London.
— *Check Programme, 1980*, Update Publications Ltd, London.
— MEQs (without answers) from previous MRCGP examinations are

available from The Membership Secretary, Royal College of General Practitioners.

References

[1] Hodgkin, K. and Knox, J.D.E. (1975) *Problem Centred Learning: The modified essay question in medicine.* Edinburgh and London: Churchill Livingstone.

[2] McGuire, C. (1980) *Medical Teacher, 2* (2), 74-79.

[3] McGuire, C. (1980) *Medical Teacher, 2* (3), 118-122.

[4] Murray, T.S., Cupples, R.W., Barber, J.H., Hannay, D.R. and Scott, D.B. (1976) *Update,* September, 523-532.

[5] Harden, R.M., Dunn, W.R., Murray, T.S., Rogers, Jill and Stoane, Cynthia (1979) *British Medical Journal, 2,* 652-653.

[6] Board of Censors (1971) *Journal of the Royal College of General Practitioners, 21,* 373.

[7] Gambrill, E.C. (1980) *Update, 20* (1), 45-47.

Appendix

Example PMQ

George Powell is 61 years old and lives in a council flat with his wife, Mary. They have a married son and two grandchildren who live nearby.

He suffers from chronic bronchitis and emphysema, but persists in smoking 25 cigarettes a day. He has had to take an early retirement because of his chest condition. Despite this problem he remains quite cheerful and enjoys life.

At about 11pm one evening, Mary telephones and tells you, in an agitated voice, that George was just going off to sleep when he suddenly 'went blank', started to shake and was unable to speak to her.

Q.1. (a) What are the three most likely conditions you would consider at this stage?

— Epilepsy (grand mal)	3
— CVA	2
— Rigor	1
— Cardiac arrhythmia	1
— Panic attack	1
— Any other reasonable suggestion	1
(Note: Only 3 answers would be marked)	max. 6 marks

(b) Would you visit immediately? If so, why?

— Yes	3
— Sounds like genuine emergency	2
— Mary is frightened	2
— Diagnosis is uncertain	2
— Signs may disappear overnight	2
	max. 11 marks

You arrive at the flat a few minutes later. George is sitting up in bed, a little confused but able to converse with you.

Q.2.   What further information would you wish to elicit at this stage? Questions relating to:

— whether he felt well during the evening?	1
— any previous attacks of a similar nature?	1
— any strange sensation before the attack?	1
— any headache before attack?	1
— any fever?	1
— any drugs taken?	1
— any alcohol?	1
— was he unconscious during attack?	1
— ask Mary to describe the attack in detail	3

— did he bite his tongue?	1
— was he incontinent?	1
— does he now feel drowsy?	1
— is his speech all right?	1
— has he a headache now?	1
	max. 16 marks

Further elaboration of the history, and a negative physical examination lead you to suspect that George may have had an epileptic fit. You decide to leave him at home for the night.

Q.3. (a) What would you say to this couple?

Explain	— possibly fit	2
	— nothing definite yet	2
	— unlikely to have another attack in the night	3
	— stress availability in case of further attack	3
Follow-up	— will see next day	2
	— advise not to drive	2
	— may need further investigation	2

(b) What medication, if any, would you give him and why?

None	— reassurance most important	3
Possible mild hypnotic		1
Because	— no firm diagnosis yet	1
	— not required	1
	— may confuse clinical situation	1
		max. 23 marks

George rapidly recovers from his isolated attack. All investigations are within normal limits except that his chest X-ray shows evidence of a small opacity in the left upper zone, which could be due to a bronchogenic carcinoma.

He comes to see you a few days later for the results of the investigations.

Q.4. What would you say to him?

— X-ray not completely clear (shadow, inflammation, etc.)	4
— diagnosis not sure	2
— will need specialist opinion	2
— should not drive	2
— how does he feel now?	2
— does he have any questions he would like to ask?	3
— be guided by his response	2
	max. 17 marks

285

43

The multiple choice questionnaire
I.M. Richardson

The multiple choice questionnaire (MCQ) is a way of testing the acquisition of relevant and classifiable knowledge. If knowledge is inappropriate or cannot be reduced to numerical or clear categories, it should not be tested by MCQ; for example, measurable levels of chemical or immunological variables in human fluids are usually precise enough to be used to discover whether a student knows the range of normal, whereas shades of colour often are not distinctive enough to be placed in clear-cut classes (how blue is cyanosis?). These conditions circumscribe the use of MCQs but once recognized they enhance the value of this technique in assessing the progress of undergraduate and postgraduate learning. Undoubtedly some of the dislike generated by MCQs is due to ignorance and carelessness in their construction and to neglect of the need to validate their use, whereas those who understand and accept the discipline involved in assembling good MCQs will soon realize their audit potential.

Should a teaching general practitioner attempt to make his own MCQs for testing the factual recall of himself or his trainee/student or should he leave construction to the experts? If he is willing to learn and apply the rules of construction, and if he accepts the need to submit his efforts to independent scrutiny, then he can and should acquire this skill; proficiency in the use of MCQs brings bonuses to learning. I want to emphasize that preparation for sitting the MCQ paper of the MRCGP (or other) examination is not the central aim of this essay; the MCQ is an aid to learning and maintaining knowledge of a kind that is essential to good general medical practice — education takes precedence over assessment.

Objective assessment

Doctors who teach must be able to distinguish between statements that are subjective and debatable and those that are objective and not disputable. The MCQ that is ambiguous, irrelevant and non-verifiable has no place in learning or assessment, because it will not accurately discriminate between those who have particular knowlege and those who do not. To say that the MCQ tests factual recall is true only if 'factual' is understood to mean something that has happened or is agreed to be the case — a 'datum of experience'. Thus the basis of any MCQ must be demonstrable by precise documentation; references to the authority of an answer are mandatory on all who claim to produce useful MCQs, otherwise the use of the term 'objective' is unjustified. It is as well to be clear about this term; objective means something external to the individual mind and therefore relatively uncoloured by the feelings or opinions of the writer. But of course 'objective' and 'subjective' are often not 'pure' terms; laboratories may show slight differences between normal ranges of values, specialists will not always completely agree on when to prescribe steroids, and not all general practitioners believe age/sex registers are essential to good clinical care. Therefore when an MCQ answer is to be marked true or false, that designation has to be the nearest to total accuracy that can be attained.

Construction

In the commonest form of MCQ there is a *stem* or introductory statement followed by up to five *items* to which the examinee is required to respond, the response being either true or false, or don't know. So the first step in construction is to choose a topic about which five true or false objective statements can confidently be made. In the context of general practice the question may refer to acute or non-acute, minor or major, physical or mental illness; any of the bodily systems; prevention, cure or care; consultations or practice organization. Against the potential of this wide resource must be set the subjective nature of much of what the general practitioner has to do. For example, before MCQ use can be made of the family doctor's wide experience of 'influenza', that condition will need to be defined and agreement reached that the stated definition applies only to demonstrable infection with the influenza viruses, a requirement that cannot be met in most cases seen outside hospital. If however the topic chosen was immunization against influenza, the current vaccines available have contents, indications, and results that are well documented and thus permit the construction of a useful MCQ on influenza prevention.

The second step for most teachers/examiners is to seek out the best authoritative text(s) on the chosen topic and to use this source for the choice of five relevant items. I must emphasize this matter of relevance; only those with thoughtful experience in general practice can judge what undergraduate students or vocational trainees should know if their performance is to be deemed adequate. That sounds easy but in fact there is frequently considerable difference of opinion between general practitioners on what constitute relevant items for an MCQ on, say, diabetes, or electrocardiography, or enuresis. The only safe course is to put relevance to the test of a small panel of active family doctors at least two thirds of whom should agree that a proposed question is pertinent (see Appendix).

The same group should be asked to judge two other critical features. If questions are too easy they will fail to detect inadequacies but if they are too difficult testers and tested will regard them as inappropriate (and tend to condemn the whole MCQ concept) so an 'about right' consensus on difficulty is important. Secondly, ambiguity must be avoided; the expressions used should state exactly and clearly what is being asked, and to achieve this end unnecessary and unfamiliar words should be rigorously pruned. Double negatives are particularly confusing (e.g. antibiotics should not be given when there is no exudate on the pharynx) but even more common are imprecise words like 'usually', 'often', 'rarely', 'commonly', or 'significantly'. If incidence or prevalence is known then it should be roundly stated: 'in more than two-thirds of patients with . . .' , 'in fewer than ten per cent of cases will the following complications be found'; if frequency is estimated only from impression, difficulties are sure to arise over accuracy. Setters must also try to find untrue items that are important and do not appear merely as such silly and obvious distractions as to be easily guessable. In passing I would like to point out that an element of guesswork comes into answering in the sense that any respondent will vary in the confidence with which items are marked as true or false, and some of this variation will depend not on knowledge but on degree of willingness to take chances.

The commonest purpose for which MCQs are used is to test factual recall, like 'the usual adult dose of oxytetracycline in bronchitis is 250 mg four times per day'. But another use is to test critical thinking, for example by asking 'failure of response to an antibiotic may be due to . . .' and this can be developed by degrees into a major problem-solving MCQ where the stem consists of a full clinical history and examination, including photographs, followed by five items of interpretation of the given information. This latter variety has been more often used in testing hospital trainees but can quite readily be applied to general practice provided the trainer is willing to give the greater time required to assemble this more complex type.

Examples

1. In Bell's palsy of the seventh cranial nerve:
   True (a) Platysma cannot be tensed.
   False (b) Masseter is paralysed.
   True (c) Hearing may be affected.
   True (d) Sense of taste may be altered.
   False (e) Cortico-steroids are contra-indicated.
   This question tests anatomy and pharmacology in a clinically important way, it is neither too easy nor too difficult, and it has been shown to be a good discriminator.
2. You are consulted by a previously healthy 15-year-old girl and her mother who reports that her daughter was brought home at 11.30pm the previous night after 'collapsing' at a disco. The daughter remembers 'lights flashing and feeling faint' and coming to in a side room; she now feels fine.

False (a) Stroboscopic epilepsy is a likely diagnosis.

False (b) Further enquiry into the circumstances of the collapse is unnecessary.

True (c) Failure of venous return to the heart is the commonest cause of an ordinary faint.

False (d) Carotid sinus syncope should be tested for.

True (e) Drug therapy is not indicated.

Here the items are related to a brief individual clinical picture but the question is testing ability to apply the general to the particular. It is to be noted that each item poses a question of probability — for instance, the faint might at this age very rarely be due to excessive carotid sinus sensitivity but with such a small probability the carotid sinus test is unnecessary.

3. A professional class married woman of 33, on holiday in your area for two weeks, consults because 'my thrush has recurred' and requests a prescription. She says this is her third attack in two years, her main complaints being vulval soreness, itch, and vaginal discharge which she describes as 'sticky white'.

False (a) The history makes vaginal examination unnecessary.

True (b) The nature of her discharge is not diagnostic of the cause.

True (c) Since she will be returning home before the laboratory report would be available, a vaginal swab need not be taken.

True (d) Vaginal pessaries are available which act on both trichomonas and monilial infections.

False (e) You must examine her husband.

There is room in item (c) for argument and therefore it should be referred for consensus views; (e) as it stands must be false because the husband's availability is unknown — it is there to test observation and reasoning ability. (a), too, is debatable depending on whether you regard the testimony of a professional woman as sufficiently reliable to allow a clinical shortcut or whether on principle a vaginal examination shall be done.

4. In the nutrition of elderly people:

False (a) Butter is a better source of vitamin D than margarine.

False (b) 'Meals on Wheels' is a good way to boost intake of vitamin C.

True (c) Weakness may be due to low potassium consumption.

False (d) Supplementation with vitamin and mineral preparations is usually desirable.

True (e) Household circumstances are important.

If practitioners should be interested in the food habits of elderly patients, this question in some form is worth asking; but if the topic is regarded as more in the field of the health visitor it is arguable whether these items should be included because not all general practitioners have an attached health visitor and not all health visitors are in contact with old people.

The list of examples could be extended almost indefinitely; suffice it to say that all four of these illustrations generated interest, frustration, and (finally) some satisfaction.

Further reading

Anderson, J. (1976) *The Multiple Choice Question in Medicine.* Tunbridge Wells: Pitman Medical.

Appendix

MCQ true/false test

Question

Answered by: Date:

Please tick the appropriate box opposite each item

Question

	True	False
(a)		
(b)		
(c)		
(d)		
(e)		

Please complete the following assessment by ticking the appropriate box

Relevant ☐   Too difficult ☐   About right ☐

Irrelevant ☐   Too easy ☐

Wording ambiguous ☐   Please specify:

Wording unambiguous ☐

The question should be used ☐

The question should not be used ☐

44
The clinical examination
J.H. Barber

Introduction

Medicine in general practice differs from that in hospital in a number of important ways, not least of which is the need to consider a wider range of probabilities, the frequent lack of hard objective evidence supporting a diagnosis, the broadening of both diagnosis and management to encompass other than purely physical disease and the variability of the time span within which the patient is to be managed. The decision-making process with which the student and hospital trained doctor are familiar and to which they are accustomed is inappropriate for work in general practice and the trainer has a responsibility to ensure that new essential clinical skills are learned during the trainee year in general practice.

This chapter is appropriately entitled 'The clinical examination' since what will be described are ideas on the content and method of such an examination. It is essential that every trainee is so assessed on at least one, and on preferably more than one, occasion during his trainee year; such an assessment serves not only to identify areas of difficulty but also as an educational experience for both the trainee and his trainer. This chapter is intended to apply principally to the vocational trainee in general practice; mention will be made later of the way in which the assessment process can be adapted for use in undergraduate teaching.

The clinical examination will be assumed to extend from the time of first doctor–patient contact until that episode of ill-health can be considered to be terminated. Clearly the time scale can range from a brief single consultation for some relatively simple self-limiting condition to the lifelong management of a patient with a chronic disease. The content to be discussed sub-divides into six major areas:

1. The interview component of the consultation.
2. The physical examination of the patient.
3. The laboratory investigations completed or ordered.
4. The treatment prescribed.
5. The advice that is given to patient and relatives regarding the general management and nursing care required.
6. The arrangements made for follow-up and review of the patient.

Within each area there are a number of questions that may be asked in order to assess the trainee's competence.

1. *The interview component of the consultation*
   (a) Was the patient at ease throughout the consultation despite or after taking into account the presence of a third party — the trainer — or the possibility that the patient and trainee had not previously met?
   (b) At the end of the interview did the trainee fully understand the patient's problems and the reasons for the consultation?
   (c) Has the trainee formulated a reasonable list of probabilities based on the information offered by the patient and asked of him by the trainee during the consultation?
   (d) Has the trainee obtained information of a social and psychological nature which, in view of his list of probabilities, may be of importance in his management of the patient?

2. *The physical examination*
   (a) Are the different physical examinations carried out by the trainee
       (i) appropriate in view of the probabilities selected?
       (ii) completed skilfully and considerately with reference to the individual patient's sex and age?
   (b) Are the conclusions that the trainee has drawn from his examination of the patient
       (i) accurate?
       (ii) such that they will help to confirm or refute one or more of the probable diagnoses?
   (c) Has a reasonable diagnosis been deduced as a result of the history and physical examination completed?

3. *Investigations ordered*
   (a) Are the investigations completed or ordered
       (i) necessary to help support or refute the diagnosis considered most probable?
       (ii) appropriate in respect of cost, invasiveness and the time delay that will occur before the result is known?
   (b) Are the conclusions that the trainee has drawn from the results of his investigations correct?

4. *Treatment prescribed*
   (a) If drug treatments were prescribed were they
       (i) necessary?
       (ii) appropriate to the diagnosis considered?
       (iii) correctly written on the prescription form?
       (iv) fully explained so that the patient understood how and at what times and for how long treatment should be continued?
   (b) Were there any alternatives to drug therapy and were these correctly considered and judged?

5. *General management*
    (a) Was the advice given to the patient and/or his relatives
        (i) correct?
        (ii) comprehensive and appropriate to the individual patient and his illness?
        (iii) given in a form that was clearly understood by the patient?
    (b) Were any other members of the practice team considered to have a part to play in the general management of the patient? If so were their roles explained to the patient?
    (c) Were the clinical notes written correctly, adequately and legibly?

6. *Follow-up*
    (a) What plans and arrangements has the trainee considered for follow-up with the patient?
    (b) Are these plans correct and appropriate?
    (c) Do the patient and relatives understand the follow-up arrangements and the reasons for them?

The majority of consultations and home visits require at least one follow-up attendance by the patient and the assessment of the trainee's clinical competence should continue throughout the course of the illness. At each follow-up consultation the questions asked should include:
    (a) Are the questions posed by the trainee about the patient's progress those that are most appropriate and meaningful?
    (b) Are the conclusions that he draws from his questions or examination of the patient accurate?
    (c) What criteria for cure has the trainee established and are these criteria correct and appropriate?
    (d) Are the indications for and timing of further follow-up consultations reasonable?

The format detailed above will allow the trainer to complete a detailed assessment of his trainee's ability to manage the acute short-lasting illness in general practice and the assessment should be repeated so as to include a representative number of the common problems met with in general practice. This can be achieved more readily by selecting from different age groups of patients rather than from disease categories. These should include:
1. The pre-school child with an infectious illness. Illnesses that are seen both in the surgery and at a home visit should be included.
2. The young adult with a condition such as headache, backache, dyspepsia, urinary tract infection or respiratory infection seen initially at a surgery consultation.
3. An adult with an acute and relatively serious illness such as lower respiratory tract infection, myocardial infarction or sciatica.
4. An elderly patient with an acute infection first seen at a home visit.

This assessment of clinical competence is of value to the trainee if it is completed during the first three months of the training year. Reassessment during the last few months is helpful to demonstrate changes which have resulted from the trainee's experience. It is clearly only possible to complete such a detailed assessment if the trainer sits in on each of the trainee's consultations with those patients selected for the exercise. An objection to the presence of a third party is that it so alters the whole course of the consultation as to make it atypical, but the need to put the trainee into an examination situation is so strong that the slight degree to which the silent observer alters the flavour of the consultation detracts little from the value of the exercise. The use of videotape is a reasonable substitute for the trainer while audiotape is a poor second best since it omits non-verbal communication and the content and method of the physical examination which the observing trainer is best suited to assess. The guidelines given above are comprehensive and will require a check list; a five point scoring system — very good, good, average, poor, very poor — can form the basis for a tutorial which allows the educative value of the exercise to be achieved.

While the examination detailed above is appropriate and practical for the common self-limiting illnesses difficulties can soon become apparent in applying the same formula to chronic or continuing illness. The management of chronic disease is however likely to be an increasingly important part of general practice and in the majority of instances is likely to be considerably more difficult and demanding than is the management of the common acute illnesses. The young hospital trained doctor has been exposed to and trained in the episodic management of illness and he thus requires a change in outlook and approach if he is to be able to manage chronic illness in a general practice context. An assessment of his skills in this area is thus just as important as it is with acute illness and the methods of assessment fall into two distinct varieties:

1. Prospectively, from the first consultation with a patient considered to have a condition likely to be of a chronic nature such as hypertension, rheumatoid arthritis, or cardiac failure.
2. Retrospectively and prospectively with a patient known to have an established chronic disease.

The trainee should be given a list of appropriate conditions and instructed to notify his trainer if he is consulted by a patient whom he thinks is presenting for the first time with such a condition. Examination then falls into two parts — the review of the intitial consultation which can be completed at or immediately after the consultation using the same check list as for an acute illness, and a review of the proposed prospective care which is best completed in a tutorial fashion. The assessment of the trainee's proposed future care of the patient may include the following areas:

1. *Frequency of follow-up*
   How often would the trainee intend to see that patient
   (a) During the period of development or stabilization of the illness?
   (b) Once the disease process has been controlled or has stabilized?

2. *Physical examination*
   (a) How frequently does the trainee intend to repeat a physical examination of the patient?
   (b) What aspects of the physical examination does the trainee consider as essential?
   (c) In what ways will the results of physical examination influence the pattern of management of the patient?

3. *Laboratory investigations*
   (a) What laboratory investigations does the trainee intend to repeat routinely?
   (b) How frequently should such investigations be repeated?
   (c) How might the results influence the treatment regime prescribed?

4. *Criteria for good management*
   (a) What criteria has the trainee decided upon as representing adequate management of the patient
       (i) in terms of the disease process?
       (ii) in relation to the patient's preferred life style?
       (iii) with regard to the patient's relatives and family?
   (b) What factors or occurrences has the trainee decided upon that will necessitate hospital in-patient, out-patient or specialist care in either the short or the long term?

5. *The natural history of the condition*
   (a) What is the likely natural history of this patient's condition?
   (b) What complications does the trainee anticipate and how would he identify them?
   (c) What changes in life style does the trainee anticipate for the patient?

6. *Alterations in treatment*
   (a) What alterations in drug therapy does the trainee consider likely with
       (i) progress of the condition?
       (ii) advancing age of the patient?
   (b) What alternative drug treatments has the trainee considered should present therapies fail to be effective or acceptable?

7. *Patient understanding*
   (a) What additional information will the patient require about his condition as it continues or if it should deteriorate?
   (b) What aspects of self-help or areas of nursing skill should the patient and his relatives have knowledge of now and in the future?
   (c) How does the trainee consider that compliance with patient management instructions can be monitored?

8. *Resources*
   (a) What practice and/or hospital resources does the trainee anticipate will be required for the patient in the future?
   (b) Has the trainee identified important physical or emotional resources, or lack of such resources, in the patient and his relatives?
   (c) How can these resources be developed and used to the greatest benefit of the patient and his family?

As in the assessment of the trainee's skills in managing acute illness a check list with a scoring system will allow this examination of clinical competence to be completed comprehensively, and a discussion of the check list can be used as an educational tool. It is probable however that either the trainee will not see a patient with the onset of a chronic illness during his year in practice or the opportunity may not arise for the first consultation and prospective care examination to be completed. An alternative scheme is therefore to select for the trainee a patient in the practice who is known to have an established chronic condition, to arrange an extended consultation for the patient with the trainee and to instruct the trainee to review the patient's past history, to assess the patient's present state and consider the future management. The questions that should then be asked of the trainee are:

1. *Past history*
   (a) Has the trainee identified the important and significant factors in the presentation of the patient's illness?
   (b) Has the trainee obtained a clear picture of the development of the patient's condition to the present date?

2. *Assessment of the patient's present condition*
   (a) Has the trainee correctly assessed the present state of the disease process?
   (b) Has the trainee identified the patient's understanding and acceptance of the condition and any limitations it may have had on his life style?
   (c) Does the trainee consider that the present management regime is
       (i) effective?
       (ii) acceptable to the patient?

(iii) sufficiently comprehensive?

3. *Future management*

Questions on the future management of the patient are the same as have been described above on page 295.

While the examples given above provide a format within which an assessment of the trainee's clinical competence can fulfil both educational and critical objectives, it cannot fully achieve either unless criteria have previously been set against which competence can be measured. Without such criteria the critical value of the exercise becomes reduced since it would rely on the subjective views and opinions of the trainer and would thus tend to be coloured by both intra- and inter-observer bias. The format for the examination of clinical competence that has been described depends on the trainer selecting a limited number of different patients and illnesses that are representative of broad groups of patients: a self-limiting acute illness in childhood is representative of the majority of the general practitioner's contacts with child patients; an adult with rheumatoid arthritis is broadly representative of the problems of chronic disease management.

The different questions that can be asked about the trainee's management of patients with both acute and chronic conditions have been set down in this chapter in a check-list form. Predetermined answers to such questions could represent the criteria against which the trainee's performance could be measured; such answers however should reflect a consensus of the views of acceptable and experienced general practitioners rather than those of a single trainer. Such consensus views could be obtained through consultation and agreement with all partners in a group practice, or preferably by widening the net to include all trainers within a district or region. The involvement of greater numbers of trainers would ensure first that the consensus views reached were more representative of current thought and practice and secondly, and importantly, that agreement was reached on the content of the assessment of the trainee's clinical skills and on the criteria against which competence would be measured for all trainees within the district or region.

Throughout this chapter the assessment of clinical skills has referred exclusively to the trainee in general practice rather than to the undergraduate student. With a few important variations the process is however equally appropriate to medical student teaching. The main difference in approach is the degree to which the steps taken by the learner or the opinions stated by him are appropriate to the general practice setting. Medical students need to be able to use the history taking procedure and the form of physical examination with which they are most familiar. They should thus not be unduly criticized if they tend to follow a hospital pattern of patient management. The trainee, in contrast, is in the midst of adapting his basic skills to the needs of full-time general practice and thus should be expected to be more selective in the extent of his physical examination of the patient and his use of investigations and more elaborate and wide-ranging in his consideration of both the patient and his illness.

45
The oral examination
Keith Hodgkin

Nearly 80 years ago Sir James McKenzie stressed that there were two distinct qualities of the human mind — memory and the process of reasoning. He also pointed out that the reasoning was only partially dependent on factual recall and that examinations continued mainly to encourage, and reward, factual recall.[1] This comment is still true today.

Written examinations have the advantage that the questions can be standardized so that the candidates' responses are cued in an exactly similar way. Comparison with an agreed model answer, and comparison between one candidate and another, can therefore be made with relative confidence. If, in a written examination, two examiners mark independently and all examination papers are sampled and monitored, and if a model answer is used to provide a check-list, the results of such examinations may be regarded as reasonably *reliable*. In the case of the MCQ (see Chapter 43) this reliability is very high indeed.

The drawback of such written examinations is that *validity* must be sacrificed to reliability. By validity is meant the relationship between the questions put or the problems explored, and the tasks for which the training was designed. An oral examination which is based on clinical problems from the examiner's own practice, or on clinical problems from the candidate's practice, may sensitively reflect a wide range of aspects from real life general practice.

The strength of the oral examination lies in the interaction between examiner and candidate. Questions may be asked, or rephrased in such a way as to help the candidate understand the exact intention of the examiner. In much the same way as the good general practitioner will pick up both verbal and non-verbal cues from his patient, so the good examiner may be able to follow the candidate's own exploration of his approach to a range of clinical or organizational problems. But the characteristics of this interaction not only constitute its strength but also its weakness. Examiner variability may be even greater than that which occurs in the marking of written papers. Interpersonal problems between candidates and examiners, and sometimes between one examiner and another may distort the oral examination in a number of ways. For example, the candidate may be confused, put off his stroke, or even misled by an examiner who has become displeased by the candidate's previous response. Or disagreement between one examiner and another, or rivalry or simply a failure to understand the thought processes of the fellow examiner may all distort the interaction. Finally, the judgement of the examiner may be seriously distorted by interpersonal factors — anger with the candidate who stands his ground, rejection of a candidate who has 'dared' to disagree with the examiner's opinion or warm and positive feelings for the candidate whose dress, manner and style approximate to the examiner's own, or whose sexual attractiveness speaks louder than the answers to the questions.

For these reasons the training of oral examiners, the holding of frequent examiners' conferences and workshops, the critical study of examiners' performance by a third party and so on, are an essential part of the conduct of any oral examination. However, candidates ought to be aware of one basic rule of oral examining. Examiners should always examine in pairs. They should mark independently and the marks should refer to the questions being asked by both examiners. At the end of the oral the independently given marks are compared, and are either reconciled (which is different from saying that the mean is calculated) or the disagreement is taken to an arbitrating senior examiner.

What can be assessed?

Wright (see Chapter 6) described the range of learning objectives, and in particular the difference between the medical *education* of the student and the *training* of the vocational trainee. The difference in these objectives will be reflected in the differences of the assessments made. The relationship between educational objectives and assessments is discussed in Chapter 2. In Chapters 4, 5, 7 and 16 there are discussions of the possibilities of the one-to-one clinical tutorial. Those educational objectives which can best be taught and learned in the one-to-one tutorial are best assessed by the oral examination. In this sense there is a relationship between methods of teaching and methods of assessment. For example, if the oral examiner is to use the role-play mode of examining (that is, he will for part of his questioning take on the role of a patient, putting the candidate in the role of doctor), this should occur only when the candidate has had ample experience of role-playing as a method of learning.

There are a number of ways of expressing the objectives of an oral examination. In terms of clinical decision taking and problem solving the following three aspects may be examined:

1. *The candidate's diagnostic vocabulary*
   These are the clinical patterns that the candidate has learned to recognize and use; they are the basic conceptual tools which he uses in the diagnosis and management of his patients' problems. Elstein demonstrated that when practising clinicians are presented with a clinical complaint, they recall from their 'diagnostic vocabulary' between two and four, rarely more, diagnostic possibilities, and these they rank order in terms of probability.[2] As the learner's diagnostic

vocabulary increases he becomes increasingly skilled in the use of the hypothetico–deductive method, which is described in this book in Chapter 16.

The oral examination is well suited to an exploration of the candidate's acquisition and use of such a diagnostic vocabulary. From this assessment the candidate's present and future clinical decision making can be inferred for the following reasons:

(a) An effective recall and manipulation of the vocabulary is the basis of every physician's skill. All physicians relate the ever-changing patterns of management skills to this relatively stable skeleton of past experience based on pattern recognition.

(b) The individual items of the vocabulary and the frequency with which they are used are specific within each medical discipline and provide its natural basic syllabus. Teachers, learners and examiners are therefore wise to relate their activities directly to the specific and most frequently used items in this relatively constant framework. In the United Kingdom this has been studied in the work of 11 general practitioners over four years.[3] The working diagnostic vocabulary of each of these practitoners was similar. Each chose a mean of 475 diagnostic labels. Ninety-five per cent of the work of these doctors was described by 166 diagnoses. Thirty-three per cent of all problems presented involved the following five categories: acute upper respiratory infections; tension; advice for contraception; minor trauma; and gastroenteritis. Marsland and Wood carried out a similar analysis in the USA.[4] The findings were very similar to those made in the UK.

(c) The size and quality of each clinician's diagnostic vocabulary is a measure of both previous and present clinical experience. This must of necessity be very limited in the case of the medical student, particularly the medical student who is assessed before the end of his medical school training. The student starts his training with the layman's diagnostic vocabulary of perhaps ten or so diseases; the general practitioner of five to ten years' experience manipulates nearly 500 such rubrics.

2. *Clinical method*

Here the concepts and processes of clinical decision making which are referred to in many of the chapters of this book, but particularly in Chapter 16, may be assessed. The candidate's ability in analysis of symptoms and signs, verbal and non-verbal communication and so on, his ability to integrate the component parts of the consultation into a formulation of the problem and a plan of action can all be sensitively explored, and if necessary probed in some depth.

It would be a misuse of the oral examination to explore at length the candidate's factual recall. This is much better tested by the MCQ. It is only necessary to test factual recall that relates to the diagnostic vocabulary and effective clinical decision taking. What the oral examination is perhaps best suited to assessing are the cognitive skills and the attitudes which inform them (see Chapter 6). Any attempt to conceptualize the assessments of an oral examination in terms of knowledge, skills and attitudes is likely to produce distortions, or at least the invention of unreal situations which cannot accurately reflect trainee experience or the practice of the candidate. By the same token, previous attempts to analyse the content of oral examinations in terms of the five areas of vocational training (health and disease, human development, human behaviour, medicine and society, the practice) failed to reflect the depth and subtlety of the questions and answers, which should be the mark of a good oral examination. Much more useful, because it reflects the real situations of general practice, is the concept of 'basic competencies' first suggested by Morrell.

3. *Competencies*

At various stages in education, it is possible to test in an oral examination the candidate's competence to undertake a variety of tasks. These tasks may be defined in advance by the examining body and evidence that the candidate can complete them may be regarded as a basic requirement if he is to pass the examination. Some candidates will show evidence in an oral examination that they are able to perform at a much higher level than that required by the basic competencies required. Where, however, the examiners identify shortcomings in the candidate and begin to question whether or not he deserves a pass mark, they may revert to these basic competencies which have been agreed. Some examples may help to clarify this approach.

— A candidate should be able to solve the problems presented by acute infection in general practice in a logical manner relating treatment to the cause of infection.
— The candidate should be able to interpret the common symptoms and physical signs of illness described by the examiner.
— The candidate should be able to interpret common patterns of human behaviour, e.g. negativism in a child; the presenting features of depressive illness.
— The candidate should be able to communicate with patients. The examiner may ask what he will say to a patient in a particular clinical situation or involve the candidate in a role-play.
— The candidate should be able to describe how to respond appropriately to medical emergency, e.g. acute pulmonary oedema; a child with a fit.
— The candidate should be able to understand and handle the impact

of chronic disease on the individual and his family.

The examiner presents the candidate with problems specifically designed to explore these areas of competence and designs the questions to test the candidate in terms of logical thought, clinical awareness and skills in communication.

The examples given may be considered appropriate in examining a young general practitioner. When dealing with undergraduates, considerable modification will be necessary and the competence expected must be tailored to the candidate's knowledge and experience so that the examination is related to the educational objectives of the course. The advantage which the oral examination offers compared with other methods is that it provides the examiner with an opportunity to explore in some depth the candidate's ability to think logically and critically. If it becomes apparent early in the examination that the candidate is in danger of failing to achieve the basic level of competence agreed in advance, then the questioning can be adjusted to test specifically this basic level of competence which is required to achieve a pass mark.

Oral examining

In their present form oral examinations, for both theoretical and logistical reasons, are not carried out in the candidate's own practice. Candidate skills and competencies must, therefore, be inferred not assessed directly in terms of clinical outcome.

The examiner presents each candidate with a series of appropriate 'tracer situations' in clinical, behavioural, attitudinal or practice management areas. In each situation, the examiners explore and mark the range and depth of the candidate's decision-making in relation to the following three questions:
1. Have all the safe and practical alternatives been considered?
2. Have the implications (good and bad) of each alternative been fully understood?
3. Have coherent arguments been presented for the candidate's final choice of action?

The candidate's range of possible decisions and depth of understanding are assessed and marked by comparison with those of the examiners. The reasonable assumption is made that such comparisons are a good predictor of future candidate performance in similar situations in subsequent unsupervised practice.

Examiners (and teachers) should ensure that their selection of 'tracer situations' is valid, that is to say, that they are:
1. Appropriate to primary care.
2. Demonstrate a wide range of appropriate alternative decisions.

3. Represent an appropriate balance of clinical, behavioural, attitudinal and organizational competence in common acute problems, common patterns of behaviour, common clinical pattern recognition, communication, medical emergencies, chronic disease, common problems of treatment and management, health care organization, and preventive medicine.

Such indirect oral assessments are based on assumptions similar to those made for one-to-one teaching in vocational training. No experimental work has been done which demonstrates that these assumptions and examiner predictions are sound. There are two reasons for this. First, clear, measurable standards (based on patient outcomes) for 'good unsupervised practice' have not been created. Secondly, the cost (in examiner time and finances) of exploring direct assessments in a candidate's own practice on anything but a small experimental basis is prohibitive.

Any experienced examiner will testify to the particularly tiring nature of the exercise. The reason lies in the concentration required. While in ordinary day-to-day work and consultation certain actions and responses are reflex, in oral examining attention must be focused continuously on the problems discussed and the candidate's answers and reactions.

It can be a matter of fine judgement to decide just how far to pursue a subject — too brief a discussion many not allow a slow candidate a fair opportunity to display sufficiently fully the knowledge, skills and attitudes being tested. On the other hand it is a mistake to persist with a subject when it is clear that the examinee is either out of his depth or unable to grasp fully the drift of the questioning. It is here that the presence of a sensitive second examiner, prepared to interrupt and direct questioning into other channels, is especially valuable.

Unless the pair of examiners have examined together before, it is essential that they should spend some time together in preparation before the examination. Any sense of unease between the examining pair can endanger the success and fairness of the exercise. For example, examiners will wish to come to an agreement about the division of the time available for questioning, when and how to interrupt each other if the candidate or the examiner seems to be in difficulties, and so on. The examiners, at the conclusion of each examination, will not only discuss the candidate's performance, and reconcile their marks, but ideally should also discuss each other's peformance. Examiners should value more those questions which ask 'why?' and 'how?' than questions which merely elicit the recall of facts which can be better assessed in other ways.

Perhaps the most controversial aspect of any particular examination is the question of its fairness. For example, did the questions reflect the course of training which you were meant to assess, or the sort of practice which the doctor carries out. Unless the intention of the examination is made very clear, an examination, and in particular an oral examination, may be manifestly unfair. For example, an examination which is geared to assess the effects of vocational training may be quite different from an examination geared to assess the quality of practice of an established doctor. Confusion between these two aims can result in a great deal of unhappiness, both for candidates and for examiners.

There is a particular problem in the oral examination of medical students. Students may well be examined months, or in some instances, almost two years before the completion of their medical school course. Because general practice is a generalist subject, clinical topics, which the student may have met in general practice, but may not yet have met in the specialist hospital setting, must be examined with this fact in mind: the emphasis should always be on an exploration of attitudes and cognitive skills, and not on the possession of a diagnostic vocabulary which the student has not yet had the opportunity of acquiring.

Conclusion

A good oral examination provides elements of assessment not possible by other means. The aim is to provide an assessment of the candidate's performance, it is not to submit the candidate to an ordeal by fire. Much may be asked of the candidate. Of the examiner the least that is demanded must be courtesy, concentration and a commitment to self-examination. In the absence of these the validity of what the oral examination may achieve will be defeated by the unreliability of the examiners' performance.

References

[1] Wilson, R. McNair (1926) *The Beloved Physician*. London: John Murray.
[2] Elstein, A.S., Kagan, N., Shulman, L.S. *et al.* (1972) 'Methods and theory in the study of medical inquiry'. *Journal of Medical Education, 47*, 55.
[3] Hodgkin, K. (1979) 'Diagnostic vocabulary for primary care'. *Journal of Family Practice, 8*, (1), 129–144.
[4] Marsland, D.W., Wood M. and Mayo, F. (1976) 'A data bank for patient care, curriculum, and research in family practice: 526,196 patient problems'. *Journal of Family Practice, 3*, 25.

Part VI
Planning for teaching

46
Designing and running courses
Michael McKendrick

Course design

In an ideal situation the course organizer will determine clear-cut educational objectives and then choose appropriate methods for teaching and evaluation. But things in the real world are rarely so simple. A course may begin with a rather vaguely perceived intention, for example the decision to look again at the management of certain chronic diseases in general practice. But external constraints will immediately be at work in shaping realistic objectives. How long is the course to last? Is it to be a short intensive course — one day, a weekend, a week long, residential or not? Is it to be an extended course, like that offered to vocational trainees — one or two sessions a week for between one and two years? What resources are available? What is the number and quality of the teachers who can contribute? The reader is referred to Chapter 2 which deals with the interrelationship between what is to be achieved, the methods for achievement and the settings in which the learning will take place.

A few general comments may be worth making. First, there has been a major shift in the design of courses for general practitioners from the use of the lecture (Chapter 9) to the use of small groups (Chapter 8). Second, the participation of the course members should extend beyond the interaction of the small group to a personal evaluation by each of them of the course itself, and its component parts (see below). Third, the individual teachers in the course, for example general practitioner group leaders, clinical specialists, educational advisers, should meet to discuss the course as a whole, and the contribution of its individual parts.

Much may be achieved by giving those who are to attend such a course a clear exposition of aims and methods. In addition course members should be supplied with clear instructions about preparing their own material in advance (for example the records of patients with particular clinical problems) and a small and realistic amount of preparatory reading.

Rule 1: *The course must be educationally sound.*

The application

In the UK, Section 63 of the Health Services and Public Health Act 1968 clearly lays the Secretary of State's responsibility for the provision of courses for general practitioners on the Postgraduate Deans in the

Universities. They approve courses, often after taking advice, and they have the final control of the funds. Since 1976, an annual allocation of funds has been made to each region by the Department of Health and Social Security or the Scottish Home and Health Department, out of whose funds the expenditure on individual educational sessions is made. One course, therefore, competes with another and at present is subject to the Postgraduate Dean's judgement on its merits.

Rule 2: *Apply in good time, say at least six months in advance, for approval of your course under Section 63.*

Courses, which may be a series of meetings, not necessarily with a common theme, may be supported in one of two ways:
1. Full Section 63 approval, when reimbursement of lecturers' fees and travelling, hire of rooms, costs of course materials, secretarial expenses and other legitimate related expenditure is made in full.
2. 'Zero-rating', when no financial aid is given by the regional postgraduate organization.

In both cases, course members may claim their personal expenses, accommodation and travel, by application to Family Practitioner Committees on the appropriate forms. Applications for approval of courses should include the following:
1. The title of the course.
2. The venue and the date.
3. Timetable.
4. Estimates for (a) speakers' fees and expenses,
   (b) secretarial and administrative costs,
   (c) hire of rooms,
   (d) advertisement, etc.
5. Content (programme).
6. Special features.
7. Additional information which may help the Postgraduate Dean to come to a decision about the course.

Rule 3: *Estimate as accurately as you can: it will save delay in approval and also any subsequent financial embarrassment.*

It must be noted that if a course is approved under Section 63 then outside sponsorship such as enhancing speakers' fees and the inclusion of promotional material is forbidden. Demonstrations, say, by pharmaceutical firms, or refreshments, may be discreetly permitted.

Courses approved under Section 63 must be open to all general practitioners but there will always be an optimum number who can be catered for. Some courses are specialized, so organizers may well establish some equitable method for selection of participants.

Family Practitioner Committees (FPCs) are invariably willing to distribute notices through their routine mailings to general practitioners and this can save a lot of expense, but if some form of special printing is necessary then this will be a charge on Section 63.

Rule 4: *Allow time and money for advertising.*

Management

Successful course management contributes so much to effective learning.

1. Consider the venue with care. Nothing detracts more from general satisfaction than poor accommodation either for living or working: uncomfortable seating, poor acoustics, extraneous and intrusive noise, ventilation and heating, and so on.

   In intensive and residential courses, members must have some privacy and there is no doubt that modern hotels geared to conferences provide excellent venues. So, too, are halls of residence in universities, although traditionally halls are more austere; often the older the institution the more spartan the quarters. This may be compensated for by the ambience, the sense of history and the architectural interest. Interest does stray beyond the seminar room and so it should.

2. Do not be tempted to accept more doctors onto the course than can readily be coped with, either in terms of accommodation or group size. An over-crowded meeting inevitably causes frustrations and delay.

3. Careful and detailed discussions with the staff of hotel or college are essential so that a full appreciation can be gained of the needs of the course. Experienced management can be a boon but it is unwise to make too many assumptions on this score and time spent in going through the programme well in advance will be fully repaid.

4. If teaching aids are required make doubly sure that the sheer physical necessities are there: power points, projectors that work, screens that do not collapse, blackboards with chalk — the list is a long one.

5. Do not overcrowd the programme. Allow time to socialize and see that each session is not too long. A successful course may often be judged by the volume and persistence of the informal conversations.

6. Expert resource adds fuel to educational fire. Draw on the best available within your budget but the addition of only one 'name' can add a welcome spice to even the best course.

7. Be prepared to make changes during the course, so long as they are consistent with achievement of the overall aims and objectives. This attitude is intrinsic to the concept of groups setting their own pace and providing their own education.

The time spent in this degree of planning may be considerable and happy is the organiser who has efficient secretarial help. Time-consuming

Time-consuming negotiations and checking can be delegated so that the organizer's direct action is decreased allowing time for the careful appraisal and reappraisal of content and methods of the educational sessions.

Rule 5: *Involve your secretary as much as possible in the planning and management.*

Course evaluation

Evaluation now becomes inescapable; justice to learners, organizers and teachers and the demonstration of value to others. It must be simple and be a combination of observation and opinions. Freedom for participants to voice their satisfaction and dissatisfaction betokens mutual confidence, however painful it may be. No one should be immune from critical scrutiny and the operation of this principle may be the foremost learning experience of the course. If the objectives have been clearly established then evaluation by questionnaire should not pose any great difficulty. The following points may be helpful in constructing your questionnaire:

1. Do not ask too many questions. Not everyone has a burning desire to complete questionnaires.
2. The questions should be grouped so that different aspects of the course may be evaluated: the accommodation and services available; the reading material provided; the performance of individual teachers; the appropriateness of the objectives to the doctor's practice and so on.
3. Two-tailed questions are best because they make clear the subject of the question. Allow an even number of spaces for scoring, so that the course member is not tempted to adopt a neutral position. For example:

| The reading material distributed before the course was relevant and helpful | | | | | | There was little relevance in the reading material to the work done on the course |

4. In constructing the questionnaire negative and positive statements should be randomly allocated to the left hand margin, so that the respondent is forced to read each two-tailed question with some care.
5. In all instances allow adequate space after each question or group of questions for the respondent to make his own comments. A mass of undifferentiated statements often emerges, but there will be veins of gold and insights which may be invaluable.
6. Get opinions before the course ends and allow time to do so. Memory is short and selective so quick reaction is valuable. However, follow-up questionnaires, perhaps by post, about six weeks later may provide a clue to any changes actually produced by the course.
7. Information has to be capable of analysis. Large amounts of data may

need to be handled by computer and special expertise is required. It may pay not to be too ambitious.

Rule 6: *Make evaluation simple.*

Conclusion

The good course is one in which all concerned in it grow. One of the many excitements of education in general practice is the realization that we can teach each other, or rather, learn together. Articulation of what we need to know can be arrived at by the group and an appropriate response engendered. Learning becomes firmly related to our work and just as we seek help for our patients by consultation and second opinion, so do we need the help of expert advice in our education. This is both good sense and an effective use of time and money. Increasingly, as groups of general practitioners struggle to learn together confidence is gained to approach experts — medical and educational — to ask the right questions and to learn from their special knowledge and experience. This is a most comprehensive form of education: stimulating to the learner, demanding of the teacher and highly beneficial in the end to the consumers, our patients.

47
The teaching practice
Alastair Donald

Before beginning to consider the organization of a practice to enable it to undertake a commitment to training it is essential that all partners should be in agreement that they wish to participate in a teaching programme. Although individual doctors are appointed as trainers, unless they are in single handed practice, each trainer will require the support and encouragement of his partners and indeed of the whole practice team if the training programme in the practice is to be successful, and perhaps more important, if it is to be enjoyed by all the participants. The concept of the teaching practice rather than of the appointed individual trainer has therefore emerged since the commitment within a training practice is a considerable one both in terms of material outlay, intellectual effort, and that most precious of commodities, time.

Once agreement has been reached between the partners that they wish to undertake teaching an approach should be made to the Regional Adviser in General Practice for although there are national guidelines regarding the criteria for selection of trainers in general practice, the authority for their appointment is vested at regional level, and the national guidelines are interpreted with flexibility and differing emphasis within the regions of the UK.

The doctor appointed as trainer is expected to assume the responsibility for ensuring that the practice is suitably equipped to undertake training and for the necessary administrative arrangements to enable a full training programme to be provided.

Within the practice premises it is essential that there is sufficient consulting room accommodation to ensure that when the trainee is seeing patients there is always another doctor working 'in tandem' whom he may consult if necessary. Ideally, although few practices can provide this, the trainee should have a consulting room of his own with which he can identify rather than shift to a different room on several occasions during each week. The trainee's room should be equipped to the same standard as other consulting rooms and the trainee provided with a medical bag containing essential equipment and drugs for use on home visits.

A training practice should also provide a common room where the trainee can engage in informal discussion with other members of the practice team and where teaching sessions can be held both at an informal level and for the more formal one-to-one teaching session which is an essential part of the training programme and which should occupy at least one full session of one-and-a-half to two hours each week. This tutorial is the focal point of teaching within the practice and will be discussed in more detail below.

The secretarial and reception staff of a practice have a significant role to play in training for it is important that the trainee should appreciate how these members of staff, effectively employed, can help patients, doctors and nurses in the efficient running of the practice. It is also important for the trainee to learn practice administration and modern business methods relevant to general practice. For these reasons then it is extremely important that the secretarial and reception staff of a practice understand the nature of a traineeship so that they can contribute to the teaching within the practice. When the trainee is consulting, for example, the receptionist can see that he does so at a rate at which he feels comfortable during the early months of training and can ensure that the trainee is not harrassed by pressure to consult at the same rate as the established principals. As the year progresses, and the trainee gains in confidence and experience, it is then possible for the rate to be gradually increased until the trainee is consulting at a similar rate to his more experienced colleagues. Unless receptionists and secretaries are sensitive to the learning situation unnecessary tensions can arise. As with the secretarial and receptionist staff so also do the nurses and health visitors attached to the practice have an important contribution to make to the learning experience of the trainee, not only as individuals but also as members of the practice team. Nurses and health visitors often have students attached to them and they will usually be sympathetic to the needs of the trainee who can, in turn, himself assist in the training of nursing students.

The importance of medical records for the proper care of patients and for teaching cannot be over-emphasized. It is therefore vital that any teaching practice should have clinical records of a high quality, whatever type of folder is used. These records should, at a minimum, contain letters arranged in chronological order, have a summary card listing the principal episodes in the patient's medical and social history, and should contain a therapy card listing drugs that are being taken on a long-term basis. Quite apart from the educational reasons for having adequate records the trainer will be at a risk of litigation should his trainee make a clinical decision detrimental to the interests of the patient because he was unaware of, or perhaps could not read, vital information that was contained in the record.

Night and weekend work are an integral part of continuity of care but when the trainee is judged competent to undertake out of hours responsibilities it is essential that at all times he is fully covered by one of the principals in the practice. The rota of out of hours work should not involve the trainee to any greater extent than that undertaken by the partners in the practice on average. This will, of course, apply to both weekdays and weekend duties.

A trainee will require to be released from the practice on one day each week to attend the day release course organized by the Regional Adviser and his course organizer colleagues. During vacations the trainee should be encouraged on these days to undertake some other form of educational activity. In addition the trainee should have a recreational half day on one weekday each week.

Every teaching practice should, of course, be equipped with an adequate library which contains not only current journals relevant to general practice but also essential text books concerned with the main specialty divisions in medicine as well as books relevant to the specialty of general practice. Recommendations regarding such a library may be obtained from the Librarian of the Royal College of General Practitioners or from the Regional Adviser and his colleagues.

When the arrangements discussed above have been considered and, where possible, provided, the practice will be organized to engage in a training programme. The trainer will be responsible for the engagement of a trainee and for all the contractual arrangements regarding the trainee's employment. A contract of employment should be drawn up (specimen copies are available from the British Medical Association) and the trainer will require to set aside time, or delegate responsibility, in respect of the trainee's salary, including the deduction of PAYE, the payment of car allowances, telephone rental, and any other allowances to which the trainee is entitled. Technically the trainee is employed by the trainer but his salary and allowances are reimbursed from the Family Practitioner Committee, or (in Scotland) the Primary Care Division on a nationally agreed scale.

When the trainee is duly appointed to the practice it is then necessary to consider educational aims and to construct a programme to achieve them. Some ideas concerning such a programme are set out below.

The training programme within the practice

The aim of the trainee practitioner year is to produce a more competent, more confident general practitioner more quickly than would otherwise be the case. The basis of learning in the trainee year is through the exercise of personal responsibility for individual patients and therefore the consultation will be the dominant learning situation. If learning is to achieve its full educational value, however, it must be supported by teaching. 'Teaching can never be a substitute for experience in this or any other branch of medicine, but without it experience can be misunderstood and misused.'[1]

Every trainee will have individual strengths and weaknesses and each programme should recognize the trainee's particular needs although there is obviously much material common to the training of every future general practitioner. During the first month the trainer will introduce the trainee to basic information regarding the organization of the practice and the procedures of which the patient would expect his doctor to be aware in the conduct of routine consultations. The roles of the members of the practice team should be discussed in some detail and the trainee will with advantage spend at least a day in the practice office or beside the receptionist so that he learns the problems of lay contact with patients and the differences in patients' attitudes towards them. A day spent with the health visitor and the practice nurse will also be rewarding to the trainee. During this time there will be opportunities to examine the practice records and a tutorial session might be held reviewing the alternative systems of record keeping and the opportunities that an age/sex register can provide for routine screening of at-risk groups or simply for the efficient conduct of immunization programmes. These subjects will again provide topics for more general consideration in tutorial sessions.

During this initial phase in the practice the trainee will sit in with the trainer and with the other partners and this provides an opportunity unique in the lifetime of most general practitioners to witness the style of a fellow practitioner in the intimacy of the consultation. The trainee will learn that the presence of a third party alters to some extent the doctor–patient relationship but most importantly the significance of that relationship to the management of health and disease. The trainer has the opportunity during the early weeks to assess the knowledge, skills and attitudes of the trainee and on that assessment will depend much of the emphasis within the programme developed for training within the practice. At an early stage thereafter the trainer and trainee should learn together the details of the programme within the practice as well as those supporting activities available to the trainee through the day release course and the use of attendance at selected intensive courses. These latter will be chosen to cover areas of training where weaknesses are revealed or where there have been omissions in the hospital phase of training. For example an intensive course in psychiatry might be useful if the trainee has not held a psychiatric hospital post.

The teaching programme in the practice will be both informal and formal. Informal discussions around the coffee table are invaluable in relation to the 'hot' case just seen or last night's emergency and thus enable the nurses and health visitors to participate in the discussion. This type of teaching is an essential component of training and should not be underrated. It must not, however, be regarded as a substitute for the formal tutorial session held at an agreed time each week and where the trainer and trainee will have the privacy of a one-to-one teaching period of one-and-a-half to two hours. The conduct of these sessions presents the trainer with his greatest challenge for they must allow the opportunity to raise not only clinical topics and management problems, but also behavioural matters related to the relationship of the trainee to patients, to staff and, most difficult of all, to the trainer himself.

If a problem is identified it is a problem already on the way to solution and it is important that tutorial sessions should not be confined to discussion of identified difficulties although an attempt must be made to resolve these. To allow the discovery of unidentified problems the use of random case analysis in tutorial sessions has proved particularly profitable (see Chapter 40). Here the trainer selects at random a patient from a recent surgery conducted by the trainee and asks him to present the case. Discussion can then take place on any aspect of management or on the wider aspects of the condition presenting. This method offers infinite varieties for discussion at all depths and its advantages lie in the discovery of problems not previously recognized as such as well as unrevealed insights shown by the trainee. It is therefore very useful in the ongoing assessment of the trainee which is a central part of the management of the teaching programme.

The tutorial session should also aim to cover priority clinical topics which are life threatening and which the trainee must be able to manage competently. Topics such as status epilepticus may be seen only rarely in the course of a trainee year but the trainee must be able to respond appropriately when the condition is encountered. A list of clinical topics based on their relative frequency of occurrence and their clinical importance is set out in the booklet, *Learning and Teaching General Practice* produced by the Scottish Council for Postgraduate Medical Education, 8 Queen Street, Edinburgh, from whom it is available. This booklet also contains a list of general and procedural topics which should be covered during the tutorial and discussion periods.

Trainers should be aware of the content of the local day release programme to avoid duplication of topics in discussion but also to allow these to be discussed with the trainee in relation to their application within the training practice.

The use of the modified essay question, perhaps using examples available from the Royal College of General Practitioners' examination, will provide a good learning exercise in tutorials and will also assist in assessment. In addition each trainee should be encouraged to undertake a project during his year in which he can consider in some depth an organizational or clinical aspect of practice. Local research faculties of the Royal College of General Practitioners will usually be able to encourage the trainee in the selection of a research topic and its planning.

The fundamental aim of training is to recognize education as a continuum and a training programme will not have succeeded if the trainee has not acquired a desire to examine critically his own performance either by himself or in discussion with his peers in the day release course or in the practice. Every trainee therefore must be encouraged to take part in some form of audit activity whereby he examines his performance and measures it against his own expectations and preferably shares in ongoing practice audit activity.

The programme of training in the practice year is capable of considerable variety. It should never become stale and it should provide an intellectual stimulus not only to the trainee but to the trainer and all his colleagues resulting in benefit to the quality of care the practice provides for its patients.

Reference

[1] Browne, K. and Freeling, P. (1976) *The Doctor – Patient Relationship*. Edinburgh: Churchill Livingstone.

Index